Children of Divorce:
Developmental
and Clinical Issues

Children of Divorce: Developmental and Clinical Issues

Craig A. Everett
Editor

The Haworth Press
New York • London

Children of Divorce: Developmental and Clinical Issues has also been published as *Journal of Divorce*, Volume 12, Numbers 2/3 1988/89.

The Haworth Press, Inc. 10 Alice Street, Binghamton, NY 13904-1580
EUROSPAN/Haworth, 3 Henrietta Street, London WC2E 8LU England

Library of Congress Cataloging-in-Publication Data

Children of divorce.

    "Has also been published as Journal of divorce, volume 12, number 2/3 1988/1989 — T.p.
verso.
    Includes bibliographies.
    1. Children of divorced parents — Psychology. 2. Adaptability (Psychology) in children. I.
Everett, Craig A. [DNLM: 1. Adaptation, Psychological — in infancy & childhood. 2. Child
Psychology. 3. Divorce. 4. Parent-Child Relations. 5. Sibling Relations. 6. Single Parent —
psychology. W1 JO622M v.12 no.2/3 /
WS 105.5.F2 C536
HQ777.5.C43 1989   306.8'9   88-35622
ISBN 0-86656-886-7

Children of Divorce: Developmental and Clinical Issues

CONTENTS

ABOUT THE EDITOR

Craig A. Everett, PhD, is a marriage and family therapist in private practice in Tucson, Arizona. Formerly President of the American Association for Marriage and Family Therapy, Dr. Everett's previous positions include Director of Family Therapy Training and Associate Professor at both Florida State University and Auburn University. He has been the editor of the *Journal of Divorce* since 1983 and is an editorial board member of six professional journals.

Introduction

There is little question that the children in divorcing families carry the greatest vulnerability and often sustain the greatest pain and anguish during and after the divorce process. In fact it is the adjustment crises that the children of divorce experience which may linger well into adulthood. Disillusionment, anger and fear may shape their own adult mate selection processes as well as the parenting and interactional patterns of the next generation.

The literature of the field has focused appropriately on the adjustments and experiences of these children. However, the weakness of the present state of literature lies in its failure to study, both empirically and clinically, the inextricable location and role of the children within the dysfunctional patterns of the family system which is dissolving. We cannot understand fully the pain and the adjustment dilemmas of the post-divorce children unless we recognize the roles that they played and the experiences that they survived within the dysfunctional subsystems of the pre-divorcing family. Similarly, to develop treatment strategies for disturbed post-divorce children, we must recognize the continuing roles that they play within the post-divorce single or remarried family systems as well as within the respective intergenerational networks.

I would like to say that this work breaks new ground in the above areas, but it does not. The available literature has just not evolved to that place yet. It does take a step in the direction of understanding more fully the role of the children of divorce within their own family systems. The collection of 18 articles looks at both developmental, structural and interactional issues that should benefit both practitioners and researchers.

Craig A. Everett, PhD
Editor

FAMILY WELL-BEING, DEVELOPMENT AND DISRUPTION: AN INTRODUCTION

Children of Divorce
and Single-Parent Lifestyles:
Facilitating Well-Being

Roger L. Hutchinson
Sharon L. Spangler-Hirsch

SUMMARY. Both the increased frequency of divorce and the resultant increase in single-parent households have experienced dramatic increases since World War II. In many instances, divorce is a major disruptive experience that imposes primary impact upon all family members. Characteristically, various levels of adjustment are required of family members amid experiences that are novel and for which those involved are possible not well prepared. It may be that our efforts can be best directed toward providing a reframing approach to parents and children experiencing divorce. For instance, there is evidence that children from single-parent families are good decision makers and that they have strengths and maturities associated with their experiences related to divorce. It seems to our advantage as professionals to be able to facilitate the cognitive reframing of parents and children in such a way that hopefulness and a sense of assurance and control can be implemented and sustained. The purpose of this article is (1) to integrate what is known about divorce-associated responses in children; (2) to promote a reframing approach in focusing on that which may be evaluated as positive and contributing to present well-being and future successes of those children; and (3) to guide practitioners as they work both programmatically and in direct service with children of divorce.

Both the increased frequency of divorce and the resultant increase in single-parent households have experienced dramatic in-

---

Roger L. Hutchinson and Sharon L. Spangler-Hirsch are on the faculty of the Department of Counseling Psychology at Guidance Services, TC619, Ball State University, Muncie, IN 47306.

5

creases since World War II. Incidents of divorce have tripled in the past three decades. In 1962 413,000 divorces were recorded in the United States; 845,000 occurred in 1972; 1.2 million divorces were reported in 1982. It is now a general consensus that an estimated 40% of marriages among young adults will fail (Drake & Shallenberger, 1981).

Schmid (1986) reported the percent of children from divorced homes to have been 9% in 1960 and 12% in 1970. While it was projected in 1982 (Pett) that by 1990 11% of all children would experience the divorce of their parents, more recent Census Bureau figures indicate that nearly one-fourth of children under 18 today live with only one parent. According to Hurley, Taylor, and Riley (1984), nearly one-half of today's children will experience the divorce of their parents.

Of significance to those in the fields of mental health and education is the widely held, but perhaps misleading, assumption that children of divorce often display concurrent behavioral and academic changes. Bilge and Kaufman (1983) provide a poignant and thought-provoking challenge to that assumption in examining one-parent families cross-culturally. They note that "when viewed cross-culturally, the one parent family is found to be neither pathological nor inferior. . . . Whether or not the single-parent household becomes a personal or social disaster depends upon the availability of sufficient resource materials, supportive social networks, and the tenor of culturally structured attitudes toward it" (p. 59).

The inherent complications of operating from an erroneous assumption are intensified by the rapidly increasing rate of incidence of divorce and the emanating increase in the numbers of school children who have experienced the divorce of parents. In the typical American classroom, one of five children comes from a divorce-resultant single-parent household (Drake & Shallenberger, 1984; Wodarski, 1982). In some school districts, rates of incidence may be even greater. In one California school district, it was discovered that of 1,000 students in a particular building, 90% were from single-parent families (Drake & Shallenberger, 1981).

It appears that immediate divorce-associated needs of children may affect not only the present but also long-range needs as well. Hepworth, Ryder, and Dreyer (1984) investigated the long-term effects of parental loss associated with divorce. They found that later intimate relationships are influenced and that compensatory behavior in adolescents is manifested in one of three ways. Relationships may be (1) avoided, (2) characterized by premature or accelerated courtship patterns, or (3) engaged in by "mock intimacy" in which a series of casual noncommittal relationships are exhibited.

Thus, one may speculate that it is possible, and perhaps probable, that today's children of divorce will experience divorce and single-parent realities as adults. The systemic changes brought about by escalating divorce rates have cyclical and compounding properties. Examining what is currently known about the effects of divorce on children and focusing upon specific elements of those treatment models that contribute to *healthy adjustment* in some children may enhance professional awareness and guide theorists and practitioners in further investigation and refinement of intervention techniques. Mental health professionals and educators can be directed toward providing preventive approaches and programs that address the needs of children experiencing the divorce of their parents and the resultant single-parent family lifestyles. Such programs must be administered in a positive framework that facilitates the inherent rights of all individuals (regardless of lifestyle or socioeconomic status), helps them to achieve a sense of well-being, and encourages them to go forward with optimism and hopefulness.

Most professionals agree that the school environment provides a logical place in which to provide such programs for these children. Drake and Shallenberger (1981) assert that children "spend more time in schools than in any other institution outside the family" and that "the schools would appear to provide a natural setting for supportive services for children experiencing separation and divorce" (p. 55). Williams (1984) also agrees that "schools are in a unique position to help alleviate stress among families experiencing divorce by recognizing their special needs and spearheading group support, counseling, and mediation programs for parents and students" (p. 24).

Guidubaldi, Cleminshaw, Perry, and McLaughlin (1983), however, raise a key issue and suggest that while "school-based support for children of divorce is a priority intervention," there is currently lacking "a detailed understanding of school related criteria and school environments that may promote positive adjustment'' (p. 304). School personnel may have negative expectations of children from single-parent families and thus must be guided to recognize the strengths of these families and children in order to most effectively meet their needs (Wodarski, 1982). In addition, ''the problem is indeed complicated by the immense variety of ideals and ideas about what is good for children'' (Bilge & Kaufman, 1983, p. 60).

Our intention is certainly not to overlook or to discredit the body of sound research that sheds light upon documented divorce-associated responses in children and parents. Rather, we contend that such information, viewed in an integrative fashion and in the proper perspective, should function as a tool for insight and as an informational base for the design of interventions intended to facilitate a sense of well-being in single parents and in children of divorce. Our preference is to ascribe to a diathesis stress model, whereby, given a particular set of circumstances, divorce-resultant symptomatology is viewed as potential rather than inevitable.

The purpose of our paper is (1) to integrate what is known about divorce-associated responses in children; (2) to promote a reframing approach by focusing on that which may be evaluated as positive and contributing to the present well-being and future successes of those children; and (3) to guide practitioners as they work both programmatically and in direct service with children of divorce and single parents.

DIVORCE AS A MAJOR DISRUPTIVE EXPERIENCE

It would be difficult to argue that divorce is not a major disruptive experience that imposes primary impact upon all family members. Major systemic changes result as well and need to be accounted for. Characteristically, various levels of adjustment are required of family members and experiences that may be novel and for which they are possibly unprepared. Our observation is that many changes, resulting from the integration process, can be classified within the following categories: (1) primary psychological or emotional responses with accompanying behavioral manifestations; (2) geographic changes influencing and/or compounding adjustment processes; (3) systemic alterations; and (4) economic issues affecting phenomenological adjustment. Having information that broadens one's understanding of all potential changes will most assuredly enhance the ability of practitioners to be maximally facilitative in intervention.

Primary Psychological or Emotional Adjustment Responses and Accompanying Behavioral Manifestations

It has been frequently documented in the literature that both parents and children may be subject to psychological and behavioral modifications subsequent to divorce. Levintin (1979) in summarizing previous research on the divorce process, concluded that severe stress and disorganization are frequently experienced by families in the first post-divorce year. Mothers and fathers were found to possess feelings of incompetency, loneliness, alienation, and depression. Behaviorally, it was noted that divorced parents were observed to be less likely to make maturity demands on children, to be consistent in discipline, to reason with children, to communicate effectively with them, or to be affectionate with them. From this arises the observation that lifestyle changes that impact the emotional schemata of the custodial parent and are manifested behaviorally in parent-child relationships are likely to occur.

To assess the disruptive nature of divorce on the lives of individuals, Mitchell-Flynn and Hutchinson (1988) conducted a longitudinal study of the problems and concerns of urban divorced men at three points in time: one month, six months, and one year following divorce. Finances, social relationships, and loneliness were major areas of concern for these men at Time 1 but were found to decrease over time. Men in that study thought less about how the children were doing at Time 1 then about financial matters, but those concerns were reversed by Time 2. McCabe (1981) assessed similar concerns in a longitudinal study of women post-divorce. Although the concerns differed in intensity and in timing in the Hutchinson et al. (1988) study of men and the McCabe (1981) study of women post-divorce, similar concerns were identified and the need for considerable post-divorce adjustment on the part of both men and women was indicated. Although reactions to divorce would not be expected to be identical in each situation or within each person, it is well documented that divorce-related problems do exist.

Indeed, behavioral manifestations have also been noted in some children experiencing the divorce of their parents. These behaviors are commonly attributed to changes in family structure. These children may exhibit "higher levels of dependent, disobedient, aggressive, demanding, unaffectionate, and whining behaviors" (Guidubaldi et al., p. 302). Drake and Shallenberger (1981) noted marked changes in the behavior of some children which may include restlessness, obstinate acts, disruptiveness, and impulsiveness. Magrab (1978) promoted the belief that children are stressed by divorce/separation and exhibit behaviors typically associated with anxiety.

Documented emotional responses in children indicate a potentially wide range of feelings. Confusion, anger, guilt, fear, and depression are possible as well as cognitively based notions of insecurity, isolation, shame, and a sense of being different (Kelly & Wallerstein, 1977). Magrab (1978) asserts that, emotionally, children experience a phenomena similar to that of a loss following death. Denial, anger, and eventual acceptance are thought to be part of the total schemata in the child but may be manifested differently in individual cases, depending upon a number of factors. The notion is that feelings of separation anxiety intermingled with feelings of helplessness and rejection are frequent. Depression and its associated symptomatology are likely to appear as well.

However, contrasting research (Hutchinson, Valutis, Brown, & White, 1988; Johnson & Hutchinson, 1988) found no statistically significant differences in self-concepts of children from intact, single-parent, or stepfamilies. Parallel studies were conducted with both institutionalized and non-institutionalized children in grades five through twelve.

Of particular interest and significance is the work of Warren, Ilgen, Grew, Konanc, and Amara (1985). They conceptualize divorce as a process occurring over time and requiring a series of adaptations. Attempting to account for the frequently overlooked and difficult to examine time variable data from a 15-year longitudinal study indicates that symptoms of stress may be acutely manifested in the five-year period following divorce but that no significant differences between children experiencing divorce and children not experiencing divorce remain at 15 years post-divorce. Children often show major adjustment and improvement within two and a half years post-divorce (Warren, Grew, Ilgen, Konac, Van Bourgondien, & Amara, 1984). A third frequently promoted approach is that of referring to the one-year period following divorce as the "crisis period." Such studies utilizing time as an independent variable suggest that successful adjustments by children can and do occur post-divorce.

In light of this reframing position, two primary questions are thus raised: (1) What variables are detrimental to or enhance psychological and behavioral post-divorce adjustment potential in children? (2) Should these be extrapolated, further investigated, and effectively addressed in preventive and post-divorce interventions designed to facilitate the ability of children (and parents) to make positive adjustments to change in their lives?

Geographic and Systemic Modifications

It was found that 40% of children having experienced divorce had moved to new neighborhoods (Schlesinger, 1982). Thus, divorce adjustment in children may be complicated by lateral changes associated with new environments. For children and single parents, the reality of divorce often necessitates change in schools, neighborhoods, and peers. Church and/or other affiliatory connections may be disrupted, altered, or discontinued.

Changes such as modified interaction patterns and basic structural alterations also frequently occur in the primary family unit following divorce. As noted by Schlesinger (1982), these changes extend beyond the obvious absence of one parent. It is his observation that one parent replaces two in most cases and that the noncustodial parent is seen less.

Responsibilities and duties associated with the home and family are frequently reorganized and reassigned during and subsequent to transition. It appears that compensatory efforts are made in adjustment to the absence of one parent and the modified role of the other. Extended family relationships undergo change as well. Schlesinger (1982) further noted that over 70% of the participants in his study reported decreased contact with the paternal extended family.

In homes where custody is awarded to the mother, the necessity of maternal employment may create a reality whereby she is less available for guidance and supervision (Schlesinger, 1982). As reported by older siblings, surrogate compensatory parenting behaviors may emerge in response to the modified role of the mother and the now-absent father. Cited are new sibling responsibilities such as the giving of advice, disciplining of other siblings, teaching sports, sitting at the head of the table, and teaching about and discussing sex. Some children report working part-time and paying for clothing, caring for younger siblings, playing a paternal role, and/or being a listening post for the parent. Pragmatically, children may now find it necessary to fix things around the house, to shop for food, to cook, and to clean (Schlesinger, 1982).

Economic Issues that Significantly Impact Phenomenology

While divorce may signal an end to or impasse in inter-parental conflict and battling, a new battle emerges and perhaps is sustained indefinitely as the mother struggles to survive economically. Wodarski (1982) observed that "the most critical aspect of the divorce process appears to be loss of income for the [custodial] mother with children" (p. 313). The average loss in family income sustained by a custodial mother with children in the United States is 74%, and two-thirds of divorced females report significantly lowered household income.

Glick (1979) cited divorce as the most common cause of single-parent households. Since 1970, such households have increased by 11%; in 90% of them, a female functions as head (Guidubaldi et al., 1983). One in seven families living in the United States is headed by a female with no husband present. Two-thirds of female-headed and single-parent families live below the poverty level (U.S. Dept. of Commerce, 1981).

While conducting research on the children of divorce in an attempt to provide more definitive conclusions about the impact of parental divorce upon children and to resolve earlier conflicting data, Guidubaldi et al. (1983) noted an unexpected finding: nationwide random sampling comparing intact and divorced families indicated a significant difference in income. The median income for the intact sample was between $25,000 and $29,000. The median income for the divorced sample was between $10,000 and $14,999.

Pett (1982) noted similar findings. She studied 206 single-parent families (411 children) where divorce had occurred within the past two years and found that 58% reported incomes ranging from $5,000 to $15,000 per year. Another 25% reported incomes of less than $6,000 per year. Less than 5% reported earnings in excess of $40,000 per year.

What is currently labeled "the feminization of poverty" may complicate and intensify the needs of the children of divorce in our culture. Research suggests that a 50% drop in family income is significantly related to psychological maladjustment in children and behavioral difficulties in school (Wodarski, 1982).

Being cognizant of such findings, related to the economic impact of divorce, may guide practitioners in direct service intervention as well as influencing programmatic endeavors in agencies and schools. It may be that successful post-divorce adjustment in children is more adequately facilitated with additional emphasis placed upon the employment needs of the custodial parent. Career counseling and vocational guidance, as well as support services for single parents, seem appropriate in conjunction with other types of child-focused intervention. Politically, a humanistic position assumed by professional organizations and individuals that is supportive of Equal Opportunity and concern for human welfare as priority items should be forwarded.

FACILITATING THE ADJUSTMENT OF CHILDREN TO DIVORCE

It is contended in the bulk of published research that some common identifiable factors contribute to the ability of the child to adjust post-divorce. Accounting for these identified commonalities in the design of preventive intervention strategies may best serve the needs of an emerging and rapidly growing client population known to educators and service providers as single parents and children of divorce. When viewed strategically and creatively, a variety of possibilities for effective intervention can be envisioned as is overviewed later in this work.

Wallerstein and Kelly (1980) identified seven variables as having a positive effect upon the child's ability to adjust. They noted (1) parental ability to resolve post-divorce conflict and anger; (2) ability of the custodial parent to successfully resume the parenting role; (3) ability of the non-custodial parent to keep a mutually satisfying relationship with the child; (4) personality characteristics of the child and the ability to develop coping skills; (5) the ability of the child to find and use support systems; (6) diminished depressive or angry responses by the child; and (7) age and sex of the child. Of particular significance is the assertion that children who view consequences as within their locus of control and who accurately comprehend interpersonal relationships are more likely to accomplish positive adjustment. It would seem that all children might benefit from curriculum exposing them to information addressing these two critical concerns.

Guidubaldi et al. (1983) noted the following specific characteristics in children who adjust well to parental divorce: (1) having earlier and regular bedtimes; (2) viewing less television; (3) participating in organized after school activities; (4) having more contact with the non-custodial parent; (5) being encouraged by parent and teachers to engage in hobbies and to strive for academic excellence; (6) having parents who are less likely to use strong discipline or rejecting child-rearing practices; and above all (7) attending school in safe, orderly, and predictable environments. Educating parents and future parents in sound parenting behaviors and practices may have significant potential.

Pett (1982) examined family correlates of children's social adjustment following divorce. She suggests that the most significant factor related to the satisfactory social adjustment of children is the sustaining or development of a positive relationship with the custodial parent. Further, greater social adjustment in parents is significantly related to greater social adjustment in children. However, it is interesting to note that she did not find a definitive relationship between the child's social adjustment and his/her relationship with the non-custodial parent. This differs from most other research.

Pett also charges that economic issues have an indirect effect on the child's social adjustment by virtue of their impact upon the custodial parent. She proposes that sound and timely intervention is necessary. According to her, children who resolve whatever initial conflicts they have concerning the divorce score significantly higher regarding satisfactory post-divorce adjustment.

Wodarski (1982) focused on the parent as facilitator of adjustment in children also. According to this work, a custodial parent who exhibits consistent discipline and develops a parenting strategy of warmth, clearly defined rules, and extensive verbal compromise facilitates the adjustment of his/her children. Most helpful to children is the custodial parent who does not maintain or increase his/her negative view of the ex-spouse and does not blame the partner for the dissolution. A parent who holds positive attitudes toward the ex-spouse and establishes satisfactory visitation rights will do much to enhance the adjustment of his/her children.

Considering the excellent findings of the various researchers cited and in view of our own experiences, it is our opinion that perhaps the following parental characteristics are central to the satisfactory adjustment of children to divorce: (1) low pre-and post-divorce inter-parental conflict and generally positive relations between parents; (2) general agreement between separated parents with regard to childrearing techniques; (3) the effective use of support systems and reduced level of stress with positive adjustment relative to the divorce by the custodial parent; (4) authoritative management style executed by the custodial parent; (5) availability of the non-custodial parent post-separation; and (6) open discussion between parent and child.

A variety of potential intervention strategies becomes apparent when one becomes cognizant of the critical linkage between sound parenting strategies and positive adjustment potential in single-parent families and children of divorce. Our observations indicate that a key stimulus to adjustment is the ability of service providers to instill within families in transition a sense of hopefulness, optimism, locus of control, and the ability to cope and manage.

CRITICISM OF RESEARCH

Obviously, much can be learned via the examination of what is known and written about the effect divorce has upon children and those factors common among children and families that appear to adjust well. However, it is important to note that the research upon which such notions have been based and promoted is not without criticism. Frequent and perhaps valid criticism of research methodology is found. Implications can be gleaned by those whose objective it is to provide effective intervention strategy.

While most of the research investigating the adjustment of children to divorce is based upon the assumption that it is the divorce per se or the breaking up of the family unit to which adjustments must be made, a differing perspective is offered by Emery (1982). Emery argues that "much of the association between divorce and child behavior problems may well be attributable to a frequently overlooked third variable" (p. 314). In this conceptualization, it is inter-parental conflict that is cited as the basis for compensatory adjustment behaviors in children rather than the separation of parents per se. Emery cautions that the expectation that marital turmoil causes behavior problems in children may not only create biased rating data but may also be problematic in that a self-fulfilling prophecy may result.

Magrab (1978) hints at a notion similar to that of Emery. He charges that "it is a commonly held belief that children of divorce are at a greater risk . . . but most studies in comparing children of divorce with children of intact homes rarely include the effects of living in intact unhappy homes" (p. 235).

Emery (1982) notes three of the most common problems perceived by him in the research on marital and child difficulties as they relate to one another. Cited as a primary methodological flaw is the use of biased sampling techniques. His concern is that divorce impacted families are studied with infrequent inclusion of and comparison to intact families. Non-independent data, where judges of child behavior are aware of the marital status of parents, is a second concern of Emery and is used to support the notion that foreknowledge creates a self-fulfilling prophecy effect, obscuring valid results. Called for are refined methods of measurement supported by the assertion that those in current use lack reliability and validity.

Guidubaldi et al. (1983) criticize limited data-gathering procedures, biased sampling, and inadequate controls as "serious methodology weaknesses" (p. 300). They also feel that restricted sampling is a principal methodological concern. They charge that much work in the area subject to this weakness "cannot be generalized to the total population" (p. 303). According to them, samples are frequently small, based on ambiguous criteria, and limited to specific settings or geographical areas. It is also noted that samples almost exclusively represent Caucasian, middle-and upper-class families where the mother is the custodial parent. They underscore the notion that potential environmental mediating variables are overlooked and not controlled for in methodology.

They also attribute major limitations of previous research to inadequate psychometric measurement tools. Cited specifically is a lack of "psychometrically adequate indices of school age children's cognitive and social competencies" (p. 303) necessary for comparative analysis of cognitive and social changes during the adjustment period.

More generally, the Guidubaldi et al. (1983) researchers are critical of the amount and quality of research done in the area noting that "it is surprising that so little has been done to provide an empirical understanding of the impact of parental divorce on children" (p. 300). Cited also is a lack of longitudinal research that discriminates between crises-related effects and long-term impact. However, it is noted that some work such as that of Wallerstein and Kelly (1979) is now emerging.

Of major significance is the assertion supported by the Guidubaldi et al. (1983) study that divorce adjustment in children is contingent upon a complex interactive component unique to individuals experientially. They contend that "the interaction of familial, social, cultural, economic, legal, and psychological systems with the experience and effects of divorce has not been adequately documented" (p. 301).

Similarly, the Lamb (1977) study concludes that while children of divorced parents, compared with children of intact homes are definitely "at risk [regarding psychological difficulty], it is not possible to specify flatly the effects of divorce, because there are no sequelae that can be identified as the inevitable consequences of divorce and family dissolution" (p. 171).

It is hoped that interested professionals will continue to critically examine what is written, pursue research with the objective of refinement, and attempt to further extrapolate variables and refine psychometric tools that will enhance research efforts. Meanwhile, interventions based upon what is known, tempered by critical analysis of established data, may comprise our best effort to facilitate post-divorce adjustment in children. It may be that weaknesses in previous research contribute heavily to an erroneous notion that children of divorce and single-parent families embody pathologies and that healthy adjustment is, at best, difficult to achieve.

WAYS IN WHICH SCHOOL PERSONNEL AND MENTAL HEALTH PROFESSIONALS CAN ALIGN AND PROVIDE SERVICES TO FACILITATE SINGLE PARENTS AND THE CHILDREN OF DIVORCE

As societal changes are experienced, schools must now anticipate having more pupils from single-parent, low-income families. Consideration for the individual needs of these children, and their families as well, must be given priority as continued focus is placed upon educational reform in the United States. Through this alignment, a greater number of children and their parents can be facilitated in an effective manner toward the end goals of enhanced adjustment processes and subsequent and continued well-being. Parents and children who have achieved these goals are more likely to contribute to and experience academic and personal successes that will be of benefit to society at large.

With increasing frequency, the view is expressed that schools should provide services to this identified special needs population. According to Drake and Shallenberger (1981), adults polled in a 1980 Gallup survey indicated that teachers should have special training to deal effectively with the problems of children from divorced or single-parent families. Specifically endorsed were the availability of school counseling personnel during the evening hours for parents who work during the day and the provision of after school activities so that children may avoid going home to an empty house. They emphasize that educating children to their fullest potential is jeopardized when unresolved emotional issues exist. They also observe that school-based intervention strategies are just beginning to appear in the literature and that little evaluative information is available. Based on our review of current literature, it appears that this is true.

Drake and Shallenberger (1981) assert that schools are obligated to recognize and act upon the knowledge they possess regarding children of divorce. A wider dissemination of information framed with hopefulness and optimism in mind may be in order. They suggest three general intervention strategy approaches: direct, indirect, or preventive. They contend that all effective approaches, however, are and should be based upon a primary first step, divorce-specific assessment.

Assessment at dual levels is recommended. They suggest that a focused interview should assess individual needs and dictate intervention strategy at the interpersonal level. In addition, assessment of the particular school population is necessary. The following questions should be addressed: (1) What percentage of the school population is comprised of children who have experienced parental divorce and live in single-parent families? (2) What modifications of school services and procedures are in order? (3) What, if any, special services are warranted? Our observation is that assessment of school populations is infrequently done. Our position is that needs definition is critical to the design and implementation of effective intervention strategies that are geographically specific.

Direct services can be provided through individual and group counseling. Individual counseling, provided by school guidance personnel or by referral as appropriate, may be child-focused or systemically oriented. Williams (1984) has suggested that a mediation approach, with focus upon obtaining parental cooperation in helping the child, is effective. In her work with school children and divorced parents, she claims success in working to enhance communication between the parents. She further claims that her role may be that of a "mouthpiece" for the child.

Counseling groups, in and out of school environments, may facilitate the adjustment of children as well. When difficulties are noted by school personnel, children may be referred to groups focusing upon coping during the crises period, stress-management, facing and dealing with losses, facilitating self-disclosure, and communication skills. The benefits of group counseling in general are well known to practitioners and do not warrant further explanation here.

In addition to more obvious direct services, schools are in a unique position to provide *indirect services* that may be helpful to children affected by divorce as well to those who work with these children. Drake and Shallenberger (1981) suggest training programs that are directed toward increasing the sensitivity of school personnel to the needs of children of divorce. Teacher in-service time may be appropriately used to this end (Williams & Hoffman, 1984). Mental health professionals and university related service providers could be instrumental in teaching guidance counselors to work with children individually and in groups. Skills and knowledge necessary may include the ability to recognize and address typical and atypical effects of divorce upon children, associated behavioral manifestations, factors that affect the degree of trauma experienced by the child, and appropriate and useful methods of assessment and psychometric tools. Restoration of hopefulness and optimism in the client population should be emphasized.

Modifications in school curriculum could effectively address the phenomena in an indirect manner also. Suggested possibilities are social studies units that address family dynamics as influenced by societal changes. Courses at the secondary level in child development and effective parenting are potentially useful indirect approaches.

Parental involvement and referral to appropriate service providers may also indirectly enhance the well-being of children in the school environment. Parents may benefit from support groups and parenting classes among other services. School counselors can serve as important and effective liaisons and mediaries in their role as referral agents.

Preventive services are a third avenue worthy of serious consideration by school personnel. According to Drake and Shallenberger (1981), curriculum changes and additions that facilitate the ability of children to understand change in their lives and to develop coping mechanisms for change are useful in preparing them for changes in their own lives and in the lives of others. Programs that increase self-disclosure and sensitivity to others may likewise help children cope with and understand personal and societal changes.

CONCLUSIONS

Using what each of us knows (or what we believe we know) to plan for and help children and single parents experiencing divorce and associated changes is to be encouraged. However, caution is warranted. It is the tendency in our society to view the one-parent family as pathological. Historically, the intact nuclear family has supported our values structure in society at large. Viewing the decline of the nuclear family as the cause of child pathology may be erroneous and may be subject to self-fulfilling prophecy properties that are detrimental to the goal of enhancing the well-being of these children.

Research indicates that divorce can lead to "different" but not necessarily "disturbed" patterns of development (Kurdak & Siesky, 1978). Some data indicates that the stress experienced by a child during and subsequent to parental divorce is not primarily attributable to the break up and to the resulting single-parent family experience but rather to the turmoil of parental conflict experienced before, during, and after the divorce (Emery, 1982; Schlesinger, 1982). The removal of tension and fear from the home environment subsequent to divorce may actually enhance child development (Kurdak & Siesky, 1978).

Schlesinger (1982) suggests that the "myths about divorce are distorted" (p. 6). It is noted that unhappiness, anxiety, fear, and hostility manifested by divorcing parents may affect children rather than the divorce, per se. A custodial parent with a positive social network of family and friends and a satisfactory relationship with the non-custodial parent will enhance the adjustment of his/her children.

It may be that our efforts can be best directed toward providing a reframing approach to parents and children experiencing divorce. There is evidence that children form single-parent families are good decision makers and that they have strengths and maturities associated with their experiences. It seems to our advantage as professionals to be able to facilitate the cognitive reframing of parents and children in such a way that hopefulness and a sense of assurance and control can be implemented and sustained.

School personnel and mental health professionals can be instrumental in the reframing process. As highlighted by Bilge and Kaufman (1983), whether or not the escalation of divorce incidence and resultant single-parent households become disastrous and detrimental to society at large depends upon the "availability of sufficient material resources, supportive social networks, and . . . culturally-structured attitudes toward it" (p. 17).

Bilge and Kaufman (1983) bring emphasis to our position that all individuals, regardless of marital status or familial structure, share an identified need to be nurtured and prepared to cope with the inevitable changes of life: "The well-being of children in any society can be assessed impressionistically by the adequacy of the nurturing, love and training they receive in preparation for the roles they eventually must play as adults, and by the resources and opportunities available to them for achieving dignity and respect as human beings in the society to which they belong" (p. 71). Educators and service providers can benefit from an increased awareness and understanding of the critical issues faced by a society in transition. Hopefully, they will develop an adequate and solidly grounded approach in service provision that communicates optimism and hope to those who experience a disrupting modification in family structure.

REFERENCES

Bilge, B., & Kaufman, G. (1983). Children of divorce and one-parent families: Cross-cultural perspectives. *Family Relations, 32,* 59-71.

Brown, B. F. (1980). A study of the school needs of children from one-parent families. *Phi Delta Kappan,* p. 547-550.

Cantor, D. W. (1977). School based groups for children of divorce. *Journal of Divorce, 1,* 183-187.

Drake, A. E., & Shallenberger, S. (1981). Children of separation and divorce: A review of school programs and implications for the psychologist. *School Psychology Review*, *10*, 54-61.

Emery, R. E. (1982). Interparental conflict and the children of discord and divorce. *Psychological Bulletin*, *92*, 310-330.

Epstein, Y. M., & Bordwin, C. M. (1985). Could this happen?: A game for children of divorce. *Psychotherapy*, *22*, 295-299.

Guidubaldi, J., Cleminshaw, H. K., Perry, J. D., & McLaughlin, C. S. (1983). The impact of parental divorce on children: Report on the nationwide NASP Study. *School Psychology Review*, *12*, 300-323.

Hepworth, J., Ryder, R. G., & Dreyer, A. S. (1984). The effects of parental loss on the formation of intimate relationships. *Journal of Marital and Family Therapy*, *10*, 73-82.

Hurley, E. C., Taylor, V. L., & Riley, M. T. (1984). Therapeutic interventions for children of divorce. *Family Therapy*, *11*, 261-268.

Hutchinson, R. L., Valutis, W. E., Brown, D. T., & White, J. S. (1988). The effects of family structure on institutionalized children's self-concepts. *Adolescence* (in press).

Johnson, M. & Hutchinson, R. L. (1988). The effects of family structure on children's self-concepts. *Journal of Divorce* (in press).

Kelly, J. B., & Wallerstein, J. S. (1977). Brief interventions with children in divorcing families. *American Journal of Orthopsychiatry*, *47*, 23-36.

Kurdak, L. A. & Siesky, A. E. (1978). Divorced single parents' perceptions of child-related problems. *Journal of Divorce*, *1*, 361-370.

Lamb, M. E. (1977). The effects of divorce on children's personality development. *Journal of Divorce*, *1*, 163-173.

Levintin, T. E. (1979). Children of divorce. *Journal of Social Issues*, *35*, 1-25.

McCabe, M. E. (1981). Coping strategies of urban divorced women at the time of divorce and six months later. *Dissertation Abstracts International*, *42*, 4608a. (University Microfilms No. 81-25736)

Magrab, P. R. (1978). For the sake of the children: A review of the psychological effects of divorce. *Journal of Divorce*, *1*, 233-245.

Mitchell-Flynn, C., & Hutchinson, R. L. (March, 1988). *A longitudinal study of the problems and concerns of urban divorced men*. Paper presented at the American Association for Counseling and Development Annual Convention, Chicago, Il.

Pett, M. G. (1982). Correlates of children's social adjustment following divorce. *Journal of Divorce*, *5*, 25-39.

Schlesinger, B. (1982). Children's viewpoints of living in a one-parent family. *Journal of Divorce*, *5*, 1-23.

Schmid, R. (1986, Dec. 14). Women postponing marriage longer. *The Anderson, IN, Herald* (AP), 18.

Wallerstein, J. S., & Kelly, J. B. (1979). Children and divorce: A review. *Social Work*, *24*, 468-475.

Warren, N. J., Grew, R. S., Ilgen, E. R., Konanc, J. T., Van Bourgondien,

M. E., & Amara, I. A. (1984). Parenting after divorce: Preventive programs for divorcing families. Paper prepared for NIMH Workshop, "Children and Divorce," Washington, D. C., June 14-15.

Warren, N. J., Ilgen, E. R., Grew, R. G., Konanc, J. T., & Amara, I. A. (1985). Time since separation: Another perspective on the NASP study of divorce. *School Psychology Review*, *14*, 373-377.

Williams, M. B. (1984). Family dissolution: An issue for the schools. *Children Today*, July-August, 24-29.

Wodarski, J. S. (1982). Single parents and children: A review for social workers. *Family Therapy*, *9*, 311-320.

Sequelae to Marital Disruption in Children

Martin L. Levin

SUMMARY. Using nationally representative surveys (The Health Examination Survey, Cycles II and III) this project attempts to assess the impact of marital disruption on children and youth in the following broad areas of human development: emotional development, physical health, moral development, peer group relations, school adjustment, cognitive achievement and intellectual development. It is argued that mechanisms by which marital disruption might produce effects can be summarized in three models—the trauma model, the structural model and the deficiency model. For the most part, the impact of marital adjustment on the study population is small, generally indirect and, where differences are found, about as likely to improve the development of the child from the divorced household as to retard it. The results are interpreted as providing mild support to the structural model.

In both absolute and relative terms, the number of children reared during a significant portion of their childhood in the absence of one natural parent is increasing. The number of divorces granted in the United States has increased dramatically since 1962, more than doubling between 1966 and 1975, exceeding one million for the first time in history in 1975. The divorce rate rose annually from 1966 to 1979 and after declining slightly in the early 80s started back up in 1984. The number of children involved in divorces and annulments has also increased steadily since 1960, topping one million per year since 1971 (National Center for Health Statistics,

Martin L. Levin, PhD, is on the faculty of the Department of Sociology, Emory University, Atlanta, GA 30322.

The research reported in this paper was supported by the National Institute of Mental Health NIMH Research Grant 5ROI MH 34450.

1986). According to some estimates, over the next few decades perhaps one-third of all children born in the U.S. will be directly affected by divorce (Bane, 1976; Bumpass and Rindfuss, 1978). Add to these estimates children affected by parental separation of the death of a parent and the prospect seems to be that between 33 percent and 44 percent of the children in the United States will, at one time or another, be reared in the absence of a parent.

There is an extensive yet contradictory literature on the significance of the absence of one of the parents — generally the father — for such pathological effects upon the child as: low school achievement (Duetch, 1960; Duetch and Brown, 1965; Duncan, 1967; Blanchard and Biller, 1971; Hess and Camara, 1979; Kinard and Reinherz, 1986), poor personal adjustment (Nye. 1957; Landis, 1960; Siegman, 1966; Felner et al., 1975; Wallerstein and Kelly, 1975, 1976, 1980; Hetherington et al., 1977; Levinger and Moles, 1979; Zill and Peterson, 1986), gender-role identification (Pederson, 1966; Biller, 1969; Hetherington and Deur, 1971); and dampened cognitive development (Hetherington and Deur, 1971; Jordan and Spaner, 1974).

On the one hand, Walters and Stinnett (1971) report a general consensus in the field that factors such as academic achievement, leadership and creative thinking of children are positively related to a warm, accepting and understanding parent-child relationship — a relationship likely to be affected negatively by the process of marital disruption. Divorce has been linked to stress and disequilibrium in the family (Hansen and Hill, 1964; Rosenberg, 1965), and it is generally assumed that the process of divorce itself and the withdrawal of one parent is damaging to the child (Burchinal, 1964). Herzog and Sudia (1970), in their review of over 40 publications on the effect of father absence in the family, note the repeated conclusion that single parent families tend to be deficient in such apparently important pedagogic qualities for adequate child development as authority patterns, appropriate role models, parental support and attention, and a sufficient level of income to meet the physical needs of the child.

On the other hand, a number of studies have found no relationship between parental absence and child development. In a study of the characteristics of adolescents from unbroken, broken and reconstituted families, Burchinal (1964) found no adverse effects due to divorce or separation. In their literature review, Walters and Stinnet (1971) reported they found no significant differences in achievement between children from one-parent and those from two-parent homes. Further, in her review, Bane (1976) notes that studies which adequately control for economic status show little or no differences between children from one- and two-parent homes on school achievement, school adjustment and delinquent behaviors.

Divorce does not necessarily produce psychological damage in the child in every case, nor is the presence of both parents always beneficial. Studies by Goode (1956), Nye (1957), Burchinal (1964), Hetherington et al. (1976) and Kelly and Berg (1978) indicate that a happy one-parent family is less stress producing for the child than an unhappy two-parent one. Landis (1962) found no difference between divorced parents and unhappy two-parent homes. Brandwein et al. (1974) reports that children who appear to be distressed most by divorce are those whose parents are not in the home after the divorce. It is the nature of the home environment that appears critical in determining the impact of divorce on the child's emotional and intellectual development (Herzog and Sudia, 1970; Hetherington and Deur, 1971).

Furthermore, where effects of marital disruption upon the child have been demonstrated, the mechanisms by which the effects come about have not always been identified. Generally, one of three models has been implicitly employed to interpret effects where they are observed—the trauma model, the structural model, and the deficiency model.

The first of these models concentrates upon the stress and disequilibrium caused by the disruption of the marriage and the events leading up to it. These trauma are seen as disturbing to the child to the extent that both performance and development are affected (Hansen and Hill, 1967; Burchinal, 1964; Rosenberg, 1965; Hetherington and Deur, 1971). The second of these models emphasizes the structural constraints surrounding child rearing in broken marriages subsequent to the disruption. The breakup of the household is seen as affecting the social and economic status of the family and in turn the development of the child (Herzog and Sudia, 1970). The third model, like the second, places emphasis on family situation subsequent to the breakup of the household and concentrates upon the deficiencies in the child's socialization and development brought about by the permanent absence from the home of one of the family socializing agents (Bohannan, 1971; Brandwein et al., 1974; Nye, 1957; Marsden, 1969). Duberman (1977), on the other hand, challenges the deficiency model.

The literature on the impact of marital disruption on child development is inconsistent, contradictory and inconclusive. Much of the research has failed to employ proper controls both in terms of variables which might directly affect the development of the child and those which might simultaneously affect the development of the child and the propensity of the parents to separate or divorce. The lack of conclusiveness also results from restricted study population and samples. Walters and Stinnet (1971), Brandwein et al. (1974), and Bane (1976) point out that the great majority of the studies tend to compare two-parent families directly with single-parent families and fail to consider controls for socioeconomic status, age of child, and the like. Few of the studies are based upon national samples. Often only the children of disrupted parents are studied (e.g., Landis, 1960) leaving comparison to non-disrupted families to be made implicitly. Even when comparison groups are included, the sampling designs employed tend to rely on captive samples (e.g., children in a particular elementary school, high school, or university; Landis, 1960; Sutton-Smith et al., 1968; Blanchard and Biller, 1971; Burchinal, 1964; Bowerman and Irish, 1962) or self-selecting samples (e.g., families seeking counseling adjustment or participating in particular programs; Felner et al., 1975; Ryker et al., 1971).

This research attempts to overcome certain of these difficulties in that the study populations are nationally representative, of sufficient size to enable the simultaneous control of several variables and contain appropriate comparison populations. Specifically, an attempt is made to determine in the following broad areas of human development the impact upon children of being reared in households where one parent is absent: emotional development, physical health, moral development, peer group relations, school adjustment, cognitive achievement and intellectual development. Mediating variables controlled in this analysis include: SES of parent(s), age order of child in household, age of mother at birth of child, place of residence, household size, current marital status of rearing parent(s), race of child, sex of child, and age of child.

DATA SOURCE

The data analyzed are from the Health Examination Survey, Cycles II (children aged 6 to 11) and III (youths aged 12 to 17). These surveys, part of a major program of the National Center for Health Statistics (NCHS), are based upon a representative, probability sampling design. The data were gathered carefully and rigorously and must be considered to be of very high quality. The sampling designs, data collection techniques, instruments, and the quality control procedures have been well documented (NCHS, 1967, 1969, 1971, 1972).

The universe consisted of all non-institutionalized children residing in the United States excluding Hawaii and Alaska between the ages of 6 and 11. Residents of American Indian Reservation Lands were also excluded. Data were collected for each respondent in the Surveys through a wide array of procedures including interviewing, paper and pencil tests, and direct physical examination and testing by professional medical personnel. Parents or guardians completed a demographic and a health history questionnaire in the homes. The physical examination was conducted in special mobile vans to which the child or youth was brought. A medical examination was conducted by a physician and a nurse, a psychological examination by a psychologist, and a dental examination by a dentist. In addition, several measurements and other medical data were collected by trained technicians, including audiometry examination, EKGs and photocardiograms, vision examinations, body measurements, X-ray, height-weight and blood samples. A Health Behavior and Health Habits and History questionnaire was also filled out by the Cycle III youths.

The field work for Cycle II took place during the period July 1963 through December 1965. Of the 7,427 children selected for the sample, examinations were completed for 7,119 or 96 percent. The Cycle III field work took place during the period March 1966 through March 1970, and of the 7,514 sample youths identified, examinations were completed upon 6,768 or 90 percent. Of the

6,768 youths examined by Cycle III, 2,177 had also been examined in Cycle II. The standards of quality control in the data collection and measurement procedures of the Health Examination Survey were high. Pretesting of instrumentation, standardization of techniques and the surveillance and evaluation of residual measurement errors were all carefully and systematically accomplished (NCHS, 1972).

A minor limitation of these data is that they exclude mortality and institutionalization as possible consequences of being reared in a disrupted household. Another limitation of the Health Examination Survey data would seem to be their age, Cycle II data being collected between 1964 and 1965 and Cycle III data between 1966 and 1970. It is difficult to know to what extent time has changed the patterns by which consequences for the child of being reared in a broken or reconstituted household come about. Clearly, rather significant changes have taken place in the U.S. with respect to divorce and remarriage during the past 15 years and one of these changes has been a dramatic increase in the numbers of children in such households. Yet it would seem that given what is really a relatively small time differential, the application of proper controls and the drawing of appropriate comparisons, the problem of the time difference is small.

RESEARCH METHODS

When working with data as rich and varied as those in the Health Examination Survey, some data reduction procedure is necessary to obtain a meaningful analysis. Several stages of reduction were employed to arrive at the variables finally employed in the analysis. Every attempt was made to include as much of the information in the data as possible. Specifically, the following steps were followed. Preliminary reduction was done by eliminating variables where the marginal distributions indicated that the variation in response was not suited for further analysis. Other items were eliminated because the nature of the information was not related to the research question. After appropriate transformations, the remaining items were correlated with each other within certain theoretically derived subsets. The correlations were examined and additional items were examined and additional items were eliminated to satisfy the criterion of non-multicollinearity. An orthogonal rotation factor analysis was then applied to each of the subsets.

From each of the subsets factors were selected in terms of generally accepted criteria provided they had an eigenvalue greater than 1. All variables loading at more than .25 were then employed to create factor scores which were based on the linear combination of the codes for the variables weighted by the square of the appropriate factor loading.

These procedures created a score on each factor for each child or youth in the sample. The factor scores were organized in terms of the theoretically derived subsets and names were assigned to the factor scores for convenience in the presentation of the analysis to follow. These names are defined by the scores, but their intuitive meaning parallels to a degree their technical meaning. The computed score for each case was matched and merged with the original data record. The resulting factors, arranged by the theoretical subsets, are listed in Figure 1.

There was one addition to this procedure regarding cognitive development and achievement. Each child and youth had been administered the Weschsler Vocabulary and Block Design Subset and the Reading and Arithmetic Subsets of the Wide Range Achievement Tests. These scores were age-sex normalized to have a mean of 50 and a standard deviation of 10. Additionally, within each test the raw scores were summed and similarly normalized to have a mean of 100 and a standard deviation of 15. These normalized scores were then used to measure cognitive development and achievement.

STRATEGY OF DATA ANALYSIS

The assessment of the impact of being reared in a disrupted household was made through multiple regression analysis with the factor and normalized scores as dependent variables. The results for children ages 6 through 11 are presented in Table 1 and for youths ages 12 through 17 appear in Table 2. Within each table, the results for each factor are grouped according to the theoretical subsets. For some of the classes of dependent variables, data were available only

FIGURE 1. Extracted Factors

Cycle II   Cycle III

Prenatal and Natal Condition

                                          Birth Context
                                          Prematurity

Prematurity with no Complications
Prematurity with Complications

                    Early Growth and Development

Health During Infancy
Infant Independence and Weaning

                              Health History

Childhood Diseases

                                          Extremity Problems
                                          General Health
                                          Childhood Diseases

Growth Development and Current Health (Males)

Neuro-locomotive Problems
Size and Strength
Heart Problems
Acute nose and throat Problems
Chronic Nose and Throat Problems
Reported Eye Problems
Blood Pressure Problems
Extremity Problems Resulting from Accidents
Oral Hygiene
Ear and Hearing Problems
Abnormal lower face cavities
Severe Chronic Respiratory Problems
Discovered Eye Problems

Obesity Problem
Size, Strength and Sexual
    Development
Oral Hygiene
Hearing and Ear Problems
Acne and Blood Pressure
Heart Problem
Slimness
Sexual Maturation
Neurological Problems
Muscular/Skeletal Problems
Overall Health
Activity Restriction
Extremity Problems
Chronic Health Problems
Eye Problems
Facial Cavities
Discovered Orthodontic
    Problems
Blood Pressure
Corrected Orthodontic Problems

FIGURE 1 (continued)

Growth Development and Current Health (Females)

Cycle II

Size and Strength
Heart Problems
Neuro-locomotive Problems
Acute Nose and Throat Problems
Chronic Nose and Throat Problems
Sexual Development
Reported Eye Problems
Oral Hygiene
Extremity Problems Resulting from Accidents
Severe Chronic Respiratory Problems
Abnormal Lower Face Cavities
Ear and Hearing Problems
Blood Pressure Problems
Discovered Eye Problems

Cycle III

Obesity Problems
Maturity of Menstruation
Oral Hygiene
Ear and Hearing Problems
Slimness
Heart Problems
Neurological Problems
Size and Strength
Overall Health
Blood Pressure
Secondary Sexual
  Characteristics
Activity Restriction
Muscular/Skeletal Problems
Extremity Problems
Chronic Health Problems
Eye Problems
Facial Cavities
Discovered Orthodontic
  Problems
Corrected Orthodontic Problems
Backache Problems

Intellectual Development

Academic difficulty
Precociousness
Exceptional Performance

Exceptional Performance
Academic Difficulty
Mental Development Problems

Emotional and Psychological Adjustment

Hostile Behavior
Night Problems
Retirement Problems
Serenity
Finger Problems
Eating Habits

Delinquency
Psychological Problems
Overeating
Speech Problems
Night Problems
Emotional Adjustment
Sociability
Parental Control
Self-centeredness

FIGURE 1 (continued)

Cycle II	Cycle III
	Social Adjustment
	Social Contacts
Popularity	
Individual Activities	
Social Activities	
Peer Activities	
	Childrearing Practices
Parental Monitoring	
Parental Control of Bedtime	
	Family Relations and Family Life
	Parental Decisions
	Youth Decisions
	Health Care Decisions
	Paid Work
Work Responsibility	

36

Parent and Youth Agreement

    School Compliance
    Complete Compliance
    Close Compliance

Family Values

    Parental Values on Personal
        Qualities
    Youth's Values on Personal
        Qualities
    Youth's Values on External
        Control

TABLE 1. Impact of Parental Marital Status on Various Outcomes for Children Ages 6 Through 11 Controlling for Sex and Age of Child (Cluster A) and for Race, Birth Order, Income, Education, Household Size, Age of Mother at Birth, and Ecological Factors (Cluster B) and of the Interaction as Between Marital Status and Variables in Cluster B Plus Age

Percents

Outcome Factor	(A) ΔR^2 for Marital Status, Cluster A Controlled	(B) ΔR^2 for Marital Status, Cluster A&B Controlled	(C) Total R^2 Cluster A and B Only	(D) ΔR^2 for Interactions, Cluster A, B and Marital Status Controlled	(E) Total R^2 Marital Status, Clusters A, B & Interactions
Prenatal & Natal Conditions					
Prematurity with no complications	0.16	0.07	3.71**	1.48*	5.26**
Prematurity with complications	0.06	0.03	0.35*	0.84	1.23

Early Growth & Development

Health during infancy	0.04	0.04	0.91**	1.10	2.04**
Infant independence and weaning	0.18	0.13	3.63**	0.79	4.55**

Health History

Childhood diseases	0.13	0.16	4.19**	0.87	5.22**

Growth, Development and Current Health--Males

Neuro-locomotive problems	0.27	0.25	0.25	2.20	2.71
Size and strength	0.55*	0.27	5.15**	2.10	7.51**
Heart problems	0.19	0.18	0.36	0.37	0.91
Acute nose and throat problems	0.54*	0.49	0.69*	3.14**	4.32**

TABLE 1 (continued)

Outcome Factor	(A) ΔR² for Marital Status, Cluster A Controlled	(B) ΔR² for Marital Status, Cluster A&B Controlled	(C) Total R² Cluster A and B Only	(D) ΔR² for Interactions, Cluster A, B and Marital Status Controlled	(E) Total R² Marital Status, Clusters A, B & Interactions
Growth, Development and Current Health--Males, cont'd.					
Chronic nose and throat problems	0.72**	0.68**	0.58*	3.24**	4.50**
Reported eye problems	0.29	0.18	0.78**	2.85	3.80**
Blood pressure problems	0.16	0.25	0.56*	0.90	1.71
Extremity problems resulting from accidents	0.06	0.05	0.10	1.22	1.37

40

Oral hygiene	0.90**	0.33	5.86**	1.60	7.80**
Ear and hearing problems	0.23	0.24	0.05	1.64	1.92
Abnormal lower face cavities	0.16	0.18	0.31	2.58*	3.06**
Severe chronic respiratory problems	0.12	0.10	0.76**	0.96	1.81
Discovered eye problems	0.30	0.18	0.82**	2.87**	3.96**

Growth, Development and Current Health--Females

Size and strength	0.16	0.20	6.68**	2.20	9.08**
Heart problems	0.07	0.14	1.35**	1.32	2.81
Neuro-locomotive problems	0.12	0.12	0.64*	1.00	1.76

41

TABLE 1 (continued)

Outcome Factor	(A) ΔR^2 for Marital Status, Cluster A Controlled	(B) ΔR^2 for Marital Status, Cluster A&B Controlled	(C) Total R^2 Cluster A and B Only	(D) ΔR^2 for Interactions, Cluster A, B and Marital Status Controlled	(E) Total R^2 Marital Status, Clusters A, B & Interactions
Growth, Development and Current Health--Females, cont'd.					
Acute nose and throat problems	0.93**	0.89**	0.76**	2.18	3.83**
Chronic nose and throat problems	1.32**	1.35**	0.21	2.71**	4.26**
Sexual development	0.12	0.11	0.37	0.63	1.12

42

Reported eye problems	0.07	0.06	0.48	2.16	2.70
Oral hygiene	0.62*	0.13	6.56**	1.77	8.46**
Extremity problems from accidents	0.12	0.12	0.43	1.00	1.56
Severe chronic respiratory problems	0.23	0.19	0.49	1.65	2.33
Abnormal lower face cavities	0.27	0.28	0.60*	2.62**	3.50**
Ear and hearing problems	0.35	0.32	0.21	2.45*	2.97
Blood pressure problems	0.35	0.28	1.55**	2.13	3.96**
Discovered eye problems	0.08	0.07	0.46	2.20	2.72

TABLE 1 (continued)

Outcome Factor	(A) ΔR^2 for Marital Status, Cluster A Controlled	(B) ΔR^2 for Marital Status, Cluster A&B Controlled	(C) Total R^2 Cluster A and B Only	(D) ΔR^2 for Interactions, Cluster A, B and Marital Status Controlled	(E) Total R^2 Marital Status, Clusters A, B & Interactions
Intellectual Development					
Academic difficulty	1.41**	0.60**	12.36*	1.69*	14.66
Precociousness	0.15	0.23	4.90*	1.08	6.21**
Exceptional performance	1.13**	0.52**	11.17**	1.46*	13.14**
Cognitive Development and Achievement					
WISC vocabulary	1.74**	0.57**	31.99**	0.71	33.28**

WISC block design	1.62**	0.28*	18.29**	0.98	19.55**
WRAT arithmetic	1.91**	0.32**	19.30**	0.97	20.60**
WRAT reading	2.12**	0.18	23.05**	1.01	24.25**
Combined WISC	2.24**	0.50**	33.06**	0.84	34.40**
Combined WRAT	2.36**	0.27**	23.05**	1.00*	26.32**

Emotional and Psychological Adjustment

Hostile behavior	1.48**	0.92**	7.60**	2.31**	10.83**
Night problems	0.54**	0.51**	4.98**	1.39	6.88**
Retirement problems	0.32	0.26	1.20**	1.45	2.92**
Serenity	0.40*	0.34*	2.97**	1.84**	5.16**
Finger problems	0.15	0.18	1.94**	1.62*	3.73**
Speech articulation	0.46**	0.32*	2.70*	1.47	4.49**
Eating habits	0.12	0.07	2.24**	1.39	3.69**

TABLE 1 (continued)

Outcome Factor	(A) ΔR² for Marital Status, Cluster A Controlled	(B) ΔR² for Marital Status, Cluster A&B Controlled	(C) Total R² Cluster A and B Only	(D) ΔR² for Interactions, Cluster A, B and Marital Status Controlled	(E) Total R² Marital Status, Clusters A, B & Interactions
Social Adjustment					
Popularity	0.49**	0.44**	3.92**	1.40	5.74**
Individual activities	0.19	0.21	9.40**	1.73**	11.35**
Social activities	1.03**	0.26*	27.85**	1.06	29.17
Peer activities	0.35*	0.16	10.35**	1.40*	11.91**

Childrearing Practices

Parental monitoring	2.60**	0.51**	32.99**	1.15**	33.94**
Parental control of bedtime	0.19	0.15	0.85**	1.26	2.26**

Family Relations and Family Life

Work responsibility	0.65**	0.30*	13.30**	1.08	14.67**

*significant beyond the .05 level
**significant beyond the .01 level

TABLE 2. Impact of Parental Marital Status on Various Outcomes for Youths Ages 12 Through 17 Controlling for Sex and Age of Youth (Cluster A) and for Race, Birth Order, Income, Education, Household Size, Age of Mother at Birth, and Ecological Factors (Cluster B) and of the Interactions Between Marital Status and Variables in Cluster B Plus Age

PERCENTS

Outcome Factor	(A) ΔR^2 for Marital Status, Cluster A Controlled	(B) ΔR^2 for Marital Status, Cluster A&B Controlled	(C) Total R^2 Cluster A and B Only	(D) ΔR^2 for Interactions, Cluster A, B and Marital Status Controlled	(E) Total R^2 Marital Status, Clusters A, B & Interactions
Prenatal and Natal Conditions					
Birth context	1.40**	0.50**	20.68**	2.69**	23.87**
Prematurity	0.27*	0.27*	1.12**	1.28	2.68**

Health History

Extremity problems	0.17	0.07	2.42**	0.97	3.46**
General health	0.22	0.18	2.48**	1.55	4.21**
Childhood diseases	1.12	0.51**	2.41**	1.88**	4.80**

Growth, Development and Current Health--Males

Obesity problems	0.16*	0.14	4.91*	1.52	6.58**
Size, strength and sexual development	0.56	0.18	4.47**	1.50	6.15**
Oral hygiene	2.88**	1.44**	13.76**	3.76**	18.95**
Hearing and ear problems	0.77**	0.75*	1.15**	2.21	4.12*

TABLE 2 (continued)

Outcome Factor	(A) ΔR^2 for Marital Status, Cluster A Controlled	(B) ΔR^2 for Marital Status, Cluster A&B Controlled	(C) Total R^2 Cluster A and B Only	(D) ΔR^2 for Interactions, Cluster A, B and Marital Status Controlled	(E) Total R^2 Marital Status, Clusters A, B & Interactions
Growth, Development and Current Health--Males, cont'd.					
Acne and blood pressure	0.40*	0.17	38.48**	1.72	40.37**
Heart problems	0.10	0.09	0.90**	2.40	3.39
Slimness	1.17**	0.82**	1.56**	3.08*	5.46**
Sexual maturation	0.26	0.24	1.09**	2.49	3.81*
Neurological problems	0.15	0.17	0.55	2.20	2.92

50

Variable					
Muscular/skeletal problems	0.16	0.18	2.09**	2.08	4.36**
Overall health	1.94**	0.86**	9.97**	2.36	13.19**
Activity restrictions	0.36	0.17	1.59**	1.03	2.79
Extremity problems	0.52	0.44	0.50	2.11	3.06
Chronic health problems	0.32	0.27	2.68**	1.56	4.51**
Eye problems	0.61*	0.56*	0.34	2.99*	3.89**
Facial cavities	0.33	0.33	1.19**	3.02*	4.55**
Discovered orthodonic problems	0.80**	0.77**	0.51	2.63	3.91**
Blood pressure	0.38	0.30	21.98**	1.14	23.42**
Corrected orthodonic problems	0.15		1.99**	1.68	3.86*

TABLE 2 (continued)

Outcome Factor	(A) ΔR² for Marital Status, Cluster A Controlled	(B) ΔR² for Marital Status, Cluster A&B Controlled	(C) Total R² Cluster A and B Only	(D) ΔR² for Interactions, Cluster A, B and Marital Status Controlled	(E) Total R² Marital Status, Clusters A, B & Interactions
Growth, Development and Current Health--Females					
Obesity problems	0.27	0.31	1.38**	2.56	4.24**
Maturity of menstruation	0.28	0.24	27.75**	1.16	29.15**
Oral hygiene	2.06**	0.29	13.74**	3.50**	17.54**
Ear and hearing problems	1.08**	0.88**	1.30**	2.68	4.85**

52

Slimness	0.15	0.13	0.66*	1.85	2.64
Heart problems	0.34	0.17	1.86**	3.19**	5.22**
Neurological problems	0.63*	0.61*	0.20	3.96**	4.77**
Size and strength	0.39	0.49	2.54**	1.96	4.99**
Overall health	2.01*	0.60*	12.31**	3.17**	16.08**
Blood pressure	0.37	0.43	3.89**	1.92	6.24**
Secondary sexual characteristics	0.27	0.28	1.77**	2.18	4.23*
Activity restrictions	0.47	0.44	1.26**	3.31*	5.02**
Muscular/skeletal	0.95**	0.53	1.60**	2.58	4.71**
Extremity problems	0.61	0.56	0.73*	2.80	4.09*
Chronic health problems	0.50	0.39	2.17**	2.31	4.88**

TABLE 2 (continued)

Outcome Factor	(A) ΔR^2 for Marital Status, Cluster A Controlled	(B) ΔR^2 for Marital Status, Cluster A&B Controlled	(C) Total R^2 Cluster A and B Only	(D) ΔR^2 for Interactions, Cluster A, B and Marital Status Controlled	(E) Total R^2 Marital Status, Clusters A, B & Interactions
Growth, Development and Current Health--Females, cont'd.					
Eye problems	0.28	0.17	0.52	2.41	3.10
Facial cavities	0.42	0.16	3.74**	3.05*	6.95**
Discovered orthodonic problems	0.55	0.39	1.50**	2.03	3.92*

Corrected orthodonic problems	0.36	0.34	2.15**	2.21	4.70**
Backache problems	0.14	0.09	3.55**	2.17	5.80**
Intellectual Development					
Exceptional performance	2.82**	0.21	16.90**	0.91	18.02**
Academic difficulty	1.71**	0.21	11.20**	1.42*	12.83*
Mental problems	2.32**	0.20	15.68**	1.03	16.91**
Cognitive Development and Achievement					
WISC vocabulary	4.02**	0.34**	35.24**	0.92*	36.50**
WISC block design	2.58**	0.08	19.98**	0.87	20.94**
WRAT arithmetic	4.15**	0.15	26.30**	0.86	27.29**

TABLE 2 (continued)

Outcome Factor	(A) ΔR² for Marital Status, Cluster A Controlled	(B) ΔR² for Marital Status, Cluster A&B Controlled	(C) Total R² Cluster A and B Only	(D) ΔR² for Interactions, Cluster A, B and Marital Status Controlled	(E) Total R² Marital Status, Clusters A, B & Interactions
Cognitive Development, cont'd.					
WRAT reading	4.18**	0.13	30.80**	1.33**	32.25**
Combined WISC	4.24**	0.22*	34.88**	0.84	35.94**
Combined WRAT	4.93**	0.16	33.57**	1.03**	34.76**
Emotional and Psychological Adjustment					
Delinquency	0.73**	0.78**	11.98**	1.53**	14.28**
Psychological problems	0.78**	0.81**	1.29**	1.22	3.32**

Overeating	0.11	0.14	2.30**	0.63	3.07**
Speech problems	0.13	0.12	2.39**	0.71	3.22**
Night problems	0.26	0.21	3.31**	1.06	4.58**
Emotional adjustment	0.44**	0.35*	2.38**	1.68*	4.42**
Sociability	0.46**	0.26	0.87***	1.47	2.60**
Parental control	0.46**	0.73**	20.38**	1.37**	22.48**
Self-centeredness	0.58**	0.58**	1.06***	1.25	4.42**
Social Adjustment					
Social contacts	0.43**	0.57**	24.52**	1.12*	26.21*
Family Relations and Family Life as Reported by Youth					
Parental decisions	0.84***	0.52**	13.65**	0.66	14.84**
Youth decisions	0.67**	0.58**	7.51**	1.09**	9.18**

TABLE 2 (continued)

Outcome Factor	(A) ΔR² for Marital Status, Cluster A Controlled	(B) ΔR² for Marital Status, Cluster A&B Controlled	(C) Total R² Cluster A and B Only	(D) ΔR² for Interactions, Cluster A, B and Marital Status Controlled	(E) Total R² Marital Status, Clusters A, B & Interactions
Family Relations and Family Life as Reported by Youth, cont'd.					
Health care decisions	1.48**	0.10	20.45**	1.60**	22.15**
Paid work	0.43**	0.12	5.34**	1.36*	6.82**
Family Relations and Family Life as Reported by Parent					
Parental decisions	1.26**	0.56**	9.44**	1.24	11.25**

Youth decisions	1.07**	1.06**	8.91**	1.49**	11.46**
Health care decisions	0.71**	0.23*	16.30**	1.53**	18.07**
Parent and Youth Agreement on Educational Plans					
School compliance	0.34*	0.18	3.36**	1.43	4.97**
Complete compliance	0.49**	0.51**	4.79**	1.16	6.46**
Close compliance	0.47**	0.49**	1.59**	1.31	3.38**
Family Values					
Parental values on personal qualities	0.70**	0.46**	1.08**	1.75**	3.29**
Youth values on personal qualities	0.22	0.21	2.92**	1.70**	4.83**

TABLE 2 (continued)

Outcome Factor	(A) ΔR² for Marital Status, Cluster A Controlled	(B) ΔR² for Marital Status, Cluster A&B Controlled	(C) Total R² Cluster A and B Only	(D) ΔR² for Interactions, Cluster A, B and Marital Status Controlled	(E) Total R² Marital Status, Clusters A, B & Interactions
Family Values cont'd.					
Youth's values on external control	0.10	0.13	1.29**	1.73**	3.15**

*significant beyond the .05 level
**significant beyond the .01 level

for children or only for youths; thus some outcomes appear only in one table.

The analysis was conducted in a modular fashion. Each row in a table represents the results of the analysis for a given dependent (outcome) variable. Five different models were evaluated and the number in each column of a row is the contribution to Multiple R-squared of a particular model. The logic of each model is the same: first, for each dependent variable, a regression equation was computed with a specific set of control variables. For example, the first column of Table 1 (Model A) reports on the factor named "prematurity with no complications." Model A was constructed as follows: First, the prematurity variable was regressed on the sex and age of the child and Multiple R-squared computed for that equation. (R-squared, of course, is the proportion of variance in the dependent variable explained by the variables in the equation.) The marital status of the household in the form of a series of dummy variables (see below for a discussion of the nature of these dummy variables) was then added to the equation and a new Multiple R-squared computed. By subtracting the new R-shaped from the first one, a measure of the percentage of variance explained by the marital status variable after the effects of the other variables have been removed was obtained. For "prematurity with no complications," this was 0.16 percent and is the number entered in Column A. A test of significance (Fisher's F test) was computed on this measure and in this instance, the difference was not significantly different from zero.

Since the contribution to explanation was small and not significant, one can conclude that nature of the parental configuration had no independent effect on that particular outcome variable given that the effects of the other variable in the equation had been removed. On the other hand, if it did appear to have important impact, the regression coefficients for each of the various household configurations should reflect both the direction and magnitudes of the effect and indicate where the effect is greatest. The five models examined were as follows.

Model A—As indicated above, this model assesses the effect (contribution of R-squared) of parental marital status with the effects of the child's age and sex removed. Since there is no reason to expect that marital disruption affects the sex and age of the child, this may be thought of as the simple or inclusive effect of the household configuration. In the Tables, the variables sex and age are referred to as Cluster A.

Model B—This model measures the effect of marital status on the outcome variable after a set of variables likely to be related with marital status are controlled. We know, for example, that children of young mothers are more likely to be first rather than later born children, and that mothers who give birth at a very young age may be unable to complete their education, and thus are likely to have a low educational level and a low income. Such mothers are also more likely to divorce than women who marry later. Model B, by removing the effects of age-of-mother-at-birth of child, of birth order, education, income, and the other variables listed in Cluster B, assesses the effect of marital status on the child independent of these variables. The variables included in Cluster B were: race of child, birth order of the child, household income, educational level of the best educated parent present in the household, the age-of-mother-at-birth of the child, the number of persons residing in the household, and a factor score indexing certain ecological and geographical characteristics. Generally, we would expect Model A to show a greater contribution of the marital variables than Model B.

Model C—This model is included to facilitate comparisons. It contains both the variables from Cluster A and B but does not include the household structure variable. This model is sometimes referred to as the reduced form model.

Model D—This model adds the effect of the interaction of the family structure variables with age and with each of the variables in Cluster B. One would wish to examine Model D when Model B shows a significant effect.

Model E—This model is also presented for comparative purposes. Like Model D, it contains all the control variables, marital status variables and all the interaction variables. The Multiple R-squared presented in Column E is thus the percentage of variance explained by all the variables in a single equation and is sometimes referred to as the saturated model.

In summary, (1) the number in Column C is the total percentage of variance explained by the control or independent variables without the family structure variables in the equation; (2) Column B is the incremental contribution to the explanation of variance measured in Column C by adding the marital status to the equation; and (3) Column A is the incremental contribution to explained variance of marital status to an equation consisting only of sex and age of the child.

THE HOUSEHOLD STRUCTURE VARIABLES

Two different schema were employed in establishing the household structure variable. The first scheme distinguished among seven marital status categories — (1) intact families (both biological parents), (2) families headed by a divorced mother, (3) families headed by a separated mother, (4) families headed by a widowed mother, (5) families in which the mother has remarried, (6) families in which the father was present but the mother absent for whatever reason and (7) families headed by a relative. The second scheme involved basically the same categories, but separated, widowed and divorced mothers (2, 3 and 4) were combined into a single category. Clearly these schema are not exhaustive of either the logical or empirical possibilities of family configurations in which children may be reared. However, the other combinations did not appear in sufficient numbers in the sample to permit their inclusion. Separate analyses were run with each of the schema. The results from the two schemes were strikingly similar — rarely would an effect be observed in one and not the other. Unfortunately, the tolerances of certain of the interaction effects for both schemes were occasionally too low for inclusion of all such effects in the saturated model. However, since the problem with the tolerances occurred only with the interaction terms, it was decided to concentrate on the finer of the two schemes, thereby enabling more precise comparisons.

STATISTICAL SIGNIFICANCE

A brief comment about statistical significance is appropriate before discussing the results. An examination of the tables shows many instances where the marital status variables have a significant effect beyond the generally employed level of five percent and frequently beyond the one percent level. However, one must be cautious in accepting these results as being of great substantive importance since generally the magnitude of the contribution to R-squared of these results is quite small. Due to the very large sample employed, very small differences can prove to be statistically significant. Thus, while the statistical significance of all the models is reported, in the discussion, only those which contribute at least one full percent to explanation will be highlighted.

FINDINGS

The results are summarized in Tables 1 and 2. Overall prediction as measured by the total amount of variance explained by the saturated model (Column E) varies considerably according to the nature of the dependent variable. For the most part, total explanation tends to be rather low on the physical and health variables, moderate on the psychological variables and highest on the cognitive and social variables. This result is not surprising. Indeed, it is somewhat reassuring for the prediction equations are comprised of primarily "social" variables, at least within the theoretical perspective employed here. Hence, one would not really expect to be able to explain physical and health outcomes. That is, there is little reason to expect variables such as income, education, birth order, and even mother's age-at-birth of child, to explain a great deal of the variance in neuro-locomotive problems, or heart problems, etc. On the other hand, one would hope that such variables would have explanatory value in areas such as the extent to which the parent monitors the child or the nature of social activities in which the child is involved. It is interesting to note that often, where the equations do show moderate explanatory power on the physical outcome variables, they tend to be in areas with a strong social component, e.g., oral hygiene and birth context (whether the child was born in a hospital, etc.).

Consistent with this overall observation is the fact that marital disruption also does not exhibit any important impact on the physical and health outcome. As a perusal of Column A will show, there are few instances where household structure explained as much as one percent of the variance in a physical or developmental variable.

Among females age 6 to 11, household structure contributes 1.32 percent to explanation for chronic nose and throat problems. Among youths, household composition had an effect on oral hygiene (2.88 percent for males and 2.06 percent for females), overall health (1.94 percent for males and 2.01 percent for females), on slimness for males (1.94 percent) and on ear and hearing problems for females (1.08 percent). With the exception of the oral hygiene variable for males, the effects are all below one percent for Model B.

On the other hand, it is of significance that marital status does appear to have some impact in the areas of cognitive and intellectual performance and development, in the area of parental monitoring and guidance and in selected social emotional areas. For children, on three of the measures of cognitive development and achievement, household structure contributed over 1.6 percent of the variance in the child's scores and contributed over two percent on the other three measures. An even stronger effect was found for the youth where household structure explained over four percent of the variance in every instance except Vocabulary where it explained 2.58 percent of the variance. The results on the standard tests among the youth were corroborated by the factor scores for the teachers' evaluations of intellectual performance. For the children, it was also found that household structure affected the extent to which the parent(s) "monitored" their offspring. For the youth, decision making in the family was also affected.

However, with but three minor exceptions, in those instances where the direct effect of household structure exceeded one percent, the effect of household dropped to less than one percent when the other independent variables were controlled (Model B). The importance of this finding lies in the suggestion that the observed effects of marital disruption are indirect rather than direct. In other words, the implication is that the effects are not directly due to the fact that the child was reared in a particular household configuration. Rather, either something occurred within the household structure affecting structural and other conditions which in turn affected the child, or that there are factors predisposing certain parents to form or disrupt a household, and these same factors affect the child's development and performance.

To separate the effect of divorce from the various other disrupted household configurations, another set of analyses were undertaken. For each factor showing a direct effect greater than one percent in Tables 1 and 2, a new set of regression equations was generated with the comparison limited to children and youths reared in intact families vs. those reared by divorced mothers living alone. This permits a direct comparison of the impact of divorce relative to residency in an intact household. These results are presented in Tables 3 and 4.

The striking result of this analysis is again negative. In no instance did being reared in a home headed by a divorced mother contribute more than one percent to explanation in comparison to children and youths reared in intact households. This suggests that the differences observed in Tables 1 and 2 were due either to comparisons other than intact vs. divorce or due to the cumulation of small differences across the various disrupted categories.

Yet, although small in magnitude, there were consistent differences observed between the divorced and intact families. Most notable were the statistically significant direct effects on all three intellectual development variables and all six cognitive variables for children. This is certainly an important, if not critical, area in which to observe differences between children in divorced vs. intact households.

But, in which direction are these effects and what are their strength? To asses the direction and magnitude of these overall effects, the mean values of the control variables were plugged into the saturated regression equations (Column E) and overall predicted means on the outcome variable computed separately for intact and divorced households. These point estimates were then compared across the groups and the results presented in Table 5 for children and Table 6 for youth.

The rightmost column of these tables contains the estimated means for the subgroups. Perusing the differences in these estimates indicates a somewhat surprising result. Among the children, those living with divorced mothers perform better on IQ tests and achievement tests, have fewer academic problems, fewer nose and throat problems, and are monitored more closely by their parent(s) than are children reared in intact households. They do however, have night problems. Among the youth the pattern is similar but not as consistent. Boys reared in divorced households have better oral hygiene, are slimmer, and have better overall health than those reared in intact homes. Girls in divorced homes, on the other hand, have poorer oral hygiene, somewhat more ear and hearing problems and have poorer overall health. Among all youth, those reared in divorced homes have more academic difficulties, require more resources for exceptional children than those in intact households, but are no more likely to have mental problems. Further, although they perform better on IQ tests, their achievement scores fall down. Interestingly, however, youths in divorced households are subject to greater health monitoring by their parent and share more in the decision-making process.

Analysis of these point estimates must be made very cautiously for the estimates are only at one point in the regression plane. That is to say, had values other than the means for the control variables been selected, very different results may have been observed. However, these results are still quite suggestive, especially the difference between children and youth with the former apparently benefiting from divorce and the latter exhibiting mixed results.

CONCLUSIONS

The results are consistent with much of the literature on the impact of divorce on children. The initial regression analysis showed that the impact of the household structure variables was primarily in the social-psychological areas and was primarily indirect. In other words, the effects of the household structure variables essentially disappeared when the background controls were applied. More unusual, perhaps, were the findings generated when children reared in divorced households were compared only with children reared by intact families. Although differences were slight and generally not significant when the background controls were applied, young children in divorced households seemed to fare better than children in intact families while older youths in divorced households fared better in some areas and worse in others. This greater deleterious impact on youths compared to children has, of course, been often noted in the literature.

TABLE 3. Impact of Being Reared by a Divorced Mother Relative to an Intact Family on Selected Outcomes for Children Ages 6 Through 11 Controlling for Sex and Age of Child (Cluster A) and for Race, Birth Order, Income, Education, Household Size, Age of Mother at Birth and Ecological Factors (Cluster B) and of the Interactions Between Marital Status and Variables in Cluster B Plus Age

PERCENTS

Outcome Factor	(A) ΔR^2 for Marital Status, Cluster A Controlled	(B) ΔR^2 for Marital Status, Cluster A&B Controlled	(C) Total R^2 Cluster A and B Only	(D) ΔR^2 for Interactions, Cluster A, B and Marital Status Controlled	(E) Total R^2 Marital Status, Clusters A, B & Interactions
Growth, Development and Current Health--Females					
Chronic nose and throat problems	0.02	0.03	0.33	0.14	7.09
Intellectual Development					
Academic difficulty	0.17**	0.01	12.15**	0.59**	12.94**
Exceptional performance	0.16*	0.01	11.60**	0.46**	12.07**

Cognitive Development and Achievement

WISC vocabulary	0.02	0.26**	29.89**	0.18	30.33**
WISC block design	0.05	0.07	16.04**	0.15	16.26**
WRAT arithmetic	0.08	0.06	16.80**	0.18	17.04**
WRAT reading	0.20**	0.01	20.48**	0.32*	20.81**
Combined WISC	0.04	0.21**	30.69**	0.16	31.06**
Combined WRAT	0.16*	0.04	22.36**	0.23	22.63**

Emotional and Psychological Adjustment

Night problems	0.00	0.02	5.06**	0.21	5.29**
Social activities	0.08	0.02	27.67**	0.07	27.75**

Childrearing Practices

Parental monitoring	0.10*	0.08*	32.24**	0.17	32.49**

*significant at .05 level
**significant at .01 level

TABLE 4. Impact of Being Reared by a Divorced Mother Relative to an Intact Family on Selected Outcomes for Children Ages 6 Through 11 Controlling for Sex and Age of Child (Cluster A) and for Race, Birth Order, Income, Education, Household Size, Age of Mother at Birth and Ecological Factors (Cluster B) and of the Interactions Between Marital Status and Variables in Cluster B Plus Age

PERCENTS

Outcome Factor	(A) ΔR^2 for Marital Status, Cluster A Controlled	(B) ΔR^2 for Marital Status, Cluster A&B Controlled	(C) Total R^2 Cluster A and B Only	(D) ΔR^2 for Interactions, Cluster A, B and Marital Status Controlled	(E) Total R^2 Marital Status, Clusters A, B & Interactions
Prenatal and Natal Conditions					
Birth context	0.04	0.20**	19.90**	0.34*	20.44**
Growth, Development and Current Health--Males					
Oral hygiene	0.03	0.15*	14.14**	0.13	14.42**
Slimness	0.55**	0.51**	0.73*	0.14	1.37*
Overall health	0.94**	0.19*	10.87**	0.12	11.18**

Growth, Development and Current Health--Females

Oral hygiene	0.01	0.11	12.47**	0.55**	13.12**
Ear and hearing problems	0.06	0.03	1.24**	0.29	1.56**
Overall health	0.06	0.06	12.01**	0.97**	13.04**

Intellectual Development

Exceptional performance	0.53**	0.03	15.06**	0.11	15.20**
Academic difficulty	0.20**	0.00	10.05**	0.46*	10.50**
Mental problems	0.17**	0.03	13.62**	0.34	13.99**

Cognitive Development and Achievement

WISC vocabulary	0.35**	0.06	31.75**	0.06	31.87**
WISC block design	0.13*	0.12*	16.27**	0.01	16.50**
WRAT arithmetic	0.51**	0.00	20.88**	0.18	21.06**
WRAT reading	0.61**	0.00	26.37**	0.13	26.50**

TABLE 4 (continued)

Outcome Factor	(A) ΔR² for Marital Status, Cluster A Controlled	(B) ΔR² for Marital Status, Cluster A&B Controlled	(C) Total R² Cluster A and B Only	(D) ΔR² for Interactions, Cluster A, B and Marital Status Controlled	(E) Total R² Marital Status, Clusters A, B & Interactions
Combined WISC	0.30**	0.12*	30.74**	0.09	30.95**
Combined WRAT	0.67**	0.00	28.31**	0.14	28.45**
Familial Decision Making as Reported by Youth					
Health care decisions	0.37**	0.00	20.28**	0.17	20.45**
Familial Relations and Family Life					
Parental decisions	0.09	0.00	8.20**	0.16	8.36**
Youth decisions	0.13*	0.20**	8.44**	0.12	8.76**

*significant at .05 level
**significant at .01 level

TABLE 5. Comparison of Regression Equations for Children Ages 6 Through 11 Reared in Intact vs. Divorced Households

Type of Household	Constant	Age of Child	Sex of Child	Age-of-Mother-at-Birth of Child	Educa-tional Level	Ecolog-ical Factors	Race	Size of Household	Birth Order of Child	Income	Estimated Mean
					Regression Coefficients (b's)						
Academic Difficulty											
Intact	.651	.000	.196	-.005	-.051	.062	-.125	.032	-.076	-.024	.033
Divorced	1.79	.005	.196	.026	.018	-.189	1.057	.101	-.006	-.100	.026
Exceptional Performance											
Intact	-.223	.000	-.065	.002	.017	-.026	.036	-.010	.025	.007	.027
Divorced	.507	.000	-.065	-.007	-.003	.044	-.022	-.031	.011	.038	-.006
WISC Vocabulary											
Intact	33.05	.010	-.380	.135	.979	-.083	5.43	-.910	.727	1.43	51.21
Divorced	13.08	-.024	-.380	.188	.382	1.64	5.34	-.446	4.13	3.09	54.82
WISC Block Design											
Intact	36.89	.005	-.095	.034	.688	.027	6.53	-.355	-.626	1.04	51.17
Divorced	28.68	.052	-.095	.240	.603	2.24	4.84	-.122	3.03	1.41	52.96
WRAT Arithmetic											
Intact	37.71	.006	-.524	.049	.776	-.087	4.28	-.414	.365	1.26	51.34
Divorced	50.80	-.062	-.524	.163	-.200	-1.77	4.48	-.751	2.59	2.54	53.07
WRAT Reading											
Intact	37.49	-.004	-.411	.101	.821	.206	3.95	-.579	1.38	1.29	51.38
Divorced	55.39	-.034	-.411	-.008	-.181	3.67	4.27	-.668	1.91	2.58	51.60

TABLE 5 (continued)

Regression Coefficients (b's)

Type of Household	Constant	Age of Child	Sex of Child	Age-of-Mother-at-Birth of Child	Educa-tional Level	Ecolog-ical Factors	Race	Size of Household	Birth Order of Child	Income	Estimated Mean
Combined WISC											
Intact	69.93	.015	-.475	.169	1.67	-.056	11.97	-1.26	.101	2.47	102.38
Divorced	71.75	.029	-.475	.428	.985	3.87	10.18	-.558	7.16	4.50	107.78
Combined WRAT											
Intact	75.20	.002	-.936	.150	1.60	.120	8.23	-.993	1.74	2.55	102.72
Divorced	106.19	-.095	-.936	.157	.018	1.90	8.75	-.142	4.49	5.12	104.66
Chronic Nose and Throat Problems											
Intact	.238	-.003	---	.008	.001	.085	.407	.020	-.116	-.128	.588
Divorced	1.81	-.011	---	-.009	.006	.004	-.608	.140	.048	.152	.542
Night Problems											
Intact	-.046	-.001	.004	-.002	.028	-.035	.146	-.039	.010	.013	.100
Divorced	-.535	-.002	.004	.019	.046	-.260	-.062	-.015	.042	-.000	.175
Social Activities											
Intact	-.384	.003	-.074	-.002	.015	-.027	.059	-.011	.007	.022	.086
Divorced	-.383	.003	-.074	-.002	.012	.013	.099	-.004	.015	.004	.086
Parental Monitoring											
Intact	-1.054	.001	-.032	.003	.070	.195	.339	-.069	.019	.090	.074
Divorced	-.754	.004	-.032	.008	.049	.084	.015	-.070	.006	.201	.222

TABLE 6. Comparison of Regression Equations for Youths Ages 12 Through 17 Reared in Intact vs. Divorced Households

Type of Household	Regression Coefficients (b's)										
	Constant	Age of Child	Sex of Child	Age-of-Mother-at-Birth of Child	Educational Level	Ecological Factors	Race	Size of Household	Birth Order of Child	Income	Estimated Mean
Birth Context											
Intact	1.06	-.000	-.006	-.003	.011	-.073	.106	-.013	-.022	.032	1.07
Divorced	1.00	-.002	-.006	.006	.012	-.071	.044	.005	.073	.027	1.10
Oral Hygiene—Males											
Intact	21.71	.043	---	.094	-1.07	.518	-8.51	.328	-.725	1.76	12.19
Divorced	22.64	.031	---	.275	-.878	2.23	-2.92	.627	-3.13	-2.26	9.10
Slimness—Males											
Intact	-.018	.000	---	-.001	.009	-.014	-.047	-.015	-.018	.005	.137
Divorced	.400	.000	---	-.006	-.005	.050	-.055	.028	-.059	-.060	.252
Overall Health—Males											
Intact	-.081	-.001	---	-.004	.027	-.145	.167	-.006	.079	.115	.079
Divorced	.333	-.006	---	-.001	.042	-.260	.136	.010	.005	.054	-.135
Oral Hygiene—Females											
Intact	17.84	.055	---	-.053	-.751	-.083	-10.01	.788	.351	-1.78	11.46
Divorced	23.18	.030	---	.532	-1.01	1.83	-23.96	-1.23	3.30	-1.95	6.30
Ear and Hearing Problems—Females											
Intact	.257	-.001	---	-.003	-.008	.103	.105	-.000	.027	-.011	.037
Divorced	1.02	-.003	---	-.010	.003	-.007	.006	-.007	.028	-.052	.158

TABLE 6 (continued)

Type of Household	Constant	Age of Child	Sex of Child	Age-of-Mother-at-Birth of Child	Educational Level	Ecological Factors	Race	Size of Household	Birth Order of Child	Income	Estimated Mean
Overall Health—Females											
Intact	.292	.002	---	.000	-.055	.167	-.144	.027	.065	-.131	.001
Divorced	-.353	.015	---	.014	-.013	.017	-.077	.239	.127	.079	3.43
Exceptional Performance											
Intact	1.32	.002	.304	-.019	-.095	-.145	-.295	.021	-.185	-.125	-.142
Divorced	2.38	-.003	.304	-.021	-.089	.083	-.339	.027	-.316	-.016	.060
Academic Difficulty											
Intact	.271	-.000	.034	-.002	.010	-.013	-.036	.005	-.009	-.019	.027
Divorced	.620	-.001	.034	-.003	-.018	.052	-.043	-.011	-.065	.022	.050
Mental Problems											
Intact	.318	.000	.012	-.001	-.008	-.009	-.029	.009	-.010	-.010	.185
Divorced	.251	.000	.012	.002	-.007	.032	-.029	.002	-.024	-.004	.185
WISC Vocabulary											
Intact	30.44	.002	-.511	.192	1.03	-1.33	4.57	-.392	2.92	1.72	51.62
Divorced	38.83	.002	-.511	.081	.824	-2.32	3.59	-.554	1.71	1.38	52.04
WISC Block Design											
Intact	34.14	.004	-.572	.074	.688	-.734	6.70	-.013	.635	1.41	51.14
Divorced	43.01	.027	-.572	-.119	.493	-1.82	5.15	-.765	-.604	1.10	51.95
WRAT Arithmetic											
Intact	34.70	-.002	.512	.097	.726	-.592	7.18	-.218	.954	1.42	51.61
Divorced	23.97	-.045	.512	.179	.978	-1.12	4.14	-4.39	1.02	.353	50.71

Regression Coefficients (b's)

WRAT Arithmetic											
Intact	34.70	-.002	.512	.097	.726	-.592	7.18	-.218	.954	1.42	51.01
Divorced	23.97	.045	.512	.179	.978	-1.12	4.14	-4.39	1.02	.353	50.71
WRAT Reading											
Intact	30.79	.005	-.489	.167	.880	-2.45	5.88	-.204	1.70	1.48	51.54
Divorced	33.88	.032	-.489	-.032	.864	-2.32	4.64	-.852	1.42	.662	50.39
Combined WISC											
Intact	64.59	.006	-1.08	.266	1.71	-2.07	11.27	-.405	3.56	3.14	102.76
Divorced	81.84	.025	-1.08	-.039	1.32	-4.14	8.73	-1.32	1.11	2.48	103.99
Combined WRAT											
Intact	65.49	.004	-1.00	.265	1.61	-3.04	13.08	-.421	2.66	2.90	103.15
Divorced	57.85	.077	-1.00	.148	1.84	-3.44	8.78	-1.29	2.44	1.02	101.09
Health Care Decisions Reported by Youth											
Intact	.887	-.001	-.083	-.007	-.047	.122	-.179	.053	-.144	-.109	-.074
Divorced	.978	-.005	-.083	.005	-.022	.152	-.131	.033	-.136	-.121	.049
Parental Decisions Reported by Parents											
Intact	1.11	-.003	.118	.009	-.105	-.116	-.534	.072	-.109	-.121	-.627
Divorced	1.77	-.000	.118	.005	-.214	-.065	-.292	.093	.205	.171	.496
Youth Decisions Reported by Parents											
Intact	-2.42	.014	.371	.006	.003	-.083	-.078	.006	-.112	.033	.112
Divorced	-2.11	.142	.371	-.016	.010	-.273	-.103	-.006	-.214	.090	.400

Since the results fail, for the most part, to demonstrate major pathological sequelae to marital disruption in children and youth, they must of necessity contribute little to resolving the differences among the trauma model, the structural model and the deficiency model. That, on the few occasions where effects were found they were ultimately shown to operate indirectly, would tend to lend credence if not support to the structural formulation. It should be borne in mind, however, that most of the children and youth from disrupted households in this sample were likely examined a year or two after the disruption took place (the interval between disruption and examination could only be determined from the data available in a small number of instances). Thus, near term effects of trauma may well have been dampened through the passage of time. In any event, it certainly appears that this nationally representative sample of children and youth demonstrates little in the way of long-term effects of marital disruption indicating that, at worst, children in disrupted households are adaptive and resilient.

REFERENCES

Bane, M. (1976). Marital Disruption and the Lives of Children. *Journal of Social Issues* 32:103-116.

Biller, H. (1969). Father Absence, Maternal Encouragement and Sex-Role Development in Kindergarten Age Boys. *Child Development* 40:539-546.

Blanchard, R. and Biller, H. (1971). Father Availability and Academic Performance Among Third-Grade Boys. *Developmental Psychology* 4:301-305.

Bohannan, P. (1971). The Six Stations of Divorce. In P. Bohannan (ed.) *Divorce and After*. New York: Doubleday & Company, Inc.

Bowerman, C. and Irish, D. (1962). Some Relationships of Stepchildren to Their Parents. *Marriage and Family Living* 24:113-121.

Brandwein, R., Brown C. and Fox, E. (1974). Women and Children Last: The Social Situation of Divorced Mothers and Their Families. *Journal of Marriage and the Family* 36:498-514.

Bumpass, L. and Rindfuss, R. (1978). *Children's Experience of Marital Disruption*. Institute for Research on Poverty, University of Wisconsin—Madison. DP# 512-78.

Burchinal, L. (1964). Characteristics of Adolescents from Unbroken and Reconstituted Families. *Journal of Marriage and the Family* 26:44-51.

Deutch, M. (1960). *Minority Groups and Class Status as Related to Social and Personality Factors in Scholastic Achievement*. The Society for Applied Anthropology, Monograph No. 2. Ithaca NY: Cornell University.

Deutch, M. and Brown, B. (1964). Social Influences in Negro-White Intelligence Differences. *Journal of Social Issues* 20:24-25.

Duberman, L. (1977). *Marriage and Other Alternatives*. New York: Praeger Publishers. Second edition.

Duncan, B. (1967). Education and Social Background. *American Journal of Sociology* 72:363-372.

Felner, R., Stalberg A. and Cowen, E. (1975). Crisis Events and School Mental Health Referral Patterns of Young Children. *Journal of Consulting and Clinical Psychology* 43:305-310.

Goode, W. (1956). *After Divorce*. New York: Free Press.

Hansen, D. and Hill, R. (1964). Families Under Stress. In H. Christensen (ed.) *Handbook of Marriage and the Family*. Chicago: Rand McNally.

Herzog, E. and Sudia, C. (1970). *Boys in Fatherless Families*. Washington, DC: U.S. Department of Health, Education and Welfare, Children's Bureau (OCD).

Hess, R. and Camara, K. (1979). Post-divorce Family Relationships as Mediating Factors in the Consequences of Divorce for Children. *Journal of Social Issues* 35:79-96.

Hetherington, E. and Deur, J. (1971). The Effects of Father Absence on Child Development. *Young Children* March:233-248.

Hetherington, E., Cox, M. and Cox R. (1976). Divorced Fathers. *Family Coordinator* 25:417-428.

Hetherington, E., Cox, M. and Cox R. (1977). The Aftermath of Divorce. In J. Stevens, Jr. and M. Matthews (eds.) *Mother-Child, Father-Child Relations*. Washington, DC: National Association for the Education of Young Children.

Jordan, B., Radin, N. and Epstein, A. (1975). Paternal Behavior and Intellectual Functioning in Pre-school Boys and Girls. *Developmental Psychology* 11:407-408.

Jordan, T. and Spaner, S. (1974). Biological and Ecological influences on Development at 48 and 60 Months of Age. *Psychological Reports* 34:119-126.

Kelly, R. and Berg, B. (1978). Measuring Children's Reactions to Divorce. *Journal of Clinical Psychology* 34:215-221.

Kinard, E. and Reinherz, H. (1986). Effects of Marital Disruption on Children's School Attitude and Achievement. *Journal of Marriage and the Family* 48:285-293.

Landis, J. (1960). The Trauma of Children When Parents Divorce. *Marriage and Family Living* 22:7-13.

Landis, J. (1962). A Comparison of Children from Divorced and Nondivorced Unhappy Marriages. *The Family Life Coordinator* 11:61-65.

Levinger, G. and Moles, O. (eds.) *Divorce and Separation: Context, Causes, and Consequences*. New York: Basic Books.

Marsden, D. (1969). *Mothers Alone: Poverty and the Fatherless Family*. London: The Penguin Press.

National Center for Health Statistics. (1967). Plan, Operation and Response

Results of a Program of Children's Examination. Vital and Health Statistics, Programs and Collection Procedures, Series 1, 8, D.H.E.W., 80.

National Center for Health Statistics. (1969). Plan and Operation of a Health Examinations Survey of U.S. Youths 12-27 Years of Age. Vital and Health Statistics, Programs and Collection Procedures, Series 1, 8, D.H.E.W.

National Center for Health Statistics. (1971). Sample Design and Estimation Procedures for a National Health Examination Survey of Children. Vital and Health Statistics, Data Evaluation and Methods Research, Series 2, 43, D.H.E.W., 40.

National Center for Health Statistics. (1972). Quality Control in a National Health Examination Survey. Vital and Health Statistics, Data Evaluation and Methods Research, Series 2, 44, D.H.E.W, 22.

National Center for Health Statistics. (1986). Advance Report of Final Divorce Statistics. *Monthly Vital Statistics Report.* 35, No. 6, Supplement (September 25, 1986).

Nye, F. (1957). Child Adjustment in Broken and in Unhappy Unbroken Homes. *Marriage and Family Living* 19:356-361.

Pederson, F. (1966). Relationships Between Father Absence and Emotional Disturbance in Male Military Dependents. *Merrill-Palmer Quarterly* 12:321-331.

Rosenberg, M. (1965). *Society and the Adolescent Self-Image.* Princeton, NJ: Princeton University Press.

Ryker, M., Rogers, E. and Beaujard, P. (1971). Six Selected Factors influencing Educational Achievement of Children from Broken Homes. *Education* 91: 200-211.

Siegman, A. (1966). Father Absence During Early Childhood and Antisocial Behavior. *Journal of Abnormal Psychology* 71:71-74.

Sutton-Smith, B., Rosenberg, B. and Landry, F. (1968). Father Absence Effects in Families of Different Sibling Compositions. *Child Development* 39:1213-1221.

Wallerstein, J. and Kelly, J. (1975). The Effects of Parental Divorce: Experiences of the Preschool child. *Journal of the American Academy of Child Psychiatry* 14:600-616.

Wallerstein, J. and Kelly, J. (1976). The Effects of Parental Divorce: Experiences of the Child in Later Latency. *American Journal of Orthopsychiatry* 46:256-269.

Wallerstein, J. and Kelly, J. (1980). *Surviving the Break-up: How Children Actually Cope with Divorce.* New York: Basic Books.

Walters, J. and Stinnett, N. (1971). Parent-Child Relationships: A Decade Review of Research. *Journal of Marriage and the Family* 33:70-111.

Zill, N. and Peterson, J. (1986). Marital Disruption, Parent-Child Relationships, and Behavior Problems in Children. *Journal of Marriage and the Family* 48:295-307.

The Impact of Divorce on Children
at Various Stages
of the Family Life Cycle

Judith Stern Peck

Two decades age, divorce was relatively rare; today an estimated 50% of couples will choose divorce as the solution to marital dissatisfaction (Glick, 1984). Although approximately 45% of divorces occur between childless couples, the majority involve children (National Center for Health Statistics, 1984a). Official statistics notwithstanding, therapists need only look at their caseloads to understand the dimensions of this problem. More and more parents must negotiate the transition from marriage to single-parenthood, and from single-parenthood to remarriage, and in many cases, a return to single-parenthood. Meanwhile, there are the children—the children whose developmental needs continue despite the vicissitudes of coupling, uncoupling, and recoupling.

Divorce creates a crisis in the family life cycle—a state of disequilibrium experienced by all members throughout the nuclear and extended family system. The disruption is associated with myriad shifts in membership, roles and boundaries that require a major reorganization of the family system (Ahrons, 1981). Despite the considerable wealth of divorce research published in the professional literature, and a healthy volume of self-help books on the subject, individuals often come to therapy bewildered by the tasks at hand. The loss of the spouse alone may precipitate the most serious emotional upheaval experienced to date by the divorcing person. It is the children who witness first hand the individual struggle of their

---

Judith Stern Peck, MSW, is Director of Clinical Services, The Family Institute of Westchester, 147 Archer Avenue, Mt. Vernon, NY 10550.

parents to survive—both economically and emotionally. Although children can make a satisfactory personal adjustment to parental divorce, many children may become symptomatic at some point during the divorce process.

Carter and McGoldrick (1980) offer the family life cycle paradigm as a therapeutic tool in working with both intact and divorcing families. In contrast to individual theories of growth and development (Erickson, 1963; Levinson, 1978; Gould, 1978), the family life cycle postulates a group of individuals related by blood and marriage moving through time in concert. If any one member falls "out of line," chances are the family has failed to successfully negotiate its present or previous life cycle tasks, with difficulties becoming most visible during the transition from one phase to the next. Problems in negotiating the present family life cycle stage may mirror difficulties in the parental families of origin (Bowen, 1978), as unresolved conflicts tend to be repeated from one generation to the next. From a systems viewpoint, both predictable changes (e.g., a child leaving for college) and unpredictable crises (e.g., divorce) create stress that is passed up and down through the generations, affecting all members of the family system.

Notably, the stages of the family life cycle are loosely framed around the stages of child development—recognizing that it is the changing needs of children that often provide the impetus for evolution and adaptation in a family's day-to-day functioning and form. The three-generational life cycle model maintains that grandparents continue to play a significant role in the lives of their adult children and grandchildren, while emphasizing the family's primary role in the nurturing of its youngest members. Divorce irrevocably alters the shape of a family, yet the divorcing family continues to perform this primary function in a new form. Research indicates that the family system requires 1 to 3 years to complete the divorce process and restabilize in its new form (Hetherington, 1982). If a family moves through the crisis satisfactorily, the result can be a more fluid system that will facilitate the "normal" family developmental process as well, and perhaps better, than the previous intact family. For example, Ahrons (1980) points out that, at least for young adult children, divorce can offer the benefit of an individual relationship with each parent. However, each ensuing life cycle phase is affected by a divorce, and subsequent symptoms in all family members must henceforth be viewed within the dual context of the stage itself and the residual effects of the divorce experience.

Research and clinical observations have yielded some general guidelines for how parents can best consider the needs of their children during the divorce process. With the goal of shifting our therapeutic orientation towards the empowerment of divorcing families, the discussion will begin with a brief examination of the factors that help children to adjust. The second part of the paper will focus on the family life cycle stage-related issues and dangers for the children of divorce. In the clinical section, the emphasis will be on therapeutic efforts to facilitate coparenting. The genogram and the family life cycle will be discussed as therapeutic tools.

SATISFACTORY ADJUSTMENT TO PARENTAL DIVORCE

While parents may perceive divorce as a solution to their problems, few children seem to want divorce. This holds true regardless of how much marital tension preceded the split (Wallerstein & Kelly, 1980). However, when divorce is about to become a new "fact of life," two elements contribute to the satisfactory adjustment of the children: the ability of the parents to make the transition from a conflictual spousal relationship to a cooperative coparenting arrangement, and the ability of the children to have free access to both parents. For obvious reasons, these may seem Herculean goals at the time of separation. Both require not only the satisfactory resolution of the emotional divorce, they also demand a high degree of flexibility from the ex-spouses.

The Coparental Relationship

Several studies have found a strong correlation between poor adjustment in children and parental conflict, regardless of marital status (Hess & Camera, 1979; Raschke & Raschke, 1979). The results of many different studies indicate that the post-divorce relationship between the parents is the most critical factor in the functioning of the family. In fact, the level of interparental conflict may be more central to post-divorce adjustment than parental absence or the divorce itself (Hetherington, 1977; Emery, 1982). One study (Luepnitz, 1982) of nonclinical families with different types of custody arrangements found that ongoing conflict was the sole predictor of poor adjustment in children.

For the couple, the process of terminating the marital relationship while maintaining interdependent roles as parents is difficult. With few useful role models to guide them, people are generally more clear about what they *don't* want, than what they *do* want from a coparental relationship. Both ex-spouses — or their future partners — may view any continuing relationship as a form of "holding on." Still, a recent 5-year study examining the nature of post-divorce relationships around parenting issues found that: 12% were "perfect pals," 38% "cooperative colleagues," 25% "angry associates," and 25% "fiery foes" (Ahrons, 1986). The good news appears to be that about half the couples studied were able to create a satisfactory coparental relationship.

Typically the first year is the hardest, with another study reporting 95% of ex-spouses as seeing gradual improvements over the course of that time in the ability to communicate (Goldsmith, 1980). Kelly (1986) found that child-focused communication was significantly better than discussion around marital issues, another encouraging indicator for cooperative post-divorce parenting.

According to Ahrons (1980a), it is the redefinition process that takes place when spouses can separate the parental role from the marital role that allows the family to restabilize. In a functional coparenting relationship, a combination of positive and negative feelings coexist, though neither to an extreme. Most discussions center around issues of parenting, with the major areas of disagreement revolving around finances and child-rearing practices. Some former spouses get together as a family for children's birthdays, school plays, graduations and other such events (Ahrons, 1981; Goldsmith, 1980). However, the most important characteristic of a successful coparenting relationship is mutual respect. Respect — and respect alone — seems to insure the flexibility required for the ongoing negotiation of child-related issues.

Access to Both Parents

Based on the assumption that it allows greater and more na
access to both parents, joint custody is emerging as a possible replacement for the traditional sole custody arrangement. While
most, if not all, studies report a high degree of satisfaction with
joint custody (Greif, 1979; Abarbanel, 1979; Ahrons, 1981), this
research has been conducted on the response of early enthusiasts of
the concept, rather than on the actual experience of children in these
situations. One study, however, found that a third of children feel
intense loyalty conflicts and great concern over being fair to both
parents (Steimnan, 1981). A slightly more recent study (Luepnitz,
1982) examined all types of custody arrangements, interviewed all
household members, and concluded that joint custody at its best is
superior to sole custody.

For the former spouses, joint custody arrangements may tie them
together in a way that impedes forward movement in their own
lives. Kelly (1986) reports that mothers are less positive about
shared parenting arrangements and often want more time with the
children than their ex-husbands. This may be due to the difficulty
women experience in sharing their primary roles as parents, and the
fact that many men feel inadequate to manage the daily demands of
young children. Notably, most children are dissatisfied with traditional, every-other-weekend visitations with their fathers, and report feeling cut off from noncustodial parents (Wallerstein & Kelly,
1980; Ahrons, 1981). Yet joint physical custody in the presence of
continuing, intense conflict may often be more harmful than no
contact with the absent parent. In short, each parent's ability to
support the children in maintaining a qualitative relationship with
the other parent appears to be more important than the particular
form of custody.

In practice, free access can take many different forms and may be
defined best in terms of a child's developmental needs. For example, physical joint custody may be ideal for adolescents, yet be
wholly inappropriate for an infant. Where more traditional custody
arrangements are in place, free access can still be provided. A child
who has the freedom to call Daddy any time, even though he lives

across the country, can be considered to have free access to his/her father. Similarly, the parents need to feel that they have some flexibility within the agreed upon visitation schedules. For example, under optimum circumstances, a father's request to have his children for an additional day on a Monday holiday can be negotiated quickly and easily between the ex-spouses. Each parent's commitment to foster the children's relationship with the ex-spouse establishes the groundwork for family growth after divorce. As children grow older and become more involved in peer friendships and activities, their schedules also become an important consideration. This may be of greater concern to the noncustodial parent, who may interpret a child's desire to attend a party or play soccer on Saturday as a personal rejection rather than a healthy interest in the outside world.

Although flexibility is the key to free access, it is important to recognize children's needs for structure in their environment. Again, structure means different things at different stages. For example, an adolescent might play a more active role in choosing when he or she will visit a father who lives nearby, yet teens need a clear set of limits about parental expectations in each household. With younger children, a set routine of visitation seems to provide the best solution. For very young children who have not yet developed a mastery of time, it can be helpful to display a calendar in the kitchen or in their bedrooms that marks off the days until they see the other parent. A well-defined plan for visitation and contact with both parents reassures even the very youngest children that they will be loved and cared for (Wallerstein & Kelly, 1980). In summary, if the coparental relationship necessitates mutual respect between the parents, free access requires respect for the child at his or her particular stage of development.

STAGE-RELATED PROBLEMS
IN CHILDREN OF DIVORCE

Divorce itself may be conceived of as a process involving beginning, middle, and end stages (Herz, in press; Ahrons, 1980a). Ahrons's theoretical framework (1980a) suggests that the process begins prior to the actual separation, with one spouse's deliberation about the viability of the marriage and the subsequent anxiety of family members around the possibility of separation. At the point of separation, the family's experience can be compared to a volcano; while the post-divorce may best be described as a period of waiting for the dust to settle. Each and every member of the nuclear and extended family is affected in ways that influence the process for all, depending in part on the life cycle phase of the family. For example, there is evidence that close grandparent/grandchild contact is of value to all three generations following a divorce (Kivnick, 1982). This, too, may require considerable effort, as there is a tendency for the families of origin to close ranks and blame the other party.

The adjustment process ends when some sort of homeostasis has been established within the new single-parent household or with the single parent's remarriage (Hetherington, 1977; Ahrons, 1980a). During this transition, triangles may develop around the mother's efforts to pull others into the "empty space" left by the father's absence (Herz, in press). Grandparents, the ex-spouse, siblings, a child, and even a therapist are likely candidates to fill the vacuum. However, Issacs (1982) suggests that restabilization is achieved only when a new person is brought into the family system (e.g., extended family member, housekeeper, babysitter, lover, etc.), although the functional level of the restabilized family unit depends on many factors (Herz, in press). Children may experience many difficulties related both to their own losses, the economic and sociocultural factors affecting the entire family, and the distress associated with parental conflict. Money is a serious problem for many single-parent families (Spanier & Casto, 1979; Weitzman, 1985), and ethnic issues surrounding the morality of divorce and grandparent/parent roles may also play a major role in adjustment (McGoldrick, 1982).

Children may become symptomatic at any stage during the divorce process, and these symptoms may often be the presenting problem in therapy. In fact, those ex-spouses who succeed in creating a flexible and cooperative relationship often do so with a push from a troubled child. Certainly careful planning prior to separation can do much to ameliorate the impact of divorce on the children, yet the inevitable upheaval at the time of separation and the necessary trial-and-error efforts to rebalance the system may serve as a catalyst for stage-related problems in children.

The nature of the impact of divorce on children is directly related to the family stage at the time of the divorce. By virtue of their dependence on their parents, children at earlier stages of the life cycle represent those most vulnerable to the effects of the family's crisis. Yet, as will become apparent in the discussion, even adult children of divorcing parents may experience serious setbacks in their own life cycle tasks.

The Newly Married Couple

This phase can be used to describe not only couples in the first few years of marriage, where the incidence of divorce is quite high, but also those couples who have sustained a marital relationship for some time without children. Often couples in this latter group experience conflict around issues concerning one spouse's desire to become more established (e.g., have a baby, buy a house, or become more career-oriented). In a sense one spouse wants to "grow up," while the other presses to preserve the carefree ways of youth.

Following a separation, family once more means being a child to one's parents, and a sibling to one's brothers and sisters. Without children, it seems that adult status has not yet been fully achieved, especially in the eyes of the older generation who may quite naturally seek to pull in the reins. Indeed, marriages that end during this stage were often precipitated by one or both parties' desire to escape the family nest.

> Denise, 24, and Juan, 26, had married after a 2-month courtship filled with passion and romance. The oldest of six siblings, Denise held an overresponsible role in her family of origin. Her parents' marriage was a constant battleground and she was continually called upon to restore peace. Cultural mores dictated that marriage was the only acceptable way for a daughter to leave the house. After the intense emotion waned, the young couple was faced with their inability to negotiate a satisfactory sharing of work and household responsibilities, which led to intense conflict. A psychosomatic illness brought Diane to therapy, where she decided to leave Juan and move back home to reorganize her plans for the future.

The absence of children eliminates the necessity of continued contact between ex-spouses, although some do become friends. Starting over is less difficult, as financial independence, career issues, and socialization tasks are unhampered by the demands of children. The danger of divorce for these "adult children," is that they will either become enmeshed in their families of origin, or cutoff from them. Treating the divorce as a nonevent (a common occurrence) discounts the emotional process that often manifests itself in anger, shame, loss and confusion. Given that they have already sought to break family ties in a radical way, the cutoff may be a more prevalent coping mechanism. At the same time that a single adult may need to be encouraged to develop community ties and peer friendships, work on relationships with the family of origin may be required to avoid a continuing pattern of failure with intimate relationships.

Families with Young Children

With the median age of marriage being 7 years, and the average age of spouses at the time of divorce between 25 and 34 (National Center for Health Statistics, 1984a), families are at an especially high risk for divorce during this stage of the family life cycle. In the current social milieu, negotiating the transition to parenthood is a formidable task and one that many previously satisfied couples fail to resolve together. For the sake of clarity, this discussion will focus separately on the impact of divorce on preschool and school age children.

Pre-School Children

Babies under 2 years old at the time of divorce often have little memory of the intact family. Ultimately, this may prove advantageous as they alone may be relieved of the obligation to mourn what was, and babies are self-centered enough not to feel more complex human emotions, such as guilt. They are totally absorbed in the drive towards mastering the basics of independence, such as walking, talking, and feeding themselves, and rudimentary social behaviors.

The chief danger for infants centers around their strong dependence on their parents for their basic survival and security. As

Erikson's (1963) psychosocial stages suggest, through basic attachment to their adult caretakers, babies learn to trust their environment. Consistency, so vital to the young child's optimum development may be difficult to maintain during a divorce. Mother may be overwhelmed with the burden of caretaking, and father may be either unavailable or uninvited to participate. The upheaval in the family system may create a demanding, or withdrawn child who clings tenaciously to his or her primary caretaker.

When babies and very young children sense parental distress, they lack the ability to articulate their concerns (Wallerstein & Kelly, 1980). The resultant anxiety may well become deep-seated and unconscious as postulated by Freudian theories. Since babies are preverbal, the parents in turn have no means to explain the comings and goings of adult caretakers. They may also interpret the infants's normal behaviors as stemming from divorce-related causes: for example, reporting that a teething baby is fretful because "Daddy deserted us." The following case serves as an illustration:

> Julie, 28, came to therapy complaining of depression and overall fatigue. After her separation from Tom, 29, she moved in with her parents, who now contributed significantly to her support. She allowed her ex-husband only limited contact with their son, Jason, 18 months, because the child cried whenever she was out of sight. She blamed the infant's behavior on the divorce, citing that he had been a happy baby before the separation. By her report, Tom did not know how to handle the child. She was angry that Tom had not helped much with Jason prior to the separation and furious that the child support awarded was insufficient to provide her with a "decent apartment." While she expressed some interest in pursuing a nursing degree, she hesitated to follow through with career plans because she was unable to leave Jason with her parents or for that matter, any other caretaker. The child's typical response was to cry unceasingly when she left, stopping only to sleep when he became fully exhausted.

Fathers as well as children do better when there is continued contact (Jacobs, 1982; Grief, 1979). As this case implies, a related danger for very young children is that without frequent contact, bonding with the absent parent never occurs. Bonding develops as the parent shares in the day-to-day routines, such as feeding, bathing and bedtime rituals. Many men view themselves as inadequate for the caretaking role post-divorce, especially if this has been the wife's domain during the marriage. As the single-parent family boundary forms around the mother, the father becomes alienated (some may withdraw altogether) and the mother's burden increases. The tremendous task overload experienced by the single mother diminishes her ability to adjust in all areas (Ahrons, 1981; Hetherington, Cox & Cox, 1978). This chain of events creates more distress and dysfunction for all participants (Ahrons, 1980).

For the same reasons, divorce is also very hard for preschoolers (Wallerstein & Kelly, 1980). Developmentally, they are starting to move away from home, towards peers and nursery school (Erikson, 1963). They begin to see themselves as a "cause" capable of having an "effect" on the world around them, and need parental encouragement to pursue new areas of competence. They have the beginnings of a sense of morality and are especially vulnerable to guilt and confusion. In the turmoil of parental divorce, they may regress developmentally in a number of ways, including: separation anxiety, sleep disturbances, bed wetting, clinginess, fear of any leave-taking, and aggressive fantasies (Wallerstein & Kelly, 1980). The parents' inappropriate response to these common reactions can interfere with the healthy development of the child's sexual identity as well. When this occurs, the child may become vulnerable to sexual acting-out behavior in adolescence.

Elementary School Children

The impact of divorce on children this age is more profound. Wallerstein and Kelly (1980) found that those in the 6 to 8 age group seem to have the hardest time, as they are old enough to realize what is happening, but lack adequate skills to deal with the disruption. They frequently feel a sense of responsibility, experience tremendous grief, and have a pervasive sadness and yearning for the departed parent. At the same time, they experience recurring fantasies of reconciliation and often believe that they possess the power to make it happen.

According to Erikson's framework (1963), children at this age are primarily engaged in developing their competency in the outside world. The disruption at home endangers the child's efforts to move forward. School performance can be severely affected by day-dreaming or acting-out behaviors, problems with peers (a child may become either a "victim" or a "bully") may occur as the child acts out internal conflicts, and somatic illnesses can develop from the inherent anxiety of the home situation (Wallerstein & Kelly, 1980). The following case is typical of children at this age:

> Michelle, 34, brought Aaron, 6, into the session. Her husband Daniel, 33, had been having an affair with a co-worker, and the couple were contemplating separation. Aaron was very articulate for his age, and demanded to know from the therapist, "What 'bad stuff' has my Daddy done?" He expressed concern that Mommy was angry with his father, and didn't know if he should go out with him as planned on Saturday. When asked about his other problems, he complained that Chris "beat him up all the time." He had refused to go to school on several occasions, and wanted his mother to find him a new school.

In summary, loyalty conflicts represent a major danger for children in latency. With a rudimentary sense of "right" and "wrong," and a concrete approach to all events, these children can easily be hooked into parental feuds. They may at this stage be drawn into parentified roles as confidantes or caretakers of smaller children-adult responsibilities that are damaging emotionally.

The Family with Adolescents

Erikson (1963) proposed that the major adolescent issues revolve around the development of a positive identity versus role confusion. To be certain adolescence is a stage filled with many changes—both physical and emotional—as children begin the process of leaving home and forming an identity separate from their parents. This family life cycle phase requires a new definition of children and the establishment of more permeable boundaries. Parents are no longer the complete authority, yet the children still need parenting and the stability that the family represents.

Divorce upsets the expected sequence of family events at this stage. It is a parent, and not the child, who leaves the nest. The process is further complicated because of the convergence of many similar issues for adolescents and parents — dating, dealing with one's own sexuality, learning to be independent. When the need for a secure "home base" is threatened, the typical adolescent reaction is anger. They may fight with parents around such issues as sexuality, dating, and household responsibilities.

Two negative scenarios are possible. Some teenagers, especially those already having difficulties, may engage in self-destructive behavior such as truancy, substance abuse, and sexual acting-out. Other serious problems, such as suicide and eating disorders, may also be precipitated by the family disruption. In short, the risk of emotional problems and their consequences increases. On the other hand, some adolescents take an opposite tack. They become parental confidantes, coparents to younger siblings, and household assistants. Although they might wish to be left alone, one or both parents may seek their companionship to fill their own loneliness. When children do fill that void, it isolates them from peers and prevents them from moving on.

> Cheryl, 16, had been an honor student throughout her school career. Her father, Walter, 40, left after many years of parental conflict, and after a quick divorce, he remarried. Her mother, Beverly, 37, was depressed and spoke often of suicide to Cheryl. Cheryl took on primary responsibility for managing the home and her two younger brothers, Keith, 13, and Carl, 10. In the school year following the divorce, Cheryl failed geometry and received only average grades in her other subjects. Notably, her father was a mathematician.

Managing teenagers is difficult, even when a marriage is intact. Handling adolescents without the support of the other spouse compounds the difficulty, especially for mothers with sons (Hetherington, 1982) who may accept the social myth that boys can only be controlled by "men," or the psychoanalytic myth that the mother-son relationship is prone to becoming eroticized without the husband/father around. Continually confronted with new situations, the single parent can feel overwhelmed and have trouble feeling "in charge" of her teenage children. Coparenting may become especially nasty. When the teenager's behavior is problematic, neither parent may know what to do, and they may compound the difficulty by blaming each other.

Launching Children and Moving On

As a result of smaller families and greater longevity, this phase of the family life cycle has emerged as the longest phase in the family history. With children no longer the major focus of their relationship, many couples may reassess the continued viability of their marriage. Faced with the necessity to restructure the marital relationship, and with tension exacerbated by career issues and the need to care for the elderly parents, increasing numbers of couples at this stage decide to divorce.

Divorce after a long-term marriage creates a tremendous upheaval due to the couple's long history together, and the fear that it may indeed be "too late" to start over. The latter may be of particular concern to divorcing women in this age group, who may feel ill equipped to enter the workforce at this age and doomed to spend the rest of their days as single persons.

Although young adult children depend less on their parents for day-to-day support, divorce can be very stressful for this age group. They may experience a sense of increased responsibility for their parents and are vulnerable to loyalty conflicts (Ahrons, 1986; Cooney, Smyer, Hagestad & Klock, 1986). Often much anger is directed at the father for leaving mother in their care, even when he did not initiate the divorce (Ahrons, 1986). The father-daughter relationship seems particularly at risk (Cooney et al., 1986). In addition, young adults may experience sadness over the loss of the family home, abandonment by their parents and a concern about their own marriages (Ahrons, 1986). There is also evidence of an increase in alcohol abuse (Cooney et al., 1986).

The biggest danger for young adult children is that they will be unable to leave. Their parents may hold onto them in various and subtle ways, and they may assume the role of substitute spouse. As with adolescents, young adult children may engage in self-destructive behavior that serves to block efforts towards personal growth.

Matt, 21, was a college junior and a member of a prominent fraternity. Always known as the "life of the party," Matt's drinking increased following the separation of his wealthy parents. While his mother had taken off on an extended tour of Europe, his father was left to manage the family business. The older man frequently drove the 40 miles from the family home to campus. Typically, he would take Matt to dinner and spend the evening complaining about his inability to manage the company. Matt began to drink every afternoon, holding "happy hours" in his room for anyone who cared to join him. As his drinking problem progressed, Matt began to become more aggressive and violent when he drank, and there were several episodes involving fights with members of a neighboring fraternity. Ultimately he was arrested for a sexual attack on a co-ed, and Matt was forced by school authorities to obtain treatment for his alcohol problem.

While Matt may have been assisted greatly by the intervention of school authorities, the fact remains that many other young adults may experience difficulties in establishing their careers, maintaining intimate relationships, and establishing new boundaries between themselves and their parents. As Erikson (1963) suggests, this is a time when the individual needs to commit the self to others and a career. Given the competitive nature of contemporary society, they may be at a serious disadvantage. A general lack of purpose in life can lead to isolation from others. In addition, these are the young adults who may marry hastily as a solution to the need for a secure home base, and may begin the cycle of divorce in their own lives.

The Family in Later Life

Divorce in the last stage of the family life cycle reverberates like a shock wave throughout the entire family system, with every problematic aspect of the last phase greatly exaggerated. Three generations of family members are impacted, as those who sit at the helm of the family system separate.

Because the individuals identify themselves in relationship to roles that emerged from the marriage, the process of redefinition is very difficult. It is especially hard to find meaning in one's life (Erikson, 1963), as divorce may precipitate feelings of complete failure. Loneliness is a big problem, as the spouses may feel unable to seek new friendships because of their fear and humiliation. Additionally, people in this age group grew up in a time when divorce was less accepted, making the transition that much more difficult. Even if the marriage was an unhappy one for many years, few family members are prepared for its ending prior to the death of one parent.

> Audrey, 48, was referred by her internist for therapy. High blood pressure had emerged as a health problem, and the physician was concerned about her overall well-being. Her parents, now in their mid 70s were in the process of a divorce. Audrey's father, Tony, 76, seemed to be coping with the support of his brothers and sisters, who had carried long-term resentment towards his wife anyway. However, her mother, Ellen, 74, had only one living sister who had refused to speak with her, citing the "sinfulness" of the divorce as her reason. The older woman called Audrey frequently in tears over problems ranging from doing her income taxes to finding an object she had lost somewhere in the house. Over the years, Audrey and her husband, Bob, 52, had cancelled several plans for a much needed vacation because Audrey was afraid to leave her mother alone. She also was experiencing difficulty with her 26-year-old daughter, Kate, who was angry at Audrey's failure to be more involved with her new baby.

At this case illustrates, the brunt of the hostility and bitterness may be felt by the younger generations (Ahrons, 1986). Adult children are now in middle age, with its attendant crises (Erikson, 1963). They are likely to feel pressed between numerous conflicting demands, as they must now resolve personal issues, renegotiate their own marital relationships, accommodate to the changing needs of their teenage and young adult children, and assume more responsibility for their parents. The burden of care for aging parents may seem premature because it does not develop as a natural result of death or physical illness, but rather because the parents are divorcing. Anger, worry, and guilt are common reactions.

CLINICAL IMPLICATIONS

Parents may present in therapy at any stage during the divorce process and with a variety of reasons, not all of which relate to their children. However, given the general concerns of this paper, the two cases presented here will describe therapeutic efforts to improve the coparental relationship, and address the developmental needs of the dependent children involved.

A therapist will frequently find the ex-spouses have been unable to negotiate a mutually satisfying coparental relationship even years after a separation, and that the children are somehow embroiled in the continued parental conflict. Children may or may not be described as "the problem," but in all cases, their ages indicate the developmental risks involved. The grandparents may be either direct participants in the current struggle, or unresolved conflicts within the family of origin may be contributing indirectly to the single parent's inability to resolve the emotional divorce and restabilize the family.

The genogram provides a three-generational map of the family (see McGoldrick & Gerson, 1985), and creates a graphic record of family membership, ethnic background, gender and occupational roles, significant events, and patterns of closeness and distance. While a full explanation of the genogram is beyond the scope of this discussion, taking a family history in this manner offers a way for the therapist to scan the family tree at a glance. By keeping the entire cast of characters in mind, the therapist extends the view of the family to extended family members who may exert considerable influence on the current situation. Nonfamily members, such as a parent's present or former lover, or other individuals mentioned as playing some important role in family functioning (e.g., a regular babysitter, a close friend, even family pets) can be added when appropriate. Additionally, the sequence of births, deaths, and other family events and crises occurring before or after the divorce, may offer further insight into the family's difficulties. For example, the serious illness or death of a grandparent, the loss of a job, a family move, or upcoming family event (e.g., wedding or graduation) might provide valuable information.

Case I

Ruth, 38, contacted the therapist concerning a behavioral crisis with her daughter, Jane, 13. For the past month, Jane had refused to attend religious instruction to complete studies for her upcoming Bat Mitzvah. Ruth and Jane had engaged in a series of hysterical battles. The celebration was already planned and Ruth called not knowing how to handle her usually obedient daughter.

In a session with Ruth and Jane, the therapist learned that Ruth had been divorced for 3 years from Jane's father, Don, 40 (see Figure 1). She reported herself as very dissatisfied with her financial settlement and acknowledged that she had initiated a suit against him for more money. Jane and her younger brother, Justin, 9, saw their father irregularly. Both were good students and this was the first major difficultly reported by Ruth. When questioned by the therapist, Jane said that she did not want to go through with

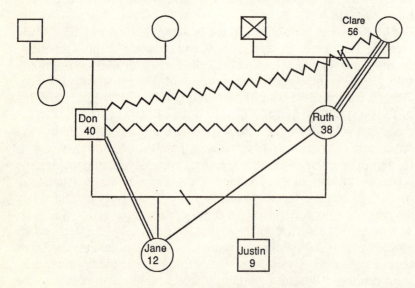

FIGURE 1. Genogram of Post-Divorce Case

the celebration because her father and his family were not going to be invited. She also admitted to being angry at her mother for initiating the divorce. Ruth was somewhat surprised at these revelations, but said that her reason for not inviting Don involved her own mother's statement that she would not attend if he or his family were on the guest list. Since the older woman was paying for the affair, she felt entitled to make this stipulation. The entire family was clearly in an uproar.

The therapist recognized that while Jane's behavior had all the earmarks of adolescent rebellion, the family crisis had less to do with the Bat Mitzvah than unresolved parental conflicts. The separation had been sudden and the children were not adequately prepared to expect the subsequent changes in residence, schools and life-style. Access to their father was hampered by Don's discomfort at being around Ruth. The grandmother, Clare, 56, was directly involved as she subsidized Ruth's alimony and child support income and painted Don as "the villain" in front of the children. This was an old family pattern extending back to Ruth's father, who had "deserted his family." Although Ruth wanted the divorce, she had not been prepared to manage on her own. Ruth stated that she admired Jane's devotion to her father and her efforts to change this pattern; however, she felt caught between her own mother and her daughter.

The therapist formulated three immediate goals from the initial contact. First, Ruth had to separate her own fears and anxieties about the future from the current situation. Second, the pending legal battle needed to be put aside to allow Ruth to include Don in planning the celebration. Third, Ruth had to deal with the more complicated issue of Clare's involvement in the divorce.

The first task the therapist gave Ruth was to identify her own priorities for the celebration, and then to call Don and describe to him how she felt the event should be handled. Jane agreed to return to Hebrew school, confident that her mother was now going to include her father in the plans. Ruth, who had also said that Don "intimidated" her, was instructed to ask for his input and consider any protests carefully. By the second session, the therapist was seeing Ruth alone. She had done her homework, and reported that she felt more in control and less like her mother was orchestrating the event. She and Don had agreed with few difficulties and he had offered to pay for his family and certain related expenses. Jane had kept her promise to return to Hebrew school, and the mother-daughter battles had ceased. While Ruth was relieved about these improvements, she expressed great anxiety about approaching her mother, who she feared would keep her promise to boycott the affair.

The therapist encouraged Ruth to speak with her mother, and to expect that an initial negative reaction would resolve itself if Ruth held firm to her position. Both the therapist and Ruth realized that this was an important first step towards Ruth's realigning her relationship with her mother and helping the entire family adjust to the divorce. The therapist suggested that Ruth tell Clare that she had seen an "expert" in divorce because she was concerned about Jane's welfare. Ruth was also instructed to acknowledge that she knew Clare had always had Ruth's best interests at heart, and that as a "mother" she knew that Clare would understand her predicament. Clare did react negatively, but several days later she agreed to attend.

Subsequent sessions were held with Ruth and Don to give them an opportunity to discuss the divorce process, work out legal differences, and resolve coparental issues.

Case II

Jeff, 32, made the appointment for he and his wife, Susan, 30, to work out the divorce agreement and custody arrangements for their 2-year-old son Todd (see Figure 2). Both were academics living in a southern university town. Neither party had engaged a lawyer and they were still living together. Susan was planning to move out of state at the end of the month.

In the first session, the therapist learned that Jeff had begun an affair soon after Todd's birth, which Jeff perceived as a displacement. The crisis erupted because Jeff, still involved in the affair, had asked for a divorce. Susan's mother had also died 6 months before. Devastated and confused, she felt unable to handle this second shock in so short a time. Jeff hoped therapy would "prepare her emotionally for the separation." When the therapist attempted to

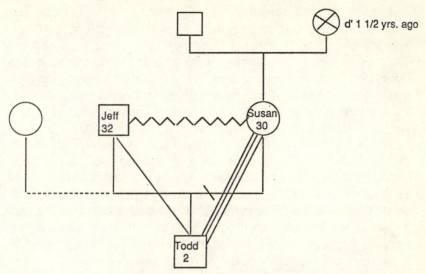

FIGURE 2. Genogram of Custody Case

explore Jeff's reasons for his decision, he made it clear that he was unwilling to discuss the marriage. His concern was Susan's threat to use her custodial rights to withhold visitation as retribution for his behavior. He had agreed to Susan's move, but wanted continued contact with his son.

Because of Susan's difficulty in accepting the divorce, the initial intervention was to define the move as a trial separation in order to give her time to adjust. Jeff agreed, and provisional financial and parenting plans were worked out. Susan chose to move back north with her father to save money; however, she recognized that this move would also help her deal with her ongoing grief over her mother's death.

During the 4-week course of treatment, the therapist identified the issues that led to the breakup, and placed the affair back in the context of the marriage so the couple could have a clearer understanding of the forming of that triangle. Susan developed some insight into Jeff's dissatisfactions. Jeff took more responsibility for his behavior, but remained adamant that he thought it was "too late to change."

A major focus of treatment was to help the couple work out their long-term coparenting arrangements. Susan remained hurt and angry; however, the therapist helped her to see that this, and not Todd's well-being, was the reason she wanted to withhold visitation rights from Jeff. Confronted with research findings, Susan accepted that Todd needed both his parents for at least the next 16 years. Taking into account the distance between the two parental homes and the fact that a 2-year-old cannot be away from his primary caretaker for too long, they agreed to a plan whereby Todd would visit with Jeff at his parents' home in Washington, D.C. Susan liked Jeff's parents and was encouraged by the fact that they would be there to help Jeff care for Todd. Susan anticipated that separations from Todd might be painful, but she understood that this was important for Todd and would provide her with some time for herself. They agreed that visiting arrangements would change as Todd grew older and was able to sustain longer separations.

Susan accepted the therapist's recommendation to seek a new therapist after her move to help her work through her grief and the possibility that the trial separation might well end in divorce. Jeff was also advised to seek therapy, but in a session alone confirmed that he was too invested in his new relationship to see the need.

The family life cycle itself can be a useful psychoeducational tool in dealing with the problems that develop during the divorce process. Within the nuclear family, assisting the parents in understanding the changing needs of their children, and their own related needs vis-à-vis the life cycle, can give them a new perspective on their problems. For example, parents with adolescents might be helped by the knowledge that family boundaries at this stage need to become more permeable, and by the recognition that even intact families experience the stress associated with mid-life issues that often parallel the child's quest for identity. The divorce can be framed as complicating family growth, rather than permanently damaging family members. Parenting education around the child's age-related development can be a valuable part in helping parents approach necessary changes. Discussing the continued importance of the grandparents can also lead spouses to dealing with their issues with the older generation more effectively.

Many parents do not seek therapy during the actual crisis precipitated by the separation. Some years later, after the family has seemingly restabilized, a youngster may develop stage-related difficulties. For example, a child who experienced parental divorce as a preschooler may not be viewed as a problem until school performance falls below the child's measured abilities. Or a child who experienced parental divorce during latency may become "out-of-control" only when the mother remarries in adolescence. As the therapist takes the family's history, it is worthwhile to include on the genogram events related to the divorce process itself — the shifts in residence, custody arrangements, and lingering resentments — in order to determine appropriate intervention.

CONCLUSION

To say that divorce therapy is a difficult business may well be an understatement. The therapist must maintain a position of neutrality while joining with each member, even those who do not appear in family sessions. In order to explore the problems of children, who can easily be seen as the "victims" of divorce, the therapist needs to be very clear about his/her own issues and biases. It is probably not possible for a therapist who "doesn't believe in divorce" to assist people struggling with this adjustment. Similarly, a therapist who has unresolved issues around the family life cycle stage in question (e.g., a therapist who functioned as a parentified child during his/her adolescence) may be hard pressed to work effectively with the client family. Regarding the stages of divorce, a therapist still going through his/her own divorce may have equal difficulty being objective and coping with the pain triggered by the client's issues. Under all circumstances, peer group or colleague support will be helpful.

As divorce becomes a part of the culture, we are seeing more and more discussion in the media about its attendant problems. Many parents already come to therapy seeking "a good divorce" for their children, despite their own marital disappointment. Children in many school districts now receive education in psychosocial issues. They are being taught that they have "feelings," and are being encouraged to express themselves. Children of divorce are often enrolled in small discussion groups where their issues are brought

out in the open, and teachers are developing the awareness necessary to spot problems that may once have gone unnoticed. Grandparents are becoming more accepting of the circumstances and
more vocal about their rights and needs for continued contact with
grandchildren. These signs all bode well for the future of the children of divorce.

On the other hand, the incidence of second divorces indicates that
outward signs of stability in the single-parent family may mask unresolved issues (Herz, in press). The necessity to blend families,
each with their own idiosyncratic approaches to preceding stages of
the life cycle and the divorce process, appears to be beyond the
reach of many people. As therapists, we might easily be tempted to
throw up our hands in collective despair. The only alternative is to
take each family where we find them, and work to enhance the
functioning of all family members.

REFERENCES

Abarbanel, A. (1979). Shared parenting after separation and divorce. *American
    Journal of Orthopsychiatry. 49*, 320-324.
Ahrons, C. R. (1980). Divorce: A crisis of family transition and change. *Family
    Relations. 29*, 533-540.
Ahrons, C. R. (1980a). Redefining the divorced family: A conceptual framework.
    Social Work. 25, 6, 437-441.
Ahrons, C. R. (1981). The continuing co-parental relationship between divorced
    spouses. *American Journal of Orthopsychiatry. 59*, 415-427.
Ahrons, C. R. (1986). Divorce when the children are older. Presentation to the
    American Family Therapy Association Conference, Washington, DC, June
    1986.
Bowen, M. (1978). *Family therapy in clinical practice.* New York: Jason Aronson.
Carter, E. A. & McGoldrick, M. (Eds.). (1980). *The family life cycle.* New York:
    Gardner.
Cooney, T., Smyer, M. Hagestad, G., & Klock, R. (1986). Parental divorce in
    young adulthood: Some preliminary findings. *American Journal of Orthopsy-
    chiatry. 56*, 470-484.
Emery, R. (1982). Interparental conflict and the children of discord and divorce.
    Psychological Bulletin. 91, 12-20.
Erikson, E. H. (1963). *Childhood and society.* New York: Norton.
Glick, P. C. (1984). Marriage, divorce, and living arrangements: Prospective
    changes. *Journal of Family Issues. 5*, 7-26.

Goldsmith, J. (1980). Relationships between former spouses: Descriptive findings. *Journal of Divorce. 4,* 1-20.

Gould, R. (1978). *Transformations: Growth and change in adult life.* New York: Simon & Schuster.

Greif, J. B. (1979). Fathers, children, and joint custody. *American Journal of Psychiatry. 49,* 311-319.

Herz, F. (in press). The post-divorce family. In E. A. Carter & M. McGoldrick (Eds.), *The family life cycle.* (2nd ed.) New York: Gardner.

Hess, R. & Camara, K. (1979). Post-divorce family relationships as mediating factors in the consequence of divorce for children. *Journal of Social Issues. 35,* 79-96.

Hetherington, E. M., Cox, M., & Parker, R. D. (1977). Beyond father absence: Conceptualization of the effects of divorce. In *Contemporary readings in child psychology.* New York: McGraw-Hill.

Hetherington, E. M., Cox., M., Cox, R. (1978). The development of children in mother-headed households. In H. Hoffman & D. Reis (Eds.), *The American family: Dying of developing.* New York: Plenum.

Hetherington, E. M. (1982). Modes of adaptation to divorce and single parenthood which enhance family functioning: Implications for a preventive program. Unpublished paper, University of Virginia.

Issacs, M. (1982). Helping Mom fail: A case of stalemated divorcing process. *Family Process. 21,* 225-234.

Jacobs, J. (1982). The effects of divorce on fathers: An overview of the literature. *American Journal of Orthopsychiatry. 52,* 223.

Kelly, J., Gigy, L., & Hausman, S. (1986). Mediated and adversarial divorce: Initial findings from the divorce and mediation project. In J. Folberg & A. Milne (Eds.), *Divorce mediation: Theory and practice.* New York: Guilford.

Kivnick, H. Q. (1982). Grandparenthood: An overview of meaning and mental health. *The Gerontologist, 22,* 121-131.

Levinson, D. (1978). *The seasons of a man's life.* New York: Knopf.

Luepnitz, D. (1982). *Child custody: A study of families after divorce.* Lexington, MA: Lexington Books.

McGoldrick, M. (1982). Ethnicity and family therapy: An overview. In M. McGoldrick, J. K. Pearce, & J. Giordano (Eds.), *Ethnicity and family therapy* (pp. 3-30). New York: Guilford.

McGoldrick, M. & Gerson, R. (1985). *Genograms in family assessment.* New York: Norton.

National Center for Health Statistics. (1984a). Births, marriages, divorces and deaths, U.S. 1983). *Monthly Vital Statistics Report. 32,* March 26, 1984a. DHHS Pub. No. (PHS) 84-1120. Public Health Service, Hyattsville, MD.

Raschke, H. & Raschke, V. (1979). Family conflict and children's self concepts: A comparison of intact and single-parent families. *Journal of Marriage and the Family. 41,* 367-374.

Spanier, G. B. & Casto, R. F. (1979). Adjustment to separation and divorce: An analysis of 50 case studies. *Journal of Divorce. 2*, 211-253.

Steinman, S. (1981). The experience of children in a joint custody arrangement: A report of a study. *American Journal of Orthopsychiatry. 51*, 403-414.

Wallerstein, J. & Kelly, J. B. (1980). *Surviving the breakup: How children and parents cope with divorce.* New York: Basic Books.

Weitzman, L. (1985). *The divorce revolution.* New York: The Free Press.

CHILDREN'S PERCEPTIONS OF THE DIVORCE EXPERIENCE

Children's Definitions of Family Following Divorce of Their Parents

Linnea Klee
Catherine Schmidt
Colleen Johnson

SUMMARY. As children adapt to new, non-biologically based family forms as a result of the high incidence of divorce in the United States, new definitions of family may develop. This paper reports results from an anthropological study of children's definitions of their families following divorce of their parents. Interviews were conducted with 29 children of white, middle-class, divorced parents as part of an ongoing study of the effects of divorce on families. These children's definitions of their families fell into five, progressively more expansive types, from a limited, household definition to an expansive type including biological, legal, and non-kin. Children's use of criteria beyond biology or law to define their reconstituted families after divorce of their parents illustrates the voluntary nature of American kinship systems.

INTRODUCTION

The high incidence of divorce in the United States has resulted in an evolution in family organization that has an impact on all members, but particularly on children, as they are socialized to an under-

Linnea Klee, PhD, Catherine Schmidt, PhD, and Colleen Johnson, PhD, are on the faculty of the Medical Anthropology Program, University of California, San Francisco, CA.

This paper results from research funded by the Academic Senate Committee on Research, University of California, San Francisco, and stems from research funded by the National Institute of Mental Health (1RO1 MH/AG 35630) and the National Institute on Aging (1RO1 AG 05348).

109

standing of family life and family structure. While some recent evidence suggests that the rate of divorce has stabilized at a very high level (Moorman and Norton, 1987), other estimates suggest that half of all recent marriages will end in divorce (Furstenberg and Spanier, 1984). More than half of these couples have children at the time of divorce, and the number of children involved in divorces doubled between 1960 and 1980 (Spanier and Glick, 1981). Eventually three of four divorced women and four of five divorced men remarry (Glick, 1984). As a consequence, 4.8 million children live in households with stepparents (Furstenberg and Spanier, 1984).

The distinctive character of children's experience of divorce and remarriages of their parents is that, unlike their parents, they maintain membership in the families of both parents. Rather than having an abbreviated family form, they are likely to have an expanded kinship network. For example, while a divorced man may lose contact with his ex-wife's family, his child will retain relationships with the mother's and father's relatives, and add new relationships with the families of one or more new stepparents (Furstenberg and Spanier, 1984; Johnson and Barer, 1987). Paul Bohannan (1970) has pointed out that our definitions of kinship, based on "blood" or genetics, have lagged behind these new family forms, so that "Americans are creating households in which more and more of the members are not kinsmen of one another," according to our cultural definitions of kinship (p. 121).

As children adapt to the inclusion of these new family forms, the question arises whether their experiences will lead to new definitions of the family as they form their own families with marriage. Such changed views of the family could have broad social, psychological and legal ramifications. New terminology may become necessary to refer to new relationships (Mead, 1970). Research has demonstrated the set of social, economic, and psychological changes that are initiated by remarriage of one or both parents (Longfellow, 1979; Wallerstein and Kelly, 1979; Wallerstein, 1985). A concentration in research on clinical populations of children may place undue emphasis on the negative impact of divorce on children. While most observers recognize these negative effects, children of divorce may have an important mediating influence in complex reconstituted families. Such a role of the child has been given almost no attention in the literature, although it may be a positive force.

Sociological and anthropological examinations of family forms have tended to develop in two directions. Family sociology has often focused on a nuclear family model based on a middle-class, white norm that neglects the role of extended family, particularly among ethnic minorities (Staples and Mirande, 1986). In addition, as Skolnick and Skolnick (1986) note, the concept of pluralism so commonly recognized in other aspects of American society, has yet to be applied to the family (p. 470). Anthropologists who study kinship either focus on the symbols and meanings of kinship relationships (Schneider, 1980) or social structural issues (Barnes, 1980).

Divorce entails major structural realignments in family, household and kinship systems; however, scant attention has been accorded to actual emerging family forms. With the rise in single-parent families, cohabitation, and homosexual unions, large numbers of the population do not live in conventional family forms. Presently, there are no identified organizing principles for such family organization and dissolution; rather choices of kin and the quality of relationships appear to be discretionary and varied (Schneider, 1980). The impact of new family forms on the socialization of children in general, and particularly on the ways in which children learn to conceptualize the family, needs greater attention.

A recent study by Isaacs, Leon and Kline (1987) of 202 children of divorce employed the Draw-A-Family Test to examine whether or not children omitted the nonresident parent from their conceptions of the family. It was found that joint custody, frequent visitation, and parents who get along well are factors that reduce the omission of the nonresident parent. The authors concluded that in their evaluations of the reconstituted family children actively assess who is responsible for them as well as the quality of the relationship between parents. This study did not report the children's exclusion or inclusion of family members other than parents in their family definitions.

Although Isaacs, Leon and Kline emphasized the importance of the nature of relationships across *all* custody arrangements, clearly children's definitions of the family are influenced by custody, which favors the mother in about 9 in 10 cases (Furstenberg and Spanier, 1984). Furstenberg and Spanier (1984) found in a longitudinal study of divorce and remarriage that contact between children and most nonresidential parents, usually the fathers, gradually diminished after divorce. National survey data also report low frequency of contact between children of divorce and the nonresidential biological parents (usually the father) (Furstenberg, Nord, Peterson and Zill, 1983). Although children may retain links to the nonresidential biological parent and his family, the low frequency of contact with the father may result in a situation after the mother remarries in which, with the presence of a stepfather, "sociological parenthood takes precedence over biological parenthood." The consequent pattern of child care has been characterized as "a system of child swapping," as, with their own remarriages, fathers refocus their attention from biological children to stepchildren and new progeny (Furstenberg and Spanier, 1984, p. 29).

This paper reports findings from research that examined children's conceptions of the new family forms resulting from divorce of their parents. Its focus is on distinctions children make among the variety of relationships consequent on divorce and remarriage. The study examined a nonclinical population of children, and viewed the child not as a victim of divorce, but as an active agent in the definition of his or her new family form.

The specific aim of the study was to determine what criteria children use to distinguish between kin and non-kin and specifically, how relatives of divorce and remarriage are either incorporated into or excluded from their definitions of their reconstituted families.

METHODS

This study derives from a larger, longitudinal project which, since 1983, has been examining the effect of divorce on three generations in 50 families involved in divorces (Johnson, 1983, 1985; Johnson and Barer, 1987; Johnson, in press). We used standard tools of anthropologists who study kinship and elicited the children's definitions of their families following the marital changes of their parents.

Sample

The majority of families were selected from public divorce records in middle-class suburbs in the San Francisco Bay Area. One member of the divorcing couple was contacted initially, and permission gained to have access to his or her mother, as the primary focus of the study was to examine the role of grandmothers in families of divorce. Opportunity sampling provided a smaller group of women who referred us to their divorcing children. Both generations were interviewed two or three times over a 40-month period. At the completion of this series of interviews, we contacted the divorced parents who had children aged 10 and older. With parental permission, we conducted 29 interviews with the third generation, the children of divorce.

There were several limitations to the study design. To control for the effects of social class and ethnicity, the sample is confined to middle-class white families. An additional constraint on the sample is that parents who refused permission for their children to be interviewed (n = 4 families) may have experienced greater disruption following divorce than those interviewed.[1] In addition, although all divorces took place at approximately the same time, five years before the interviews with children, the ages of the children at the time of their parents' separation ranged from 1-20, with a mean of 8.7. Consequently, in interpretative statements on the impact of divorce on these children one must consider their age at the time of separation and/or divorce. Accumulated evidence suggests that younger children are more adversely affected by divorce than older children (Longfellow, 1979). How age may influence children's conceptions of the composition of their families following divorce is unknown.

The characteristics of the sample of children interviewed are presented in Table 1. They ranged in age from 10 to 26 years, with a mean of 14.9 years, and by chance, two-thirds were female. More of the children had experienced remarriage of their fathers (45%) than of their mothers (28%), but three of the fathers' remarriages had also ended in divorce. Forty-one percent of the children lived with a step-parent, but step-siblings or half-siblings were present in the households of only seven children. Two of the children's mothers were cohabiting, as were two of the children's fathers.

Table 1:   Sample Characteristics

n=29

Sex

    Female: 20

    Male :   9

Age

    10-12 :   9

    13-17 :   13

    18 + :   7

Household Status

	Yes	No
Stepparent	12	17
Step sibling	3	26
Half sibling	4	25

Parents' Marital Status

	Mother	Father
Divorced	18	11
Remarried	8	10
Remarried/Divorced	0	3
Cohabiting	2	2
Divorced/Widowed	1	0
Deceased	0	3

Procedures

An open-ended interview guide was used to interview the children. In addition, two paper and pencil instruments were completed: a kinship diagram of the child's family and a set of concentric "relationship circles" on which the child wrote the names of people in his or her network, indicating social closeness or distance. The interview guide covered the following topics:

1. Demographic background: age and sex
2. Household status
3. Social adjustment to school or work, and outside activities
4. Relatives with whom holidays are celebrated
5. Definitions of family and kinship terminology
6. Numbers of siblings, half-siblings, and step-siblings
7. Contact measures for significant relatives
8. Typical activities with significant relatives
9. Measures of social support

Interviews took place in the children's homes and lasted approximately one hour. They were conducted by either an anthropologist or a sociologist who had also interviewed many of the other family members in the longitudinal study and were familiar with the families.

RESULTS

For this paper, we examined in particular children's definitions of their families. Specifically, children were asked "With whom are you living now?" and "Who is in your family?" They were also asked the kinship terms by which they address their relatives and the terms used to talk about them to others. Our major concern here was with the key relatives that result from divorce and remarriage; i.e., stepparents, step- and half-siblings, and other step-kin. We were also interested in the place in the children's family definitions of the non-custodial parent, namely the father.

Children's definitions of their families fell into five types which demonstrated a progressively more expansive pattern. In the following discussion, each type is defined and exemplified by a brief case study of one child's family. A diagram for each case study is presented in Figure 1.

1. *The Household*: Ten percent (3) of the children identified their families as the members of their household, including their mothers (custodial), stepfathers, siblings, half-siblings, and step-siblings. All three excluded their biological fathers (who were not members of the households) from the definition of their families. Mean age was 12.3.

Case Study: Julie, age 10, was four years old when her parents separated. Both of her parents have remarried; custody is maternal. Julie's household includes her mother, brother and stepfather, and on alternate weeks, her stepfather's youngest child from his former marriage. Julie's two other step-siblings live with their mother and visit their father infrequently. Julie only erratically visits her father and his new wife, who has a 22-year-old daughter from the first of her five marriages. Julie describes her father as "kinda wild and weird," and her stepfather as "all business." She is not particularly close to either one. Julie's family definition included mother, brother, stepfather, and stepbrother ("I guess, since they live with me").

2. *The Biological Family*: Twenty-eight percent (8) of the children defined their family according to biological ties, including mother, father, siblings, grandparents, aunts and uncles. Household status for these children included maternal custody with and without stepfathers and step- and half-siblings, and two adults on their own. In the three relevant cases, stepparents, step-siblings and half-siblings were *not* included in the definition of family, even when they were members of the child's household. Mean age was 17.5.

Case study: Jason, age 13, was seven when his parents separated. His mother, who has custody of her two sons, has remarried. Jason lives with his mother, younger brother, stepfather, and half-sister. Although Jason's relationship with his stepfather is friendly, he maintains a closer relationship with his father, whom he visits almost every weekend, and who has not remarried. Jason's definition of his family included his mother, father, brother and himself.

3. *The Biological with Step Family*: Seventeen percent (5) of the children defined their families to include the biological members in

the previous type, and their stepparents and half-siblings (no step-siblings existed). Households included maternal and joint custody with and without stepfathers, and one adult on his own. Mean age was 16.4.

Case study: Jessie, age 10, was two years old when her parents separated. Although her mother has remarried and maintains a bitter relationship with Jessie's father, joint custody is strictly adhered to, with Jessie spending alternate weeks in each household. Jessie has always been extremely close to her father, and in recent years has grown closer to her stepfather. There are no step-siblings as her father has not remarried and her stepfather had no previous marriages or children. Jessie describes her family as including her father, her mother, her stepfather, both sets of grandparents, maternal aunts and paternal aunts and nephews.

4. *Expansive Family with Kin*: Twenty-eight percent (8) of the children defined their families as either the Biological or Biological with Step described above, with the additional inclusion of cousins, second cousins, step-kin, aunts or uncles spouses, and affinals of the informant's spouse, including a stepdaughter. The biological father was excluded in three cases. Households included maternal and joint custody and two adult informants. Mean age was 14.5.

Case study: Jenny, age 12, was six years old when her parents separated. Jenny's father has remarried, and Jenny has a baby half-sister from this union, her only sibling. Custody is joint, and Jenny spends two weeks a month in each of her parents' households. Her mother has not remarried. Although Jenny's mother and father maintain a hostile relationship, Jenny is equally close to both parents, and Jenny's mother retains ties with many of her ex-in-laws. Jenny's family definition included her mother, father, stepmother, half-sister, aunts and cousins on both sides, grandmother, step-grandfather, stepmother's parents, second cousin, great aunts and great uncles (and her cats).

5. *Expansive Family with Non-Kin*: Seventeen percent (5) of the children defined an Expansive Family with Kin as above with the additional inclusion of informant's boyfriend or girlfriend, parents' or grandparents' cohabitants, ex-step-kin, and friends. Households included maternal and joint custody. Mean age was 13.4.

Figure 1: Kinship Diagrams*

I. Julie: THE HOUSEHOLD

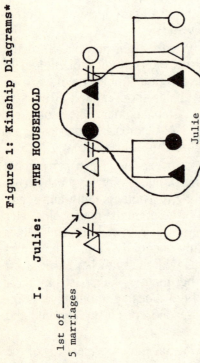

II. Jason: THE BIOLOGICAL FAMILY

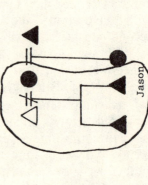

III. Jessie: THE BIOLOGICAL WITH STEP FAMILY

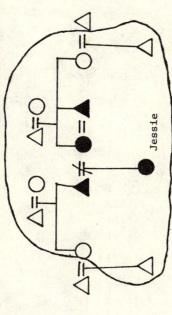

Jessie

*Relatives included in family definitions are circled;
household members are filled in.

△ male ○ female = marriage ≠ divorce ∅ ⌀ deceased

119

Figure 1: Kinship Diagrams (continued)*

IV.   Jenny: EXPANSIVE WITH KIN

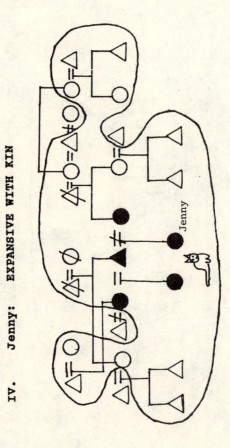

v.   Joanne: EXPANSIVE WITH NON KIN

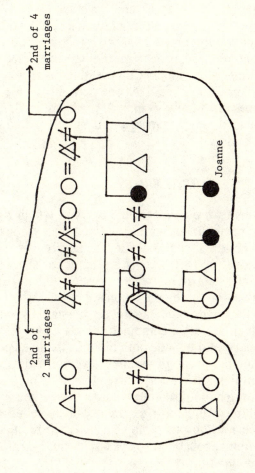

2nd of 4
marriages

2nd of
2 marriages

Joanne

*Relatives included in family definitions are circled;
household members are filled in.

△ male ○ female = marriage ≠ divorce ∅ ⌀ deceased

Case study: Joanne, age 15, was 11 when her parents separated. Her father has subsequently remarried and divorced again, but Joanne still considers her ex-stepmother and ex-step-siblings part of her family. Joanne also maintains relationships with several of her father's former cohabiting girlfriends and their children. Joanne's mother has custody of her two daughters, but Joanne and her sister see their father several times a week and have spent several summers living with him. Her mother has not remarried, but has a long-term relationship with a divorced man with grown children. Joanne's paternal grandmother has been married and divorced twice, and maternal grandfather four times. Commenting on her expansive kinship network, Joanne remarked, "At one point I had nine grandparents." She defines her family to include "All my relatives, everyone I'm related to through marriage and blood, including my Dad's ex-wife and children."

DISCUSSION

We found that there were five possible ways in which the children in this sample of divorced families defined their reconstituted families. For some children, such as Julie, the family was confined to the two-generational unit of parents and children sharing their households, including stepparents where present. Others, such as Jason, defined a two- or three-generational family linked by the biological ties of the predivorce family only; step-kin were excluded. Children such as Jessie combined these types into a more expansive family that could include both biological and stepparents of the same sex. Another group of children, exemplified by Jenny, expanded their families still further through both biological and step-kin ties, including biological and stepparents and their kin. The final group of children were most expansive in their definitions, including a network not only of biological and step relatives, but non-kin, such as parents, cohabitants, or ex-step-kin, as in Joanne's case.

With a sample this size, sex composition and age range, it is difficult to say whether there are differences by age or sex in the ways children define their families following divorce. Children defining their family strictly as the household members with whom they lived had the youngest mean age, which suggests a narrower perspective for younger children. However, the group with the next youngest mean age were those with the most expansive definition of family. We feel that differences in family definitions are more likely to be accounted for by the nature of particular relationships than by sex and age.

Sixty-nine percent (20) of sample children had at least one stepparent. Each child was asked if he/she felt related to the stepparent, and could respond "Yes," "Sort of," or "No." Seventy-five percent of those with stepmothers responded "Yes" or "Sort of" to this question, while 90% of those with stepfathers responded this way. While the difference in these responses may reflect the living arrangements of most of these children (with mother and stepfather) and the potential replacement of biological fathers by stepfathers, it may also indicate a commonly observed greater difficulty in the acceptance of stepmothers than stepfathers (Furstenberg and Spanier, 1984). In another publication (Johnson, Klee and Schmidt, 1988), we analyzed how the children perceived their fathers and stepmothers to be more distant from them and less involved than their mothers and stepfathers, irrespective of how active their fathers were. Kinship terminology did not clarify this difference in feelings of relatedness, for with the exception of only one child, all called their stepparents by their first names, rather than by "mother" or "father" terms.

Because previous studies have suggested the potential replacement of biological fathers by stepfathers in the many instances of maternal custody, we looked closely at the place of the biological and stepfathers in children's definitions of their families. Although none of the fathers in this sample of children was awarded sole custody, the majority maintained contact and visitation rights with their children, and displayed a commitment to co-parenting. In three cases joint custody was actively maintained. Only three of the interviewed children had infrequent contact with their fathers. Nevertheless, eight of the sample children excluded their biological fathers from their definitions of their post-divorce families. Table 2

Table 2: Exclusion of Father from Family Definition   n=8

Age	Sex	Family Type	Reason for Exclusion of Father	Relationship with Stepfather	Relationship with Stepmother
10	F	Household	unstable father	included in family definition	no relationship
12	M	Household	rare contact	included in family definition	no relationship
15	M	Household	contact, but gay, lives with lover	included in family definition	NA
13	M	Biological	unstable father	excluded from family definition	no relationship
9	F	Expansive with kin	absent	NA	no relationship
13	F	Expansive with kin	relies on other kin more	NA	NA
14	F	Expansive with kin	absent	NA	no relationship
14	F	Expansive with non-kin	she finds him boring and has decreased contact	Mother's boyfriend in family definition	included in family definition

illustrates these cases and their apparent reasons for exclusion of their fathers.[2]

In four of these cases, it appears that a replacement of biological father by stepfather has taken place. Three of these children define their family as the household type, including the resident stepfather, and excluding the non-resident father. In the fourth case, a 14-year-old girl includes her mother's resident boyfriend in her definition (expansive with non-kin) of her family, and excludes her father, even though he sees her occasionally. In three additional cases of exclusion of the father from family definition there is no stepfather to make a replacement. These children defined their families as expansive with kin. Apparently, lacking stepfathers, they have substituted other relatives for their biological fathers in their family definitions. In the final case of exclusion of the father, a 13-year-old boy defines his family biologically, but limits it to his mother and sister. From our interviews we have learned that he has poor quality relationships with both his non-resident father and with his resident stepfather and step-siblings.

The five ways that children in this study defined their reconstituted families after divorce offer us an initial structure for examining children's conceptions of the effect of divorce on kinship systems. Some children define their families as limited, either by the proximity and immediate support of members of the household, or by traditional biological ("blood") ties. Other children conceive of their families in more expansive ways: including step-kin along with their biologically defined families, including both step-kin and a wider expanse of biological relatives in their family definition, or finally, by including such legal and biological relatives as well as people who are not related to the child in either of these ways.

David Schneider (1980) has said that the important feature of the American kinship system is its discretionary quality. Thus American kinship systems operate on a voluntary basis depending upon attraction, friendships, proximity and a host of other factors. Such leeway and flexibility is also evident in definitions of family and kinship among both divorcing parents and their children. As relationships change with the addition and subtraction of members through additional marriages and divorces, children's definitions may become more flexible, going beyond the criteria of biology or law to the more immediate realities of relations with the people with whom they live and/or on whom they depend for the necessities provided by family life.

NOTES

1. Thirty-four families from the original sample had children of eligible ages. Thirteen of the families did not participate. Four refused permission, two because they felt the family had been interviewed enough and two because they did not want to involve their children in the study. Nine other families could not participate because two could not be reached, two were "too busy" or the children were away at college, two moved too far away to be interviewed, and the decision was made not to contact three families because of their treatment for drug or alcohol problems.

2. The children were not asked specifically why they excluded their biological fathers from their family definitions. Our familiarity with the family situations from interviews with various family members over the years, as well as questions of the children concerning contact with their fathers, shared activities, holidays, and provision of assistance to the child, provided apparent reasons for the exclusion.

REFERENCES

Barnes, J. A. (1980) "Kinship studies: Some impressions of the current state of play." Man 15(2): 293-303.

Bohannan, P. (Ed.) (1970) Divorce and After. Garden City, N.Y.:Doubleday.

Furstenberg, F. F. and G. B. Spanier (1984) Recycling the Family: Remarriage after Divorce. Beverly Hills: Sage.

Furstenberg, F. F., C. W. Nord, J. L. Peterson and N. Zill (1983)"The life course of children of divorce: Marital disruption and parental contact." American Sociological Review 48: 656-668.

Glick, P. C. (1984) "Marriage, divorce, and living arrangements: Prospective changes." Journal of Family Issues 5: 7-26.

Isaacs, M. B., G. H. Leon and M. Kline (1987) "When is a parent out of the picture? Different custody, different perceptions." Family Process 26: 101-110.

Johnson, C. L. (1983) "A cultural analysis of the grandmother." Research in Aging 5: 547-567.

Johnson, C. L. (1985) "Grandparenting options in divorcing families: An anthropological perspective," in V. Bengston and J. Robertson (Eds.), Grandparenthood. Beverly Hills: Sage.

Johnson, C. L. "Definitions of family and kinship relations with divorce and remarriage," in I. Rauch and G. Carr (Eds.), The Semiotic Bridge: Trends from California. Berlin: Mouton de Guyter, in press.

Johnson, C. L. and B. Barer (1987) "Marital instability and changing kinship networks of grandparents." The Gerontologist 27(3): 330-335.

Johnson, C. L., L. Klee and C. Schmidt (1988) "Conceptions of parentage and kinship among children of divorce." The American Anthropologist 90(1): 136-144.

Longfellow, C. (1979) "Divorce in context: Its impact on children," in G. Levinger and 0. Moles (Eds.), Divorce and Separation. New York: Basic Books.

Mead, M. (1970) "Anomalies in American postdivorce relationships," in Paul Bohannan (Ed.), Divorce and After. Garden City, N.Y.: Doubleday, pp. 97-112.

Moorman, J. E. and A. J. Norton (1987) "Current trends in marriage and divorce among American women." The Journal of Marriage and Family 49(1): 3-14.

Schneider, D. (1980) "Twelve years later: An afterward," in American Kinship: A Cultural Account. Chicago: University of Chicago Press.

Skolnick, A. S. and J. H. Skolnick (Eds.) (1986) Family in Transition: Rethinking Marriage, Sexuality, Child Rearing and Family Organization, 5th Ed. Boston: Little, Brown.

Spanier, G. B. and P. C. Glick (1981) "Marital instability in the United States: Some correlates and recent changes." Family Relations 30: 329-338.

Staples, R. and A. Mirande (1986) "Racial and cultural variations among American families: A decennial review of the literature on minority families." Pages 474-497 in A. S.

Wallerstein, J. (1985) "The overburdened child: Some long-term consequences of divorce." Columbia Journal of Law and Social Problems 19: 165-182.

Wallerstein, J. and J. Kelly (1979) "Children and divorce: A review." Social Work 24(6): 468-474.

Wallerstein, J. and J. Kelly (1980) Surviving the Breakup: How Parents and Children Cope with Divorce. New York: Basic Books.

Effects of Family Structure on Children's Self-Concepts

Melanie K. Johnson
Roger L. Hutchinson

SUMMARY. This study examined the effects of family structure (intact, stepparent, and single-parent) on children's self-concepts using Parish and Parish's Personal Attribute Inventory for Children (PAIC). One hundred and ninety-nine (199) students in grades 7 through 12 participated. Although children from stepfamilies checked fewer positive adjectives than students from single-parent or intact families, a statistically significant difference (.05 level) was not found.

American society is experiencing many changes in the makeup of family compositions. The number of nontraditional families, which includes single-parent families and stepfamilies, has been steadily increasing over the years (Touliatos & Lindholm, 1980). In a 1979 survey, Glick indicated that the number of children under 18 years of age, who reside with only one parent, has doubled since 1960. The number of children living in stepfamilies, which have also been cited in the literature as blended, reconstituted, or remarried families, has increased 1.6% over the same period. Since 1960, there has been an 11.5% decline in the number of intact families, which are families containing both biological parents (Glick, 1979). These

---

Melanie K. Johnson is a graduate student and Roger L. Hutchinson is on the faculty of the Department of Counseling Psychology and Guidance Services, Ball State University, Muncie, IN 47306.

statistics clearly indicate that the number of stepfamilies in our society is on the rise.

A study (Parish & Dostal, 1980) was conducted to determine how children's perceptions of self varied according to the family structure in which they lived (intact, divorced remarried, and divorced nonremarried). They administered Parish's Personal Attribute Inventory for Children (PAIC) to 738 children ranging in age from 11-14 years. The results indicated that children from both single-parent and stepfamilies (divorced nonremarried and divorced remarried) perceived themselves and their parents less favorably than did children from intact families. Their findings were statistically significant at the .01 level.

In a similar study, Raschke and Raschke (1979) tested the hypothesis that family structure (i.e., intact, single-parent, or reconstituted) should have no effect on a child's self-concept. Their study involved 289 children in grades 3, 6, and 8. They used the Piers-Harris Children's Self-Concept Scale to measure self-concept. No statistically significant differences in self-concept scores of children from intact, single-parent, or reconstituted families were found. Their findings lend support to the proposition that "children are not adversely affected by living in a single-parent family, but family conflict and/or parental unhappiness can be detrimental, at least to self-concept, which is also a measure of social and personal adjustment" (p. 373).

The purpose of this study was to explore how this change in lifestyle (stepfamily, single-parent) may affect the children involved. After reviewing some of the research conducted on the different family structures and the children involved in them, and from observations in our own workplaces, we became interested in developing a better understanding of children's perceptions of themselves and how they might be affected by living in various family structures. We tended to believe that children from stepfamilies would not perceive themselves as positively as children from either intact homes or single-parent homes. This pre-research assumption was based on our observations that many children with whom we have worked seem to survive their parent's divorce but have difficulty adjusting to the second emotional jolt of becoming a member of a stepfamily.

METHOD

The PAIC was administered to the students from the 3 different family structures. It was hypothesized that there would be differences in how children from stepfamilies, single-parent families, and intact families perceived themselves. Additionally, differences in relation to sex and grade were investigated. Specific adjectives that children from the different family structures chose when describing themselves were also examined.

Participants

Participants were 214 students in grades 7 through 12 attending a university-related laboratory school which enrolls a cross section of students regarding socioeconomic backgrounds. Of the 214 subjects who participated, 199 (82 boys, 117 girls) provided data which could be used in the study. Nine cases were eliminated because of insufficient or unclear information; 6 were not included because the children were in a single-parent home as a result of parental loss through death and not divorce. This left a total of 199 subjects across the 6 different grade levels. There were 37 seventh graders, 18 eighth graders, 50 ninth graders, 51 tenth graders, 24 eleventh graders, and 19 twelfth graders. Of these students, 143 (72%) were from intact families, 24 (12%) from stepfamilies, and 32 (16%) from single-parent families.

Instrument

The Personal Attribute Inventory for Children (PAIC) contains a list of 24 positive and 24 negative adjectives arranged in alphabetical order. An example of some of the adjectives are angry, fairminded, complaining, and handsome. Children are asked to select 15 adjectives which best describe themselves.

In a study (Parish & Parish, 1983) utilizing the PAIC, 426 children from intact, divorced, and reconstituted families were asked to evaluate both themselves and their families by responding to the PAIC. It was determined that the choice of a particular adjective when describing oneself was related to family structure. They concluded that the 48 adjectives on the PAIC provide a sensitive, multifaceted self-concept scale which can help to provide insight into the strengths and weaknesses of children from various family situations, and thus may prove useful to parents, counselors, educators, and other helping professionals as a tool to better understand the children's needs. (p. 657)

Parish and Taylor (1978a) in a report concerning the validity and reliability of the PAIC, administered both the PAIC and the Piers-Harris Children's Self-Concept Scale (PHCSCS) to third and sixth graders. They found a correlation of .67 (p < .001) between these two scales.

Procedure

Subjects were asked to sign a consent form before beginning the experiment. The principal investigator read the form aloud and explained the rights of the students, which included confidentiality and the right to withdraw from the study at any time. Participants were asked not to sign their names to the questionnaire, thus assuring anonymity. After consent forms were signed and collected, the testing instruments were distributed. Materials used in this study included a demographic questionnaire structured by the researchers and the PAIC, developed by Parish and Taylor (1978a, 1978b).

After completing the demographic questionnaire, subjects were asked to choose 15 adjectives that they believed best described themselves from the list of 48 included in the PAIC. The total time required for the completion of the study was approximately 20 minutes. Materials were immediately collected by the investigator.

The computer software package SPSS-X was used to analyze the data. A 3 × 3 (family structure × grade level) and a 3 × 2 (family structure × sex) factorial design analyses of variance were computed utilizing the .05 level of significance.

RESULTS AND DISCUSSION

No statistically significant differences in how children in the three different family structures perceived themselves were found. Although students from stepfamilies tended to check fewer positive adjectives on the PAIC ($\overline{X}sf$ = 11.58), their means did not differ significantly from the means of the children from single-parent families ($\overline{X}$sp = 12.16) or from the means of intact families ($\overline{X}$i = 12.45). (See Figure 1.)

Children from intact homes chose a slightly higher number of positive adjectives than the norm. Those from stepfamilies chose considerably fewer, and those from single-parent families fell at the norm.

The means found in this study were similar to the means found in Parish and Dostal's (1980) research. However, they reported statistically significant results (.10 level) between family structure and number of positive adjectives selected by children living in those various structures.

These means were also similar to those found by Rankin and Parish (1981), who administered the PAIC to 1,050 children in grades 5 to 8 from 15 different school districts across Kansas. They found that those children overall chose an average (mean) of 12.24 positive adjectives when asked to describe themselves.

As verified in previous research (Parish & Dostal, 1980), an individual's sex seems to have no bearing on the number of positive adjectives checked in self-evaluation. We, likewise, found there to be no statistically significant differences in relation to the sex of the respondent.

An interesting difference was found to exist as a function of grade level. We found that the mean number of positive adjectives checked was lowest for students in the ninth and tenth grades (see Figure 2). The seventh and eighth graders checked a mean number of 13.04 positive adjectives; ninth and tenth graders checked a mean number of 11.74 positive adjectives; and the eleventh and twelfth graders checked a mean number of 12.65 positive adjectives.

We also identified adjectives actually chosen by children in each of the 3 family structures (see Table 1). The words marked by an asterisk were found to be statistically significant at the .05 level. For example, children from stepfamilies chose lazy, mean, and dumb more frequently than did children from either intact or single-parent families.

However, a statistically significant (.05 level) difference, as measured by the PAIC, was not found in the overall self-concepts

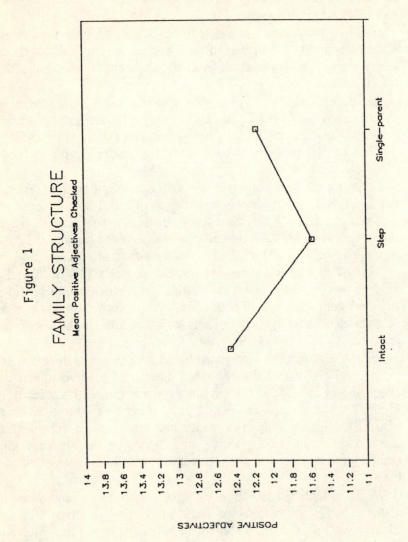

Figure 1

FAMILY STRUCTURE

Mean Positive Adjectives Checked

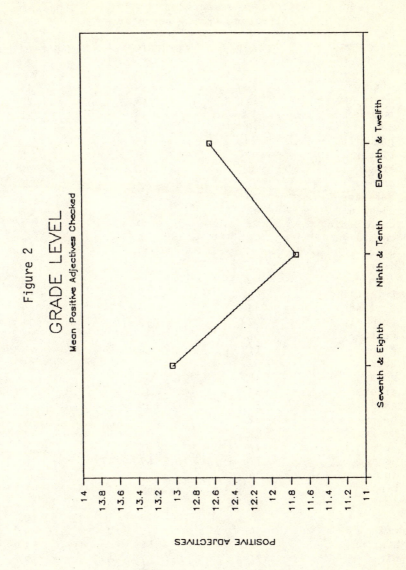

Figure 2

GRADE LEVEL

Mean Positive Adjectives Checked

Table 1
Percent of adjectives selected by children in the three
different family structures

ADJECTIVES	INTACT %	STEPFAMILY %	SINGLE-PARENT %
afraid	10	4	19
*angry	11	13	29
awkward	19	29	22
bad	3	4	3
beautiful	9	13	16
bitter	9	8	9
brave	36	46	28
calm	57	46	60
careless	24	38	13
cheerful	62	63	63
complaining	24	17	28
cowardly	4	8	0
cruel	5	17	9
dirty	1	4	6
*dumb	2	13	3
fairminded	45	33	53
foolish	11	8	3
friendly	92	83	97
gentle	56	46	50
gloomy	11	8	22
good	62	50	66
great	29	33	16
greedy	11	17	6
*handsome	26	38	9
happy	72	67	66
healthy	81	71	72
helpful	78	75	88
honest	72	67	78
jolly	24	33	28
kind	77	67	69
*lazy	38	75	34
lovely	16	17	19
*mean	4	17	9
nagging	11	4	13
nice	77	67	69
polite	78	75	75
pretty	34	25	25
rude	4	8	6
selfish	15	4	9
show-off	24	17	9

TABLE 1 (continued)

ADJECTIVES	INTACT %	STEPFAMILY %	SINGLE-PARENT %
strong	42	29	47
sweet	44	54	50
*ugly	3	13	13
unfriendly	3	0	0
*weak	5	17	0
wise	50	38	53
wonderful	29	25	22
*wrongful	0	0	6

*Significant <.05 level

of children from step-, intact, or single-parent families. This finding is in concert with that reported by several previous researchers.

IMPLICATIONS

Our society is inclined to view family structures other than the intact, nuclear family as potentially pathological. However, viewing the decline of the nuclear family as the cause of child pathology may be erroneous. Kurdak and Siesky (1978) suggest that the removal of tension and fear from the home environment subsequent to divorce may actually enhance child development. It is possible and even probable that many children of divorce and those who became stepchildren obtain strengths and maturities associated with their experiences.

REFERENCES

Glick, P. (1979). Children of divorced parents in demographic perspective. *Journal of Social Issues*, 35, 170-182.

Kurdak, L. A., & Siesky, A. E. (1978). Divorced single parents' perceptions of child-related problems. *Journal of Divorce*, 1, 361-370.

Parish, J., & Parish, T. (1983). Children's self-concepts as related to family structure and family concept. *Adolescence*, 18, 649-658.

Parish, T. & Dostal, J. (1980). Evaluations of self and parent figures by children from intact, divorced, and reconstituted families. *Journal of Youth and Adolescence*, 9, 347-351.

Parish, T., & Taylor, J. (1978a). The Personal Attribute Inventory for Children: A report on its reliability and validity as a self-concept scale. *Educational and Psychological Measurement, 38*, 565-569.

Parish, T., & Taylor, J. (1978b). A further report on the validity and reliability of the Personal Attribute Inventory for Children as a self-concept scale. *Educational and Psychological Measurement, 38*, 1225-1228.

Rankin, C., & Parish, T. (1981). The Personal Attribute Inventory for Children: Normative data. *Perceptual and Motor Skills, 53*, 273-274.

Raschke, H., & Raschke, V. (1979). Family conflict and children's self-concepts: A comparison of intact and single-parent families. *Journal of Marriage and the Family, 41*, 367-374.

Touliatos, J., & Lindholm, B. (1980). Teachers' perceptions of behavior problems in children from intact, single-parent, and stepparent families. *Psychology in the Schools, 17*, 264-269.

Family Dysfunctional Patterns During Divorce — From the View of the Children

Jolene Oppawsky

SUMMARY. This article reports the results of a case-study research project on 22 nonclinical children of parental divorce (ages 22 months to 18 years) from 16 families in West Germany. This project revealed the family dysfunctional patterns during divorce *from the view of the children*.

INTRODUCTION

The recent divorce rate in West Germany, as it is in the USA, is dramatically rising. Due to the similarities in cultures and cross-cultural divorce-specific characteristics such as parental discord, faulty interpersonal interactions within the family, awarding custody of the children in most cases to the mother and the loss in quality and quantity of the child-parent interaction with the non-custodial parent (in most cases the father), the effects of divorce on West German children, as well as their reactions to divorce closely parallel those reported in the American literature.

The majority of the literature and research studies on divorce has been written, researched and published in the USA. Due to the lack of West German literature and data on divorce and the efforts of professionals such as psychologists, therapists, court personnel and politicians to deal with the rising divorce rate and the hefty impact divorce has on a large number of children, the reception of the American literature and findings on divorce by these professionals

Jolene Oppawsky, PhD, RN, NCC edM, is a psychologist practicing at Waldstr.7, 8024 Oberbiberg, Munich, West Germany.

in West Germany has been excellent. Still, each country needs their own research data and findings to compare and contrast as well as to expose problems unique to their land and people.

The following article reports the results of a case-study research project on 22 nonclinical children of parental divorce (ages 22 months to 18 years) from 16 families in West Germany. Eight boys and 14 girls participated. The children over 3 years of age (N = 21) were given the Brem-Gräser (1980) projective test "Family as Animals" in addition to the in-depth interviews. The study, which focused when age permitted on divorce *from the view of the children* (N = 20), revealed a host of family dysfunctional patterns which characterized the divorcing family.

The interviews with the children of divorce suggested that the children were forced into faulty interactional patterns with their parents and siblings by being coerced into playing a variety of roles and serving a variety of functions within the divorcing family. *From the view of the children*, these faulty interactions produced many of their negative feelings, caused them trouble and governed their reactions to the crisis.

Four general forms of faulty interactions could be delineated: those between the child-parent and the parent-child, those between the parents and those between the siblings. A variety of expressions of dysfunction characterized these relationships.

EXPRESSIONS OF FAULTY CHILD-PARENT INTERACTION

Denunciation and Repudiation of the Parents

Eighty-two percent of the children interviewed for this study who had experienced and witnessed severe parental discord developed such frustrations and fear and experienced such intense anger and hate toward one or both parents because of their behavior that they denounced and repudiated, at least temporarily, their parents. One hundred percent of the children who denounced their parents had been subjected to severe parental strife. This denunciation led to other intense feelings such as helplessness, isolation and desire to escape or separate from the family as soon as possible.

Despite the smallness of the study and the disproportion of the age groups and the impressions that the children left who were older and more articulate, the statements of the children seemed to indicate that some age-specific cognition abilities were necessary for the children to strain against identification and denounce their parents as role models. This suggested that other powers were in force, such as age-specific development, which led to denunciation of their parents besides the power emitted from the exposure to faulty interactional patterns.

Centripetal-Centrifugal Patterns

The interviews with the children revealed that 80% of the children (100% of the 6 to 12-year olds and 67% of the 12 to 18-year olds) had an overt or secret wish that the parents would remain together or rejoin. Dislike for one parent which arose when the children felt that a parent could not change or where children saw physical or severe emotional spouse abuse, and time, seemed to be mediating factors for those older children who did not wish that the parents would rejoin. Their wish for a family however, did not seem to be subdued. Here three processes seemed to be in force: An age-specific normal binding of the child to the family of origin that remained untouched by the divorce situation; an age-specific normal binding of the family of origin that was jeopardized by the crisis and therefore strengthened; and an incessant longing for a family. The interviews suggested that one force governing the wish that the family would remain together or reunite was the fear that the children had that they were not loved or lovable. This fear was a perpetuator of many of their reactions such as sadness, anger, aggression, depression and regression. A provocative question which arose from the study was whether or not to tell the children that they were not loved by the parent who severely abused visitation privileges.

Contradictory to the evidence of centripetality as a behavioral pattern adopted by the children, most children tended to distance themselves emotionally from the family conflict. In addition, the interviews and the projection assessment "Family as Animals" revealed that many of the children were pushed into a centrifugal separation pattern by family discord and disruption. Fifty-two percent of the children tested (N = 21) were missing or outside the family nucleus. Eighty-two percent of these children related that they had witnessed severe parental discord. This centrifugality did not dampen most of these children's overt or secret wish for family reunification. (See Figure 1.)

Overlapping with the notion of centripetal-centrifugal patterns of behavior were the notions of enmeshment and disengagement. This study suggested that many children were propelled as a response to emotional pain into a disengagement mode. Disengaged from the family, these children faced loyalty conflicts, had communication difficulties and felt indifferent toward their parents, unprotected, vulnerable to hurt and isolated. Their capacity for interdependence was reduced and they felt they could no longer request support from their parents with ease. Some of the older children sought support and protection outside the family. Some formed inadequate relationships to meet their needs. Children of all ages used selective emotional disengagement to gain equilibrium in the turbulent divorce scenario and to cope with the situation.

An enmeshed interactional pattern was a characteristic of several expressions of family dysfunction such as parentification and partner-ersatz. In enmeshment the subsystem boundaries were poorly differentiated, weak and easily crossed and there was often no demarcation between the children's actions and those of the parents. This study also showed that there was often no clear-cut enmeshed or disengagement pattern because the children were thrown by the divorce situation into alternate enmeshment and disengagement inconsistencies within the family. When the children were drawn into partner-ersatz or parentification roles or coerced into overinvolvement in the parent's world, an enmeshed environment, they experienced frustrations, confusion and anger, and hate feelings toward their parents. When the parents tried to reclaim their executive function and exercise parental control, these were ineffective. This dual process propelled children into disengagement. Some of these children rebelled and acted out, others were able to cope under great duress.

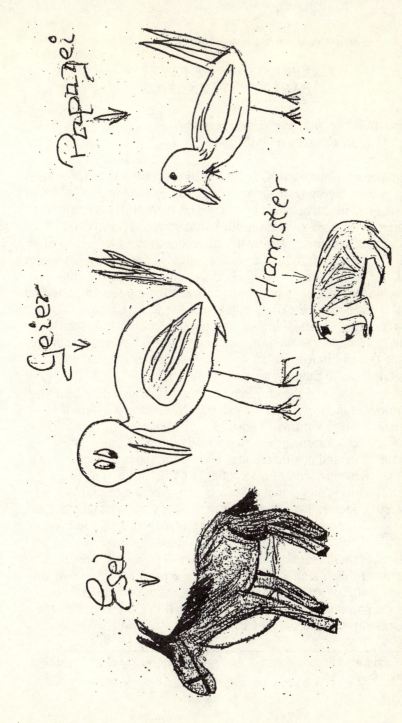

FIGURE 1. Pencil drawing by the 12-year-old Barbara. Barbara is a small hamster underneath her family. Mother is a "dumb donkey." Father is a vulture "who can eat up a hamster." Brother is a parrot who is "egotistic, colorful, small and ineffective."

143

EXPRESSIONS OF FAULTY
PARENT INTERACTION

Constant Bickering, Fighting, Screaming
and "War in the Household"

The parental interaction, fights, yelling and "war in the household,"[1] from the view of the affected children, seemed to represent the one most negative effect of divorce on them. Fifty percent of the children from 56% of the families interviewed reported that they had experienced severe parental strife characterized by one or more of the following: Hefty and constant fighting, parental fights where substance abuse was evident to the children, physical abuse between the parents, physical abuse between the parents escalated by use of a weapon, threat of parental suicide and manifested evidence of extramarital affairs of one or both parents (took place in the home or the children were taken to such encounters). Seventy-seven percent of the children reported that they had often been subjected to parental verbal fights.

From the view of the children, parental fighting and screaming, regardless of intensity, had the valence to perpetuate a host of negative reactions of various intensities and hinder adjustment. These reactions were, among others, increased crying, sadness, anger, aggression, hate and hostile feelings toward the parents, shame due to parental behavior, centrifugal patterns of behavior, fall in grades and academic achievements (86% of the school-age children who received grades and who had experienced severe parental strife experienced a drop in their academic achievements), angst and repression.

Many of these reactions such as angst, aggression, hate and hostility toward the parents, shame due to the parents' behaviors, centrifugal patterns of behavior (emotional and physical distancing from the parents and the conflict) and a fall in grades seemed to be governed by the intensity of the parental strife and were not age-

---

1. Term coined by the children of the Fayerweather Street School, Cambridge, Massachusetts.

specific or sex-specific reactions. The other reactions such as increased crying and sadness seemed to be general reactions of all children to parental divorce.

Ninety percent of the 6 to 18 year olds sought solace for their distress over the situation with peers who had had similar experiences. This seemed to be a divorce-specific reaction.

EXPRESSIONS OF FAULTY PARENT-CHILD INTERACTION

Bridge Between the Parents

Seventy-five percent of the children had been used as bridges by one or both parents to forge gaps between themselves and their former spouses. The children registered the use of themselves as bridge for four general purposes, all of which caused them feelings of insecurity and guilt and placed them in loyalty binds. These uses were:

1. The children were used as a bridge to transport messages to a partner with whom the parent only wanted minimal contact.
2. The children were used to transport messages about successes and failures which were meant by the parents to be transported to the spouse on the next visit or upon return from a visit.
3. The children were used as communication bridges between parents who were legally separated in the same living domicile. This communication modus was mainly due to circumstances which put duelling or emotionally divorced parents at the same table and in the same living room or allowed them to use the same facilities. This legal separation arrangement trapped the children in the middle of it all.
4. The children were used as a bridge to maintain partner communication which allowed the parents to deny their own problems.

One use of the children as bridge was not identified by the children themselves, but was extracted from the concurrent interviews with the parents.[2] This bridge was formed by parents who could not deal with one another directly, but who could unite in protective concern for the children, or by those who wished to win the partner's return. This communication bridge was established most often around psychosomatic symptoms of the children, real illness, and other reactions to divorce such as increased crying, aggressive behaviors or lowered academic achievements.

Parentification of the Child

Twenty-five percent of the children were grossly affected by this faulty parent-child interaction. These children reported being ripped out of their childhood by being physically and psychologically overburdened. Their privacy was invaded, their independence thwarted and they had to yield their autonomy. They reported feelings of loneliness, isolation, discrimination, vulnerability and strong animosity toward their parents. These children expressed the wish to leave home as soon as they were 18.

Partner-Ersatz

The interviews with the children showed that partner-ersatz evolved from two sources. In one, the parent-child relationship was replaced by the partner-ersatz relationship as a response to the parents' emotional needs. The other source arose from the children's feelings of protection and sense of duty toward the parents and their love for them.

The most common form instigated by the parents and found to some degree in all the families was using the child as a conversational partner. Although the study was small and there was a disproportion of age and sex groups and only 18% of the children had sole-custody fathers, the interviews suggested that older girls were used more by both mothers and fathers for conversation and household duties. These girls resented and rebelled against this and were the only children in the study that did not voice strong protective inclinations toward the custodial parent.

---

2. N = 19

The most common form of parent-ersatz instigated by the non-custodial parent was gift-giving and entertainment outings.

The children in the partner-ersatz roles were overtaxed by the burden of responsibility placed upon them at a time in which they had their own age-specific tasks to weather. These children were expected by the parents and propelled by their own self-expectations to fill the gap perpetuated by the divorce, both physically and emotionally, for which they were psychologically and emotionally ill suited. This pushed these children into a failure modus. In the parent-ersatz relationship the hierarchical parent-child relationship was forfeited and when the parents did try to regain status and control, they were ineffectual.

Scapegoating

The dominant theme in the interviews with the 30% of the children affected by this interactional pattern was the scapegoat phenomenon. Whether the child was the selected negative scapegoat, the positive paired sibling or just deeply involved in the process of scapegoating a family member or substantiating the family myth, these children seemed deeply troubled by this interaction pattern. These children felt hopeless and felt that all their attempts to change or to change others' views of themselves or to change the family's interactional pattern were snuffed out by other family members. Feelings of low self-esteem and despair characterized their interviews. Resentment and animosity toward family members also ran high. These children felt trapped in this web-like family process with no way out and were often kept busy trying to live up to or live down their label.

Some of the children were assigned the role of both good and bad scapegoat depending on the situation prevailing at the time. These double messages confused the children and rendered all their responses to the situation invalid.

The three above expressions of faulty parent-child interactions — parentification, parent-ersatz and scapegoating, which were not found in the majority, seemed to deeply trouble those children affected.

Double Bind

Ninety percent of the children seemed markedly troubled by double binds which were found in some form in all the families. The multifaceted character of divorce produced many double bind situations which were registered by the children. They were:

1. Contradictions between what was said aloud and what was communicated nonverbally.
2. When the parents tried to manipulate the children into taking sides becoming rivals for the children's attention.
3. The double bind situation produced by the custodial question.

The most common form related by the children was the discrepancy between overt actions and words and nonverbal communication. The act of separation and divorce as such, placed the children in the double bind situation and raised the question of being loved or lovable in their minds. Furthermore, the situation produced many approach and avoidance episodes. The most common revolved around the custodial decision and visitation privileges, usually between the non-custodial parents and their children. These episodes were confusing and degrading to the children and led to marked feelings of rejection. Feeling rejected, the children then responded with love-hate, approach-avoidance behavior which then characterized further dealings with their parents.

Many children reported that their parents became rivals for their attention and love which threw them into serious loyalty conflicts which resulted in guilt feelings. Guilt feelings also arose from the custodial decision placed upon the children, although most of the children had a firm opinion about with whom they should live. About 95% of the older children thought that they should participate in the decision. Both situations, one imposed upon the children by rivaling parents; the other, a legitimate form used to respect the rights and wishes of the children, placed the children in a double bind. To side with one parent, regardless of the legitimacy of the situation, was to automatically reject the other. This resulted in serious loyalty conflicts and guilt feelings. Neither age, sex nor cognitive prowess seemed to be good mediators for dealing with these feelings.

Weekend Santa Phenomenon

Thirty-five percent of the children related strong ambivalent feelings about the "Weekend Santa"[3] phenomenon which arose exclusively in this study from the children's interactions with the noncustodial parents. This phenomenon threw some of the children into double-bind situations in which they questioned the actions and motives of their parents which were so dissimilar to previous ones, but responded positively out of loyalty toward their parents and because the gifts, trips and outings were just too enticing to be rejected. Most of the conflicts however, arose when the children returned home to the custodial parents, embarrassed to "show and tell" and with enough time on their hands to evaluate the situation more closely. This closer evaluation revived their doubts about intentions of the parents as well as their guilt feelings because they liked the attention and gifts. It also rekindled loyalty conflicts which arose from loyalty to and love for the custodial parents in contrast to the loyalty and love for the parents who had, in their eyes, left them. The fear of loss of parental love or parental rejection was also kept viable.

Mystification

The children revealed three forms of mystification which arose from the divorce situation. They were:

1. Mystification of parental love for the children. No clear-cut parental stance on their love for their children. Declarations of love for their children by the non-custodial parents despite abuse of visitation privileges or loss of contact with their children.
2. The mystification of the reason for divorce by both parents and children.
3. The mystification of marital disharmony leading to certain divorce.

---

3. Term coined by the children of the Fayerweather Street School, Cambridge, Mass.

Mystification, a phenomenon in which 57% of the children were involved, regardless of the reason for it, helped them distort and deny reality. The interviews suggested that the children suspected or actually knew what was going on, but chose to maintain the status quo in the crisis situation to avoid coming to terms with the deteriorating family relationship or to face up to the realization that they may not be loved by one parent.

One of the major questions plaguing most children during all phases of the divorce process was the question of being loved and lovable. Parental separation and divorce, as well as many of the expressions of faulty parent-child interactions such as double-bind, "Weekend Santa" phenomenon and mystification helped to keep this question viable and unanswered in the children's minds.

Psychosomatic Reactions

Psychosomatic reactions were not recognized by the children as reactions to parental divorce and were not considered to be a negative effect of the crisis on them. The related findings are from the concurrent interviews with the parents and not from the view of the children.

Forty-one percent of the children[4] had had a psychosomatic disorder at one point during the divorce crisis. Enuresis was the most frequent disorder (50% of the psychosomatic reactions) and found exclusively in girls. Thirty-six percent of the girls in the study had the disorder. Other psychosomatic disorders were elective mutism, facial tics and night terrors with physical symptoms.

SIBLING INTERACTIONS

Rise in Sibling Jealousy

Forty-five percent of the children reported a rise in sibling or stepsibling jealousy or jealousy of the children of the parents' new partners. The children felt guilty, insecure, unloved, unlovable and non-unique. It was jealousy of the children of the parents' new part-

---

4. N = 22

ners, who often received, from the view of the biological children, more attention than they did from their parents, that troubled them most.

Other Sibling Interactions

The divorce crisis provoked two other sibling interactional patterns which, although not representative of the group, were worth mentioning because of the intensity of the children's reactions and interactions. They were adoration of an older brother and hostility and aggression toward an older brother by girls, both as a result of loss of interaction with the father. The sex orientation was due to the smallness of the study. Whether these findings can be reproduced in boys with older sisters who have lost interactions with their mothers remains evasive as long as sole custody is primarily awarded to mothers.

POSITIVE INTERACTIONAL PATTERNS

The family interactional patterns deemed positive or improved from the view of the children as a result of separation and divorce were few and usually particular to one child or one situation. A few examples were: Improved interaction with one parent or both; the loosening of loyalty binds and double-bind situations after the divorce; and increased sibling cohesion.

The one consistent positive finding from the view of the children was the reduction of parental fighting and yelling after the parents moved apart. This reduction in parental discord afforded the children with a release from tension and stress, peace and quiet, stability, harmony, decrease in fear and rise in academic achievements. One hundred percent of the children who experienced any form of parental strife deemed a reduction of this strife necessary to reduce the negative effects upon them. Sixty-five percent of the children suggested that the one thing their parents could do to reduce the divorce trauma on them was to stop fighting.

FAMILY THERAPY AS THE THERAPY OF CHOICE FOR CHILDREN OF DIVORCE

The results of this study strongly suggested that the majority of the negative effects of divorce on children arose from the mikro-level of their individual and social existence and suggested that family therapy, where the focus of therapy should be on changing faulty family interactional patterns to functional ones, may be more on target for treating children of divorce than individual therapy. The author suggested that all divorcing families need psychological counseling to smooth the path of divorce for children, to prevent psychological damage, to repair damage already done and to facilitate the children's normal growth from infancy into adolescence and adult years by not tapping or blocking the resources for health that these children possess.

REFERENCES

Brem-Gräser, L. (1980). Familie in Tieren. München, Basel: Ernst Reinhardt Verlag.

Children of the Fayerweather Street School (1982). Rofes (Ed.), The Kids' book of divorce. New York: Vintage Books.

Oppawsky, J. (1987). Scheidungskinder Schwerpunkt: Aus der Sicht der Kinder. München: Profil Verlag.

Divorce, Custody, and Visitation: The Child's Point of View

R. Neugebauer

SUMMARY. This paper discusses children's perceptions of the divorce experience. Specifically, it illuminates children's perceptions of divorce, custody, and visitation. Custody and visitation arrangements have been made on the basis of what is believed to be in the best interests of the child. However, the viewpoint of the child is seldom considered in decisions concerning custody and access. Moreover, a negligible amount of empirical research has explored the child's interpretation of custody and visitation. This paper is an attempt to redress this imbalance. Findings based on in-depth interviews with 40 children and teenagers reveal a preference for the post-divorce family structure and more flexible visitation arrangements. Moreover, the feasibility of father and joint-custody is addressed.

INTRODUCTION

This paper explores children's perceptions of the divorce experience. The objective of this research is to illuminate children's perceptions and evaluations of divorce, custody, and visitation, with particular attention focussed on the child's relationship with the non-custodial parent.

Custody and visitation arrangements have been made on the basis of what is believed to be in the "best interests" of the child. But,

R. Neugebauer is a PhD candidate and part-time instructor in the Sociology Department at York University, 4700 Keele Street, North York, Ontario, Canada M3J 1P3.

153

the viewpoint of the child is seldom considered in decisions concerning custody and visitation. Hence, the notion of what constitutes the best interests of the child requires careful scrutiny in light of the child's perspective. Moreover, in a society in which divorce is becoming more prevalent, this task is imminent. To date, a negligible amount of empirical research has explored the child's interpretation of custody and visitation. Thus, to conduct such an investigation is the aim of this study.

CHILD CUSTODY AWARDS

Until very recently, the awarding of child custody almost invariably went to the mother. The dominance of psychology, the myth of the "maternal instinct," and the doctrine of tender years placed divorced fathers at a disadvantage regarding child custody.

To date, the most influential and unchallenged authority for the legal profession regarding custody and visitation privileges is the book *Beyond the Best Interests of the Child* by Goldstein, Freud and Solnit (1973). This source relies heavily on the early work of Bowlby, which emphasized the significance of the normative mother-child bond. According to this "best interests" doctrine, in cases of divorce, children must be granted to the "psychological parent" — the mother. This belief acquired considerable influence due to the "tender years doctrine" which still maintains that young children invariably benefit from being with their mother. This doctrine remained a norm until fairly recently when statutory legislation replaced common law principles.

Theoretically, the fundamental statutory premise currently gives each parent equal opportunity in gaining custody (Bala et al., 1981:43). Irrespective of the adoption of this premise, decisions are ultimately left to the discretion of judges. Regrettably, the current system for settling custody is based within an adversarial framework. Children are often treated as property, that is, booty to be won in a contest between parents (Bala et al., 1981:22-25).

In its broadest sense, custody means control or full responsibility for the upbringing of the child — the mental, emotional and physical nurturing of the child. As a general rule one person, usually the mother, is granted sole custody while the other is allowed reasonable or specified visitation privileges. Thus, the effect of a sole custody order is to prevent the non-custodial parent from having any legal control over decisions related to the child's upbringing (Bala et al., 1981:43-44). These custody orders are inspired by the doctrine of "the best interests of the child" which states that the custodial parent has complete authority in deciding the conditions under which the child be raised, including the right to decide whether the non-custodial parent should have visiting privileges (Goldstein, Freud and Solnit, 1973:38).

Within our legal framework, it remains very difficult for a man to gain and secure custody of his children after divorce. For a man to succeed juridically he must demonstrate in court that his wife is an unfit parent. Clearly, a more equitable and less painful remedy to this predicament would incorporate the consideration of the child's best interests and the best interests of his or her parents.

Method

This research is based on in-depth, open-ended interviews with 40 children and teenagers between the ages of 7 and 18 whose parents had undergone a divorce. All children were between the ages of 2 and 11 years old at the time of parental separation. The parents of the participants had been apart for a minimum of 4 years.

At the time of interviewing, 31 individuals were living in mother-custody homes and 3 in father-custody homes. However, the 3 children had been in the custody of their father for less than a year. The remaining 6 children were living in a joint-custody arrangement.

PERSPECTIVES ON DIVORCE

Perceptions and Adjustments

Divorce is a multidimensional process involving the experiences of marital separation and parental separation. The latter occupies a central focus within the interpretive framework for children. To children, divorce means that they no longer reside with one of their parents. In short, divorce is operationally perceived as a loss of a significant emotional relationship. Hence, what children find most distressing about divorce is not the demise of their parents' marriage, but that one of their parents (usually the father) is no longer part of their daily lives.

In exploring the behaviour and emotional responses of children following separation, children reported feelings of anger, sadness, anxiety and depression. A few children reported difficulties in school initially following the separation. Upon closer examination, there were differences in response according to gender. To elaborate, boys exhibited more expressive behaviour of rebellion than girls. This finding corroborates other studies by Hetherington, Cox and Cox (1976; 1978; 1979a, b, c, d). These difficulties lasted approximately 1 1/2 to 2 years following the separation, as children adjusted to the new circumstances of their living arrangements and contacts with the non-custodial parent. This timetable corresponds to the post-separation adjustment period found by Wallerstein and Kelly (1980). Furthermore, younger children under 4 years of age reported little distress in their reaction to separation.

In spite of the distress experienced by children, they unanimously described the separation as a relief, that is, as a solution to their unhappy home life. Children are sensitive to their social environment — interparental conflict affects them as well as their parents.

The majority of children reported overt conflict between parents prior to separation. Many had been exposed to arguments for many years, and in a few cases even violence. Moreover, even those children whose parents argued little maintained that the distance between parents created a tense family atmosphere. Interparental conflict was quite distressing for children and affected them in a variety of ways. Children 4 years and older reported feelings of depression, and spent much time crying alone in their rooms. Some young children reported that they wet their beds, while some older children maintained that they had had behavioural problems. Some individuals had problems concentrating on their school work. Most children managed to cope alone, while others still adjusted by seeking the support of siblings during unhappy times. However, by far toddlers who were too young to comprehend what was going on appear to have been spared the distress experienced by other children. The following quotes by two individuals capture the discomfort experienced by many.

> It was awful. There was so much yelling. It was really bad for a few years . . . I was depressed and unhappy. Sometimes I wanted to hide under the bed. Things were really strained. (Carol, 16)

> It was fine until they started fighting, and they were fighting a lot. Once me and Sarah took out some knives and said we were going to kill ourselves if they didn't stop fighting. (Bobby, 10)

Prior to separation, sibling relationships can become significant during periods of marital conflict. Some children reported that although little verbal discussion about their parents' problems transpired between them, they nevertheless tended to gravitate towards one another when things were tense between parents. Sarah and Molly noted:

> . . . Me and Bobby stuck together when things were bad. (Sarah, 13)

> We never talked about it, but sometimes when they were fighting Lisa and I would gang up on them. (Molly, 14)

Siblings can become a support system for children. Since siblings confront similar circumstances within similar time-frames, they forge alliances with one another. An unexpected finding was that although some siblings provided each other with support, their relationships were more attenuated. In a few situations, however, conflict between parents appeared to be "contagious"; these siblings became more distant and antagonistic with each other. This finding suggests that the tension between parents has a wider impact on all family members.

All children noted that the social atmosphere in the home had improved dramatically after the separation. Hence, despite the absence of one parent from their daily lives, overall, children expressed a preference for the post-divorce family structure. Moreover, none of the respondents entertained the desire for parental reconciliation. The following quotes are indicative of children's feelings of relief after separation.

> Um . . . well, it was a relief. There was no more fighting. I was still unhappy because my dad was gone . . . my mom seemed happier. Well, at least it was much calmer. The knots in my stomach were beginning to clear so things were much better. (Cyril, 11)

> Slowly, but surely, I realized that they were better off apart than together so it was best to leave it that way . . . It was more peaceful at home and I was happier in the long run. (Sarah, 13)

In contrast to the children living with one parent and visiting with the other, children living in joint-custody situations suffered little distress in response to the divorce, especially since both parents were equally accessible to them. Unlike their sole-custody counterparts, none of the joint-custody children experienced the sense of loss of a parent, nor did they experience many problems adjusting to the separation.

Another arrangement which was disturbing for children was that of living apart from siblings. Although at the time of being interviewed, 3 children had been separated from their siblings, 3 others had at one time been in this situation. In addition, 2 of these respondents were separated by great distances. Consequently, living apart from one's siblings in addition to one's father created more disruption in these children's lives.

Another change occurring after divorce is that contact with relatives decreases. In particular, children tend to see relatives of the non-custodial parent on an occasional basis when visiting with their father. However, children do not appear to be bothered by this change. In some cases, the only relatives missed by children are their grandparents. This finding suggests the significance of grandparents to children. In fact, grandparents can be a source of emotional support for a child after divorce. Moreover, at a time when things seem uncertain, grandparents provide children with a sense of security and confirmation that some things stay the same following divorce.

Overall, children claimed to be closer to the parents of custodial parents, a fact due at least in part to the greater contact with them relative to the other set of grandparents following divorce. Moreover, in a few cases grandparents filled some of the emptiness caused by the absence of a father. One boy in particular had an exceptional relationship with his grandparents. Because they lived close to the school which the boy attended, he would visit them during his lunch break and even after school.

Hence, some children had managed to develop a network of individuals who provided them with a measure of social support.

Children's Understanding of Divorce

Many children interviewed experienced some confusion over their parents' divorce. Approximately two-thirds of the individuals had never been directly informed of the reasons for the divorce. Parents who apprised their children calmly sat down with them and explained that they were seeking a divorce. Moreover, these sensitive parents ensured their children that the divorce had nothing to do with them. Surprisingly, less than one-quarter of the children received advanced explicit warnings of their parents' separation and divorce.

Children soon realized that their parents were separating at a time when their fathers were getting ready to leave. Others realized this as they themselves were leaving the home with their mothers. In many cases fathers left during the night, or during the day when children were at school. These children figured out that their parents were separated when their father failed to return home. However, even without verbal communication, children 9 years of age and older at the time of separation attributed the breakup to parental incompatibility or marital problems. A few younger children adopted a victimogenic approach whereby they apportioned blame to themselves. These 3 children witnessed parental disputes, symptomatic of a problematic marriage without an adequate explanation from either parent of the actual cause of the disputes.

Consider, for example, the following comments by David, an 8-year-old who has blamed himself for the divorce since he was four years old:

They didn't tell me anything. One day my dad just left
. . . One day I rolled the car off the driveway. I wasn't sup-
posed to be in the car. After I did that my parents were always
fighting. They never fought before that. I thought it was all
because of me. I mostly felt that way.

These 3 children suffered unnecessary pain over the break-up of
their parents' marriage.

Such findings underscore the importance of communication regarding divorce. Adequate communication prior to separation prepared children psychologically for the event, and subsequently increased children's ability to cope with the separation. Moreover,
children who were able to discuss the divorce with their parents
were better adjusted. The sensitive nature of the issue of divorce
and the reluctance of parents to discuss divorce with their children
inhibit children from disclosing their thoughts, feelings and wishes
about the problematic situation. In essence, most children coped
alone. They revealed their experiences, thoughts and feelings to no
one. This state of affairs can only be remedied by improved communication with their parents.

Evaluations of Divorce

Since the meaning of divorce to children is the absence of a parent from their day-to-day lives, children's evaluations of the divorce experience depended primarily on their satisfaction with custody and visitation arrangements. Subsequently, the most positive
evaluations of divorce were expressed by respondents whose visitation arrangements met their needs. Conversely, the least positive
evaluations came from those who felt deprived of contact with the
non-custodial parent. Only 2 young children expressed a disdain for
divorce. These respondents were the least satisfied with visitation
and custody. In fact, both children conveyed the desire to live with
the non-custodial father. However, in general children viewed divorce as a necessary solution to marital problems.

Furthermore, all individuals had positive attitudes toward marriage. With few exceptions, children indicated that they hoped to
get married in the future. A few teenagers maintained that they

would co-habit prior to marriage to ensure compatibility with their partner.

However, a few others stated that they would co-habit instead of marrying. Many adolescents and teenagers maintained that their parents' divorce provided them with a good learning experience in preparing them for marriage. These individuals indicated that their approach to marriage and methods of dealing with marital problems were superior to those of their parents. The following statement by Tina, age 18, illustrates this perspective.

> It's a mistake to get married young. When you fall in love you don't really know what a relationship is. My parents, for example, didn't have much experience in a relationship because they were so young when they got married. What happened to my parents will most likely not happen to me when I get married. Their divorce was probably imminent.

In sum, although initially it may be traumatic, divorce is not usually perceived negatively by children. The majority of children expressed positive evaluations of divorce. This was the case in spite of dissatisfaction with visitation. Overall, children's discomfort with their parents' marital unhappiness and tension in the home greatly outweighed their discomfort concerning visitation. In spite of parental absence, children preferred the harmonious atmosphere of the post-divorce family structure. Moreover, the more satisfied children were with visitation and custody arrangements, the more positive were their views of divorce. Consequently, the most positive views of divorce were expressed by children living in joint-custody situations.

PERSPECTIVES ON CUSTODY AND VISITATION

At the time of the interview most children had consistent visiting patterns with their non-custodial parent. However, there were exceptions to this rule. Five individuals who were separated by great distances from their non-custodial parents visited infrequently and only during summer vacations. In fact, one young man reported that he had not seen his father in 8 years. However, the majority of the children living in a sole-custody situation visited with the noncustodial parent every other weekend. In addition to contacts made in person, children relied on telephone calls and, in some cases, letters from non-custodial parents.

Children unanimously express a very strong preference for flexible and unrestricted contact with the non-custodial parent. Depending on their emotional needs and the quality of the non-custodial parent-child relationship, children's desire for contact varied. For example, children who had very close relationships with their fathers wished to spend more time with them. In general, however, younger children had a preference for more frequent contact with fathers, while teenagers had a preference for greater flexibility of contact so that visitation schedules could be coordinated with their social life. Overall, the most content respondents were those who had continuous and flexible contact with the non-custodial parent. It was in the context of these relationships that children were ensured continuity of affection and attention of the non-custodial parent. Moreover, flexibility of contact allowed children to have a more natural relationship with their fathers — one that existed beyond the confines of a bi-monthly weekend visit. Children also preferred to have the freedom to telephone their fathers when the need arose. Many children reported that they were often forbidden to do so.

Nonetheless, as children get older they seize more control over the visiting relationship. They more freely initiate contact with their fathers and schedule visits without their mother's interference. Since this is the case, younger children expressed greater dissatisfaction with visitation and even with custody. This dissatisfaction was exaggerated among those who were separated by great distances from their fathers. Approximately 1 year prior to being interviewed, 3 respondents (2 teenagers and 1 young child) who had always preferred to live with their fathers, had been placed in their custody. Nevertheless the desires of young children to have input into custody dispositions are typically disregarded. For example, two young children like the aforementioned were closer to their fathers and wished to live with them. Three others preferred a joint-custody arrangement because they desired much more contact with their fathers than visitation allowed.

In addition to the dissatisfaction with the frequency and flexibility of contact, children expressed dismay over the lack of individual time spent alone with the non-custodial parent. Once again, teenagers were more successful in arranging to spend visits without their siblings. Children also resented being subtly forced to form an alliance with one parent over the other, or to favour one parent more than the other. Moreover, they were equally upset by the open expression of one parent's negative opinion of the other. However, by far the most disruptive and distressing situation for children was the custodial parent's indifference toward and often disdain for visitation. More than half of the respondents reported that their mothers had interfered with the visiting relationship. Some parents were uncooperative regarding access, and contacts made by telephone and mail even to the extent of sabotaging contacts between non-custodial parent and child. Some individuals revealed that they did not realize that their fathers had attempted to contact them until years later. Excerpts by Paul, Timothy, and Ryan illustrate this point:

> I used to write letters to him. But from what I've learned he never got them. Four or five years after I hadn't seen my father he told me about the letters he had written. Then I figured my mom never mailed my letters and ripped up the ones he had sent. He'd call but I never got to talk to him. (Paul, 18)

> Sometimes my mom would cancel my plans with my dad last minute just to get back at him, I guess. So to make up for it he'd meet me in the school yard at lunch. (Timothy, 12)

> I got into trouble for writing letters. . . . She didn't like it so I did it without her knowing. Once she caught me and took it away from me. . . . He knew when my mom was out and called then. When she came home, I'd hang up. (Ryan, 8)

Evidently, attempts to interfere with a child's contact with his or her parent were more successful when they were separated by great distances. Furthermore, children expressed anger at a custodial parent who deliberately moved far away from the other at the time of separation. For, the extreme efforts of one spouse to avoid the other seriously neglected the needs of children who necessarily moved with them.

In contrast, both parent-child relationships within joint-custody are free of the restrictions imposed by visitation. Six participants from 3 families were involved in a joint-custody arrangement. These children lived with each parent during alternating weeks.

The unique characteristic of joint-custody is that both parents have equal control over their children's upbringing. As such, one parent-child relationship is not subject to the same potential abuse by the other that exists within a sole-custody arrangement. In addition, both parents are required to reside within the same geographic area. Interactions with both parents are flexible so that a child may telephone or visit one parent while residing with the other. All of the joint-custody children in this study enjoyed these very freedoms. All expressed contentment with the amount of contact that they had with each parent. Furthermore, they all experienced a minimal sense of loss and distress at the time of separation. Hence, since both parents were readily accessible, children did not suffer the same deprivations of affection and attention, and adjustment problems encountered in sole-custody. The experiences of Janet and Simon stand as testimony to this fact.

> Other kids wish they were me because I get to see my daddy all the time even though they're divorced . . . My friends don't get to see their dads that much. It's too bad. I don't know how they do it. (Janet, 9)

> The funny thing is that I've never really been sad since they broke up. Well, it was weird at first going back and forth. But, if I missed my mom I could call her or even go to see her. Like, I'd see her soon anyway. And if I wanted to see my dad I could call him too . . . It's great to know that they're always around. (Simon, 11)

Such findings provide additional support for the conclusion that the adjustment problems of children could be alleviated with continuous and unrestricted contact with both parents.

After divorce the relationship between parents has a significant impact on visiting patterns. In this regard, the custodial parent's attitude towards access is crucial. Hostility between parents can negatively affect the child's opportunity to have a reasonable amount of contact with his or her non-custodial parent. In particular, custodial parents who forbid, and even prevent non-custodial parents and children from having contact with one another are necessarily hurting their children, their ex-spouses and, inevitably, themselves. Yet, all too often parents let their bitterness over their divorce interfere with the well-being of their children. Children become the ammunition one parent uses against the other.

In contrast to parents who lose sight of their children's best interests are those who recognize the necessity of a child's continuing contact with the other parent. Although they may have bitter feelings toward the other parent, these parents manage to compromise for the sake of their children. In particular, joint-custody parents display the greatest ability to compromise — to cooperate with one another to ensure their children continuous contact with both parents. Furthermore, the children living in joint-custody arrangements fared the best of all participants. Since these children experienced consistency and continuity of affection and attention with both parents, they had been spared the sense of loss of an emotional relationship and distress characterizing sole-custody arrangements. Hence, the availability of both parents to the child can only enhance the child's emotional adjustment and social development.

DISCUSSION

Data from this study support the view that it is better for children to come from a broken home than to grow up in one. In this study, the anxieties suffered by children in conflict-ridden homes have more impact than the experience of marital separation. Simply, the distress of inter-parental conflict was much more deleterious to children than separation.

With few exceptions, children viewed the divorce as a solution to a difficult home life. All children reported an improvement in the atmosphere of their homes. Thus, these children expressed a preference for the post-divorce family structure. Overall, children's perceptions of divorce were positive.

The concept of divorce for children is the absence of a parent from their daily existence. Initially, divorce is perceived as a loss of a significant emotional relationship. For most children divorce means living with one parent and visiting with the other. Hence, it is not surprising that children's evaluations of divorce are linked to their levels of satisfaction with custody and visitation. Obviously, the most positive evaluations of divorce were reported by children whose contact with both parents met their needs. Consequently, the most positive evaluations of divorce came from children living in joint-custody situations.

One very significant theme emerged from our analysis of the data—the importance of communication or information—sharing regarding divorce. The majority of children reported that their parents had not warned them of their forthcoming separation and divorce. Moreover, they did not directly explain the reasons for the divorce. Effective communication about divorce prior to the event prepared children psychologically and enhanced their ability to cope with the separation once actualized.

The data provide evidence of a child's preference for flexible and unrestricted visitation arrangements. The children who were more content were those who maintained contact with the non-custodial parent on a continuous and flexible basis. It was in the context of these relationships that children were ensured continuity of affection and attention. Children also expressed a preference for flexibility in other types of contacts with the non-custodial parent, such as communication by telephone and mail.

The testimony of children provides evidence of the willingness of children to influence custody and visitation arrangements. In this regard, accommodations in the legal system are warranted. Moreover, since our findings suggest the importance of adequate levels of parent-child interaction, the most logical solution to limited contact with the non-custodial parent would be the implementation of a programme of more flexible visitation schedules. This research indicates that this is a basic demand and need of these children. Alternatively, the implementation of joint-custody awards remains yet another logical remedy. Due to limited research on joint-custody, the assessment of its total advantages over sole-custody is admittedly inconclusive. Positive consequences of this arrangement for both parents and children are nonetheless apparent. Joint-custody offers both parents the equal opportunity for continued involvement in the child's life and upbringing. Regrettably, parent-child bonds are subject to considerable competition and conflict in traditional sole-custody arrangements. Joint-custody offers children the security of an ongoing relationship with both parents equally.

CONCLUSIONS

The institution of the family is a "socially constructed" reality shaped by the participation of a number of interacting actors. There remains a great deal of controversy about the nature of participation by children. The role of children in the family tends to be largely overlooked. In fact, a paradigm of protection exists which highlights the subservience of children and maintains the importance of parents in defining what constitutes the "best interests" of their children. A cultural hegemony is preserved which excludes children and relegates them to a marginal status. The views of those who invariably are affected by separation and divorce requires greater enlistment. Children are not necessarily a deterministically defined cohort of victims manipulated by parental values. Despite their obvious dependencies, children make sense of their worlds and are able to interpret parental influences. Social scientists can help to identify specific problems and delineate the range of possibilities. Important policy considerations include the interface between law and the family. This research provides evidence that highlights the need for the modification of current legal remedies. These remedies directed at the divorce process need to be less punitive and more corrective, that is, doing less harm to children rather than simply preserving normative assumptions about the family. In light of the changing role of the father, the legal system should be more accommodating and less discriminatory to men. Our findings repeatedly single out the significance that children attach to maintaining relations with fathers. Joint-custody, for example, is a mechanism that allows for accommodation in a manner that is not blatantly discriminatory.

The results of this study clearly indicate the need for father-custody, joint-custody, more flexible visitation and legal representation for children. A more accurate understanding of children's needs and desires regarding divorce, custody, and visitation can serve to dispel common misunderstandings regarding the "best interests" of the child.

Educating parents of children's perceptions and needs after divorce undoubtedly fosters a greater understanding of their children. This understanding, when translated into action, provides children with greater authority over their contacts with "significant others," especially with the non-custodial parent.

BIBLIOGRAPHY

Bala, N.; *The Child and the Law*. Toronto: McGraw-Hill Ryerson Limited, 1981.

Goldstein, J.; Freud, A.; Solnit, A.: *Beyond the Best Interests of the Child*. New York: Free Press, 1973.

Hetherington, E.M.; Cox, M.; Cox, R.: "Divorced Fathers" *Family Coordinator, 25*, 1976. 417-428.

_____; "The Aftermath of Divorce" in J.H. Stevens Jr. & M. Mathews eds., *Mother-Child, Father-Child Relations*. Washington D.C.: NAEYC, 1978.

_____; "The Development of Children in Mother-Headed Families" in H. Hoffman & D. Reiss eds., *The American Family: Dying or Developing*. New York: Plenum, 1979(a).

_____; "Stress and Coping in Divorce: A Focus on Women" in J. Gullahorn ed., *Psychology and Women in Transition*. B.H. Winston and Sons, 1979(b).

_____; "Family Interaction and the Social, Emotional and Cognitive Development of Children Following Divorce" in V.C. Vaughan & T.B. Brazelton eds., *The Family: Setting Priorities*. New York: Science and Medicine Publishers, 1979(c).

_____; "Play and Social Interaction in Children Following Divorce" *Journal of Social Issues, 35* (4), 1979(d). 26-29

Wallerstein, J.; Kelly, J.: *Surviving the Break-up: How Children and Parents Cope with Divorce*. New York: Basic Books, Inc., 1980.

FAMILY STRUCTURE AND INTERACTIONAL PATTERNS: POST DIVORCE

A Comparison of Children
Living in Single-Mother
and Single-Father Families

Reuben Schnayer
R. Robert Orr

SUMMARY. Research comparing children living in single-mother and single-father families has become important due to the increase in the number of parents contesting custody in divorce cases and as the number of single custodial fathers increases. The present study was designed to investigate a number of characteristics relating to children living in single-father families (SFFs) and in single-mother families (SMFs). Previous research has suggested that in the case of separation and/or divorce the mother is the more competent parent to raise the children. However, recent studies have provided some support for the idea that single fathers can be effective single parents. The subject sample included 42 single divorced custodial parents (21 single mothers and 21 single fathers) and their 62 (6- to 16-year-old) children. The measures employed were The Self-Perception Profile for Children (SPPC; Harter, 1985) and The Child Behaviour Checklist (CBCL; Achenbach & Edelbrock, 1983). One-way MANCOVA and ANCOVA procedures were performed and it was found that the overall scores of children from single-father families (SFFs) did not differ significantly from children in single-mother families (SMFs) on the SPPC and the CBCL. The implications of these findings are discussed and suggestions for future research are provided.

Research addressing the impact of living in a one-parent family (OPF) on children has become increasingly important with the increase in the number of one-parent families (OPFs) in both the United States (Lowenstein & Koopman, 1978) and Canada (Davis,

---

Reuben Schnayer, PhD, and R. Robert Orr, PhD, are on the staff of the Windsor Board of Education, 451 Park St. West, Windsor, Ontario, Canada N9A 4V4.

1985). More specifically, as more parents are contesting custody in divorce cases and as the number of single custodial fathers increases, research comparing children living in single-father versus single-mother families is needed to assess the effectiveness of each of these single parent arrangements. In addition, this information would likely prove beneficial to the legal system in the determination of custody and access issues.

While historically the general bias in childrearing favors the mother, several recent studies provide some support for the idea that single fathers can be effective single parents. For example, Rosen (1979) interviewed and administered projective instruments to subjects (ages 9-28) from single-mother, single-father, and two-parent families and found no meaningful differences in general adjustment between these three groups.

A study conducted by Ambert (1982) suggested that fathers may in some cases be the more effective parent. Ambert compared single mothers' and single fathers' perceptions of their children as well as their relationship with them. A comparison of the parents' perceptions of their children revealed that all of the single fathers reported that their children were not manifesting any significant behaviour problems whereas the single mothers listed some of the following: truancy, disrespectfulness, incidences of shoplifting and vandalism, juvenile delinquency, and poor mother-child relationships. Ambert suggested that these results may be partially attributable to socio-economic (SES) factors since mothers in the high SES group had fewer problems and reported a more satisfactory relationship with their children than did the mothers in the low SES group. However, even in the high SES group, the single fathers seemed to be functioning better than the single mothers. It may be, as Ambert suggests, that our society actually favors the single-father role over the single-mother role. The single father receives authority and respect quasi-automatically from his children and does not suffer the decline in social status that the single mother experiences. Furthermore, Ambert reported that the single father is far more likely to receive offers of help from others than the single mother.

In general, the research by Ambert (1982) and the results of other studies comparing SFFs and SMFs (e.g., Lowenstein & Koopman, 1978) suggest that it may not be the sex of the parent that is the most important factor affecting children in OPFs, but rather the psychological adjustment and financial situation of the custodial parent. Futhermore, as it appears that as a group single fathers are typically in a better financial position than single mothers (Chang & Deinard, 1982), it seems plausible that single fathers can be at least as effective as single mothers in rearing their children.

In the present study, we extended Ambert's study to include not only the parents' perceptions of their children but also the children's perceptions of themselves. Therefore, in order to assess and evaluate the similarities and differences between children living in SMFs and SFFs, we utilized measures of these childrens' self-perceptions, self-esteem, social competencies, and the frequency and severity of their reported behaviour problems.

METHOD

Subjects

Participants in this study were 42 single, divorced, custodial parents (21 single-father families, and 21 single-mother families) and their 62 (6- to-16-year-old) children. These single parents were recruited through various chapters of Parents without Partners, in the Detroit, Michigan and Windsor, Ontario areas. In addition, 4 single-father families were recruited through Fathers For Equal Rights (Detroit, Michigan Chapter). The following criteria were established for inclusion in the experimental group:

1. The child must be between the ages of 6-16 years,
2. He/she must have lived in a one-parent arrangement for at least 1 year,
3. His/her parents must be either separated or divorced, and,
4. The child must attain a standard score of at least 85 on The Peabody Picture Vocabulary Test-Revised (Dunn & Dunn, 1981).

In general, the typical single parent who volunteered for this study was Caucasian, in his/her mid-thirties, and had 13 to 14 years of education. In addition, most single parents had been in this familial arrangement for at least 2 years and had custody of 2 children on average. With respect to socio-economic status, most of the single parents fell into the lower middle- to middle-class ranges. However, it should be noted that the single mothers' incomes were substantially lower than those of the single fathers. A comparison of these groups with respect to the demographic variables is presented in Tables 1 and 2 and is further discussed in the Results section.

Measures

Three dependent measures with established norms were utilized in this study. Two of these (The Self-Perception Profile for Children and The Peabody Picture Vocabulary Test-Revised) were administered to the children, while The Child Behaviour Checklist was completed by the parent. The following is a brief discussion of these instruments.

Table 1

Demographic Variables According to Family Type

	Family Type			
	SFF		SMF	
Variables	M	SD	M	SD
Parent's age	37.0	5.0	38.4	4.6
Parent's education	14.2	2.1	13.2	1.6
Years as a single parent	3.9	2.0	6.0	2.8
Years married	10.3	4.9	10.5	4.8
Number of children	2.1	0.9	2.7	1.2
Family incomes[a]	32.0	13.0	17.8	9.0

[a]In units of one thousand

Table 2

Total Number, Gender and Age of Subjects According to Family Type

	Family Type	
Variables	SFF	SMF
Number of children	28.0	34.0
Male	17.0	16.0
Female	11.0	18.0
Age – M	11.2	11.6
SD	2.6	2.4

The Self-Perception Profile for Children (SPPC)

The SPPC consists of 36 items that include 2 statements per item. First, the child must decide which statement best suits him/her (e.g., "Some kids feel that they are good at their school work but other kids worry that they cannot do the school work assigned to them") and then he/she must indicate whether the statement that he/she selected is "sort of true" or "really true" for him/her. The subscales of the SPPC (Harter, 1983) include: (1) Scholastic Competence (i.e., perceived academic abilities), (2) Social Acceptance (i.e., perceived popularity and acceptance by peers), (3) Athletic Competence (i.e., perceived athletic ability), (4) Physical Appearance (i.e., perceived satisfaction with one's height, weight, etc.), (5) Behavioural Conduct (i.e., perceived satisfaction with one's behaviour, doing the right thing, etc.), and (6) Global Self-Worth (i.e., perceived sense of self-worth).

The Child Behaviour Checklist (CBCL)

The CBCL (Achenbach & Edelbrock, 1983) is comprised of 2 basic scales that provide information relating to a child's "Social Competence," and "Behaviour Problems." From the parents' responses, a Social Competence Profile is derived. This Profile includes 3 scores—Activities, Social, and School. The Behaviour Problem Scale consists of 118 items. Using this instrument, the parent is asked to rate each item on a 3-point scale (0 = Not true, 1 = Somewhat or Sometimes True, 2 = Very or Often True) using the child's behaviour in the past 6 months as a point of reference.

Peabody Picture Vocabulary Test-Revised (PPVT-R)

The PPVT-R (Dunn & Dunn, 1981) is a non-verbal, multiple-choice test designed to assess the receptive vocabulary skills of children and adults (ages 2 1/2 and older). This task requires the child to match a spoken work with its pictorial representation. The PPVT-R correlations with intelligence tests vary from moderate to high.

Procedure

Once the single-parent families were recruited through the various single-parent support groups, those who volunteered were contacted and an interview at the parent's home was arranged. Following this, the parent was given the CBCL and a parent questionnaire and was asked to complete these forms while the child(ren) was(were) interviewed individually. In most cases, the parent did not remain in the same room as the child unless he/she expressed a strong preference to do so or if there were no other rooms available. After these forms were completed, a semi-structured interview was conducted. The entire home visit took between 1 to 3 hours, with most sessions lasting approximately 90 minutes.

RESULTS

In order to evaluate differences in potentially confounding variables, a one-way multivariate analysis of variance (MANOVA) was performed comparing the two groups with respect to the following variables: parent's age and years of education, number of years married and years as a single parent, family income, the custodial parent's relationship with the noncustodial parent and the child's relationship with the noncustodial parent (as rated by the custodial of 1 to 3), and the child's frequency of contact with the noncustodial parent (as rated by the custodial parent on a scale of 1 to 5). Using the Hotelling-Lawley Trace Test as the criterion measure, significant Group effects were found between SFFs and SMFs ($F(9,32) = 2.73$, $p < .02$). Post hoc t-tests revealed that these two groups were significantly different with respect to two demographic variables: family income (i.e., SFFs incomes were higher than SMFs) and number of years as a single parent (i.e., single mothers had been single parents for a longer period of time than single fathers). Therefore, in order to control for the possible confounding effects of these 2 demographic variables, a one-way multivariate analysis of covariance (MANCOVA), using family income and years as a single parent as covariates, was performed for each of the dependent measures in this study. In addition, individual analyses of covariance (ANCOVA) were calculated for each of the dependent measures' subscales.

Table 3 provides the mean scores and the standard deviations for children from SMFs and SFFs on the SPPC as well as a summary of the one-way analyses of covariance (ANCOVA) that were performed comparing these two groups. The MANCOVA results comparing children from SFFs and SMFs on the SPPC yielded a significant Main effect ($F(6,52) = 2.40$, $p < .04$). The ANCOVA procedures that were performed for each of the individual subscales revealed significant Main effects on the Scholastic Competence ($F(3,57) = 2.84$, $p < .04$) and Social Acceptance subscales ($F(3,57) = 3.03$, $p < .04$). According to Table 3, a significant Group effect was obtained on the Scholastic Competence subscale. However, it also appears that this significant result may be related to the number of years as a single parent ($F(1,59) = 5.62$, $p < .02$). The significant Main effect on the Social Acceptance subscale appears to be attributable to family income ($F(1,59) = 5.45$, $p < .05$).

The children's scores on the SPPC were compared with the overall sample mean scores and standard deviations for each scale. Individual scores that were at least one standard deviation below the mean for that scale were identified as a problem area for that child. A review of the frequency and percentages of the child's identified problem areas by group (see Table 4) did not reveal any substantial

Table 3

Mean Scores and Standard Deviations on the SPPC and the CBCL by

Group and a Summary of the One-Way Analyses of Covariance

(ANCOVA) between Children from SFFs and SMFs

	SFF (n=28)		SMF (n=34)		
	M	SD	M	SD	F (df=1,59)
SPPC[1]					
Scholastic Competence	15.63	4.1	17.12	3.4	5.40*
Athletic Competence	16.07	4.7	15.94	3.7	0.20
Social Acceptance	18.26	3.9	17.97	3.8	3.50
Physical Appearance	18.67	3.6	17.56	3.2	1.61
Behavioural Conduct	17.00	4.4	16.32	4.2	0.05
Global Self-Worth	19.70	3.1	18.20	3.2	1.79
CBCL					F(df=1,58)
Behaviour Problems[2]					
Raw Score	21.56	16.4	25.74	17.0	0.01
T Score	51.44	10.8	54.11	9.0	
Social Competence[3]					
Raw Score	19.57	2.9	19.15	3.6	0.32
T Score	48.21	8.3	46.74	10.0	

(Table continues)

TABLE 3 (continued)

1   The scores on the six subscales of the SPPC from 6 to 24. The higher the score, the higher the perceived self-competence on the subscale.

2   The Behaviour Problem raw scores range from 0-226. The higher the score, the more behaviour problems identified by the parent.

3   The Social Competence score is the sum of 3 variables (Activities, Social, and School) and the raw scores range from 0-30. The higher the score the higher the parent's ratings of their children's social competence.

* p < .05

differences between these two groups with the exception of the relatively lower number of children from SFFs who scored significantly below the average on the Global Self-Worth and Behavioral Conduct subscales. However, it must be considered that since this procedure does not statistically control for the effect of the sex of the child and the family income, it is possible that these differences are attributable to these two variables and not the sex of the single parent. Nonetheless, in both cases these children were more likely to be living in a single-mother arrangement.

Table 3 provides the mean scores and standard deviations for children from SMFs and SFFs on the CBCL as well as a summary of the one-way analyses of covariance (ANCOVA) that were performed comparing these two groups. The results of the MAN-

Table 4

Frequency (f) and Percentages (%) of Children's Identified
Problem Areas on the SPPC and CBCL by Group

	SFF		SMF	
	f	%	f	%
SPPC				
Scholastic Competence	7	26	6	18
Athletic Competence	7	26	5	15
Social Acceptance	5	19	6	18
Physical Appearance	3	11	5	15
Behavioural Conduct	3	11	8	24
Global Self-Worth	2	7	10	29
CBCL				
Social Competence T Score	4	15	7	21
Behaviour Problems T Score	4	15	8	24

COVA comparing SMFs and SFFs on the CBCL did not yield any significant overall Group effects ($F(6,56) = 0.13$, $p < .88$). Although these results reveal a significant Main effect for the Behaviour Problem score, a closer inspection of the sources of this difference suggests that this effect is attributable to family income ($F(1,59) = 8.10$, $p < .006$) and not the sex of the single parent.

According to the CBCL norms, a T score of less than approximately 28 or 29 (depending on the age and sex of the child) on the Social Competence Scale is considered a problem area. These results (Table 4) indicated that the percentage of children scoring below a T score of 30 on the Social Competence Scale was roughly equivalent for both SFFs and SMFs. On the Behaviour Problem Scales, a T score of 62 or 63 above (depending on the child's age and sex) is considered clinically significant. These scores indicated that the percentage of children who could be classified as a "behaviour problem" was slightly higher in the SMF group than the SFF group. However, this procedure does not control for the effects of the sex of the child and family income and therefore it is possible that these variables are contributing to this result.

DISCUSSION

The purpose of this study was to examine whether there are any significant differences between children reared in SMFs and SFFs with respect to their self-perceptions regarding self-esteem, social competencies, and the frequency and severity of their reported behaviour problems. In general, these results are consistent with the findings of other studies (e.g., Ambert, 1982; Fry, 1983; Lowenstein & Koopman, 1978; Rosen, 1979) and do not support the historical assumption that single mothers are more effective parents than single fathers. Therefore, it follows that the traditional belief that in the case of child custody, children be placed with their mothers (e.g., "the tender years doctrine") is not supported. These results suggest that both single mothers and single fathers can be effective parents.

A significant finding to emerge in this study was that children from SMFs scored higher than children from SFFs on a measure of perceived scholastic competence. This finding also appears to be related to the number of years that a child has lived in a single-parent home. In this regard, Wallerstein and Kelly's (1980) research suggests that during the first 2 years after the parents' divorce, children generally become more defiant, negative, and depressed. Further, the work of Mitchell, Hammond, and Bee (1983; cited in Bee, 1985) found that school performance also decreased after the divorce. Therefore, as the single mothers tended to be single parents for a longer period of time than single fathers, this finding may be more related to length of time since separation/divorce rather than by the sex of the single parent.

A second noteworthy finding was that socio-economic status

(i.e., family income) was significantly related to both the children's perceptions of their social acceptance and to the parents' ratings of their children's behaviour problems. This latter finding suggests that socio-economic status may be a better predictor of children's behaviour problems than the sex of the single parent. Futhermore, it is possible that the frequently reported conclusion that children in OPFs tend to exhibit more behaviour problems than children from intact families, with the implication that the problem behaviours are directly related to living in a OPF, may be inaccurate (e.g., Brown, 1980). In support of this, Blechman (1982) concluded that many studies investigating the negative consequences for children living in OPFs failed to control for the SES variable.

In order to avoid some of the common criticisms of the research on OPFs (e.g., Blechman, 1982), this study has attempted to refine some of the methodological shortcomings that have confounded previous research. In this regard, statistical procedures were utilized to control for the possible confounding effects of certain demographic variables (e.g., family income) and well-developed and validated dependent measures were selected.

Based on the results of this study, a number of suggestions for future research in this area seem appropriate. First, the importance of controlling for SES factors cannot be overemphasized. Failure to do so seriously restricts the validity of the research findings. In addition, much of the research on OPFs involves volunteers from single-parent support groups. Although this is likely the easiest single-parent group to recruit, this limits the generalizability of the findings to other single-parent groups. Therefore, other methods of recruitment directed at different single-parent populations may provide a different perspective of the OPF. Television and radio campaigns or personal contacts in various communities may prove effective in this regard.

Second, as sex of the parent does not appear to distinguish between successful and unsuccessful single-parent families, other criteria are needed to assess the prognosis for success of single parents. Therefore, research addressing the qualities or characteristics of successful single-parent families may prove helpful. Some preliminary research has been undertaken in this area (e.g., Barry, 1979).

In conclusion, the results of this study suggest that both single mothers and single fathers can be effective parents and that the presumed assumption that the mother is the more competent parent to raise the children in the case of separation and/or divorce may not be a fair or an accurate assertion. With respect to child custody, these results imply that the decision as to which parent should receive custody should not be determined merely by the sex of the child and/or the parent. It is recommended that the decision as to which parent should receive custody should be based on an assessment of the parents (e.g., financial situation, emotional adjustment, and individual qualities) and what they each have to offer their children, rather than being predetermined by their sex.

REFERENCES

Achenbach, T., & Edelbrock, C. (1983). *Manual for the Child Behaviour Checklist and Revised Child Behaviour Profile*. Burlington, Vt.: Department of Psychology, University of Vermont.

Ambert, A. (1982). Differences in children's behaviour toward custodial mothers and custodial fathers. *Journal of Marriage and the Family, 44*, 73-86.

Barry, A. (1974). A research project on successful single-parent families. *American Journal of Family Therapy, 7*, 65-73.

Bee, H. (1985). *The developing child* (4th ed.). Philadelphia: Harper & Row Publishers.

Blechman, E. A. (1982). Are children with one parent at psychological risk? A methodological review. *Journal of Marriage and the Family, 44*, 179-195.

Brown, B. F. (1980). A study of the school needs of children from OPFs. *Phi Delta Kappan*, 537-540.

Chang, P. W., & Deinard, A. S. (1982). Single father caretakers: Demographic characteristics and adjustment processes. *American Journal of Orthopsychiatry, 52*, 236-243.

Davis, L. (1985). The one-parent family in Canada: The quantitative background. In B. Schlesinger (Ed.), *The one-parent family in the 1980's*. Toronto: University of Toronto Press.

Dunn, L. M., & Dunn, L. M. (1981). *Peabody Picture Vocabulary Test-Revised Manual*. American Guidance Service.

Fry, P. S. (1983). The kid's eye view: The OPF and children's perceptions of personal needs and concerns for the future. *Journal of Child Care, 1* 31-50.

Harter, S. (1983). Supplementary description of the Self-Perception Profile for Children-Revision of the Perceived Competence Scale. University of Denver.

Hetherington, E. M., Cox, M., & Cox, R. (1978). The aftermath of divorce. In H. H. Stevens, Jr. & M. Mathews (Eds.), *Mother/child, father/child relation-*

ships. Washington, D. C.: National Association for the Education of Young Children.

Lowenstein, J. S., & Koopman, E. J. (1978). A comparison of self-esteem between boys living with single-parent mothers and single-parent fathers. *Journal of Divorce, 2*, 195-207.

McFadden, J. (1974). *Bachelor fatherhood: How to raise and enjoy your children as a single parent*. New York: Walker.

Rosen, R. (1979). Some crucial issues concerning children of divorce. *Journal of Divorce, 3*, 19-25.

Santrock, J. W., & Warshak, R. A. (1979). Father custody and social development in boys and girls. *Journal of Social Issues, 35*, 112-125.

Wallerstein, J. S., & Kelly, J. B. (1980). *Surviving the breakup: How children and parents cope with divorce*. New York: Basic Books.

Comparing the Effects on the Child of Post-Divorce Parenting Arrangements

Rebecca J. Glover
Connie Steele

SUMMARY. Comparisons of the impact on the child of parenting arrangements as a result of parental divorce were examined. Twenty-four children were matched in eight triplets consisting of one joint-custody child, one single-custody child, and one child from an intact family. Results of this exploratory study revealed that shared parenting in joint custody was at least as beneficial, perhaps a more beneficial parenting arrangement than the solo parenting arrangement for children in custody due to parental divorce.

INTRODUCTION

Currently, it is estimated that 40 to 50 percent of children born during the 70s will spend some portion of their childhood in a single-parent family (Santrock, 1986). Concern for these children dictates that attention be focused on parenting arrangements after divorce. While custody of approximately 90 percent of the children continues to be awarded to the mother, joint custody is being touted as a viable option by the courts, by the states, by family service units, by film awards, by the popular press, and by the individuals themselves (Dean, 1983; Steinman, 1981; Trombetta, 1980-81;

Rebecca J. Glover, MS, is a graduate student and Connie Steele, EdD, is on the faculty of the Department of Human Development and Family Studies, Texas Tech University, Lubbock, TX 79409.

Vander Zander, 1985; Ware, 1982). Even so, investigation of the comparative merit of joint custody over other custodial arrangements of children of divorce has been remarkably minimal.

Single Custody

Research regarding the effects of single custody on the child's emotional development has centered around the comparison of this parenting arrangement with intact families. Children of divorced parents living in single custody (usually with the mother) have evidenced strong feelings of sadness and grieving, fear, a sense of loss in regard to the departed parent, anger, and other problems (Freed, 1979; Hess & Camara, 1979; Kelly & Wallerstein, 1976; Parish & Dostal, 1980). Perhaps the usual maternal parenting in single custodial families predicts problems since it is the product of divorce and its subsequent psychological difficulties; if that be so, then any parenting arrangement would suffer from the psychological and economic impact of divorce. However, since divorce today results in the necessity of attending to the children affected by this legal and social event, it seems worthwhile to attempt to find alternative methods for providing parenting arrangements after divorce that might be least psychologically harmful to children and their healthy development. An alternative to be considered might be joint custody of the children by both of the divorcing parents.

Joint Custody

While only a few states have enacted laws authorizing joint custody, some divorcing couples have employed informal, cooperative agreements that give both parents responsibility and decision making as well as frequent interactions with their children (Trombetta, 1980-81).

Critics of joint custody have suggested that the increased interactions of divorced parents inherent in joint custody would increase parental display of friction, conflict, and dissension with the child as the central focus of both parents—to the detriment of the child (Levy & Chambers, 1981). Furthermore, others have alleged that the joint-custody arrangement creates feelings of instability and confusion for children as they move from one house to another and back again (Goldstein et al., 1979; Miller, 1979).

A few studies have investigated the effects on the children of joint custody. Analyzing interviews with six parents and their children using joint custody, Abarbanel (1979) found that the children appeared "well-adjusted" with no severe behavioral problems; none of the children seemed to experience the sense of loss of one parent, and all appeared well adapted to living in two homes. Following up the effects of joint custody on 24 divorced families, Steinman (1981) concluded that the joint-custody children had a strong attachment and loyalty to both their mothers and fathers. The process of shifting homes did not appear to be a negative factor, and most of the children adapted to each household of the father and the mother with a minimum of conflict and confusion. One study compared the effects of maternal custody in 16 families, paternal custody in 16 families, and joint custody in 18 families on 91 children's self-concept and other measures of psychological adjustment and found that these scores did not differ according to custody type; the conclusion was drawn that joint custody at its best was superior to (or as good as) single custody at its best (Luepnitz, 1982). Another study looked for differences in emotional adjustment of boys in joint custody, single custody, happy/intact families, and unhappy/intact families; both joint-custody boys and happy/intact families were better emotionally adjusted than boys from single-custody and unhappy/intact families (Pojman, 1981). The conclusion was drawn that joint custody was at least as satisfactory a parenting arrangement for the emotional adjustment of children of divorce as other post-divorce parenting arrangements.

Children's Perceptions of Their Parents and the Divorce

Inasmuch as maximum cognitive sensitivity to interpersonal stimuli occurs between ages seven and eleven, the effects of divorce on the social and emotional development of children will be most apparent at those ages (Piaget & Inhelder, 1969). Comparisons have been made of the child's self-concept, the child's emotional adjustment to the divorce, attachment and loyalty to both parents, and feelings of anger, loss, instability, and confusion in parenting arrangements following divorce (Abarbanel, 1979; Freed, 1979; Hess & Camara, 1979; Kelly & Wallerstein, 1976; Levy & Chambers, 1981; Luepnitz, 1982; Parish & Dostal, 1980; Pojman, 1981; Steinman, 1981). In addition, children's feelings about their two divorcing parents may affect their emotional adjustment and have been examined, but outcomes regarding selection of a better parenting alternative for divorcing parents have been inconclusive as children have shown positive feelings almost equally divided between the custodial and non-custodial parent (Freed, 1979). Family relationships after the divorce have tended to affect the child as much or more than the divorce itself with the child's relationship with both the mother and father being of equal importance to the child's emotional well-being (Hess & Camara, 1979). Divorce has been seen as least traumatic when freedom of access to the custodial and non-custodial parent has been permitted with the strength of the parent-child attachment as most crucial (Rosen, 1979). Children's most negative feelings have centered on loss of the non-custodial parent; but, in one study, frequent visitation with this parent led to more negative divorce adjustment (Kurdek et al., 1981). In general, children seem to adjust better to their parents' divorce when they have continued involvement with both parents.

Purpose of This Study

If nurturance from both parents seems to aid in the emotional adjustment of the child of divorce, then study of joint custody as a viable alternative for parenting arrangements after divorce is warranted. This study investigated whether or not custodial arrangements of selected families seemed to be the factor relating to differences in the children's emotional and social behaviors. It was hypothesized that the child's self-concept, locus of control, emotional perceptions of each parent, and reaction to divorce of the parents would be more positive for children in joint custody than for those in single custody. Comparisons of both single and joint custody with intact families were predicted to show both parenting arrangements to be less positive than parenting children in intact families.

METHOD

Subjects

Three homogeneous groups of Caucasian, middle- to upper middle-class children were selected for the study: (1) children whose parents shared their joint custody, (2) children who resided solely with the mother, and (3) children from intact families, used as a comparison group. The children ranged in age from 6 to 15 years, and all were the natural children of the parents. Parents of the children from the joint-custody and single-custody groups had been divorced for a period of at least six months, but not longer than two years. Only custodial parents who had remained single were selected in order to avoid change of parenting relationships due to step-parent involvement.

Joint-Custody Children

The joint-custody children were sought initially; children in the other two groups were matched individually to this group. In an attempt to locate all of the available joint-custody families in the area, local judges and attorneys were visited and appeals were made to local divorce adjustment groups, schools, and the community. Seven children residing in "joint custody" were found in the West Texas area; an additional child was located in Albuquerque, New Mexico, making a total of eight joint-custody children. Joint-custodial arrangements varied from child to child—some residing six months with each parent, some changing homes on a weekly or biweekly basis, and some rotating parental homes. All joint-custody arrangements had been agreed upon by the parents prior to finalizing the divorce.

Single-Custody Children

Children in single custody were sought for matching the joint-custody sample by examining public divorce records within Lubbock County, Texas. Letters were mailed to persons identified by these records that requested parent and child's participation; only one individual's response was returned. Appeals for participants in the study were made to local single-parent and divorce-adjustment groups as well as telephone contacts to single parents whose names appeared in the directories of local schools.

Intact-Family Children

The children from intact families were those whose parents had never separated or divorced. Children were located through personal references and were matched to those in joint custody for age at time of assessment and gender.

After the three groups had been as closely matched as feasible, analysis of variance showed no significant difference among the three groups' ages nor between the length-of-time-since-parental-divorce for the single- and joint-custody families. Intact families were matched to joint-custody families — each having 5 males and 3 females, but single-custody families had 3 males and 5 females. (See Table 1.)

Measures

Children of each custodial status were administered the following measures: (1) the Nowicki-Strickland Locus of Control Scale for Children (1973), (2) the Piers-Harris Self-Concept Scale (1964), and (3) the Anthony-Bene Family Relations Test (1957). Those children from divorced families also completed the Structured Divorce Questionnaire (Kurdek & Siesky, 1983). These instruments were selected as they have frequently been cited as assessing characteristics affecting children's emotional adjustment to parental divorce.

Locus of Control

The locus of control scale, a paper and pencil measure consisting of 40 Yes-or-No questions, assessed the extent to which the child perceived experiences as being internally or externally controlled (Nowicki & Strickland, 1973). Possible scores could range from 40 to 80, the higher score indicating more external control. The range of scores for this sample was 41 to 55.

Table 1.

Comparison of Joint-Custody, Single-Custody,

and Intact Family Groups of Subjects

	N	Gender M	F	Mean Age $_a$	Mean Time Since Divorce $_b$
Joint Custody	8	5	3	10.6	2.05 years
Single Custody	8	3	5	11.1	2.09 years
Intact Family	8	5	3	10.3	

a. F-value = .155; p = .85.

b. F-value = .002; p = .96.

Self-Concept

The self-concept scale consisting of 80 first-person, declarative, Yes-or-No sentences was scored so that a higher score indicated a higher level of self-concept (Piers-Harris, 1964). The possible range of scores for this measure was 80 to 160; scores for the children of this study ranged from 123 to 154.

The Family Relations Test

Designed to give a concrete representation of the child's family, the Family Relations Test has 20 figures stereotypically representing members of any child's family (Anthony & Bene, 1957). In addition, a figure symbolizing "Nobody" permitted responses that did not apply to anyone in the family (e.g., "Sometimes I hate this person in the family"). The child placed cards containing messages with the figure of the person for whom the message best applied.

Only figures representing Father, Mother, and Nobody were utilized for this study. Strong positive incoming and outgoing feelings were valued at 2 points; mild positive incoming and outgoing feelings were given 1 point. Strong negative incoming and outgoing feelings were scored -2 points; mild negative incoming and outgoing feelings were scored -1 point. Responses regarding each father and each mother were totalled individually with possible scores ranging from -50 to 50; the sample's scores ranged from -19 to 45, with the higher scores reflecting more positive relations with the parent.

Post-Divorce Adjustment

For this study, only 38 items of the 69-item Structured Divorce Questionnaire (Kurdek & Siesky, 1983) were administered to children in joint and single custody. These items were utilized as they categorized children's perceptions of divorce regarding News of Divorce, Acceptance of Parents, Loss of Parent, Changes in Family Relationships, Post-Divorce Conflict, Emotional Responses, and Peer Reactions. For purposes of this study, the scoring system was reduced from a five-point spread to a forced choice of Agree or Disagree. Possible scores ranged from 38 to 76; a higher score indicated less adjustment to the divorce. Scores for this sample ranged from 38 to 67.

Procedures

Visiting the parent and the child in the home, the researcher provided the child with instructions for completing each measure. The younger children were asked if they preferred to read the instruments individually or to have the items read to them. All except one joint-custody child and one single-custody child elected to read the instruments independently. The measures were administered in random order with the parents not present during the evaluation.

RESULTS

Group Responses

One-way analysis of variance procedures showed no significant differences among the groups' responses to the measures of locus of control, self-concept, father relations, mother relations, and divorce adjustment. (See Table 2.)

As the sample population was so small for comparison by ANOVA procedures, other methods were employed to examine the eight matched sets of three persons (hereinafter referred to as "matched triplets"). The children from intact families scored higher than children in joint and single custody in internality, self-concept, and father relationships. Children from intact families evidenced the highest level of internality in locus of control, Mean (M) = 48.12, followed by the single-custody children, M = 48.81, as children in joint custody showed the least internality score of the

Table 2.

Group and Population Means of Children in Each Custodial

Arrangement for Each Measure

	Joint	Single	Intact	Difference Probability
Locus of Control	49.87	48.81	48.12	n.s.
Self-Concept	144.06	143.43	146.50	n.s.
Father Relations	22.50	13.75	23.87	n.s.
Mother Relations	27.50	22.00	25.25	n.s.
Divorce Adjustment	47.50	51.87		n.s.

For all variables, df (1,23); level of significance, $p < .05$.

three groups, $M = 49.87$. Children from intact families also achieved the highest self-concept scores, $M = 146.50$, followed by the children in joint custody, $M = 144.06$, with single-custody children registering the lowest self-concept, $M = 143.43$. Children from intact families reflected the most positive father relationships, $M = 23.87$, followed by children in joint custody, $M = 22.50$, with children in single custody scoring considerably lower, $M = 13.75$, than the other two groups.

Evidence of positive relationships with their mothers shows a somewhat different pattern. A "t-test" indicated that children in joint custody reflected a more positive attitude toward their mothers than did children in single custody (F-value $= 4.78; p < .056$) and surprisingly more than children from intact families (F-value $= 2.88; p < .186$). As Table 2 reports, joint-custody children were somewhat more positively adjusted following their parents' divorce than were the single-custody children.

Comparisons of the Individual Triplets

Raw scores of the three children in each of the eight matched triplets — one joint-custody child, the matching child in single custody, and the matching child from an intact family — were compared for each measure.

Locus of Control

Though only a trend, joint-custody children compared favorably to matched single-custody children in regarding themselves as controlling their environment. On the locus of control measure of internality/externality, children in joint custody and in the intact families scored more internality in three of the eight triplets, while children in single custody achieved the most positive scores in the remaining two triplets. Children in single custody received the least positive scores in four of the triplets; joint-custody children achieved the least positive scores in two of the triplets, and a child from an intact family in one triplet responded with the least positive score. In one triplet, the least positive score was shared by the child in single custody and the child from an intact family.

Self-Concept

Joint-custody children fared at least as well as or higher in self-regard than their matching single-custody children. Joint-custody children achieved the highest scores in four of the eight triplets, children from intact families scored highest in three triplets, while only one single-custody child achieved the highest score in his triplet. On the other hand, the single-custody children held the lowest scores in four of the triplets, while the joint-custody children scored lowest in two triplets, and the child from the intact family received the lowest score in only one triplet. In the remaining triplet, the lowest score was shared by the child from the intact family and the child residing solely with the mother.

Father-Mother Relationships

Especially in response to questions about their relationships with their fathers and mothers, joint-custody children reflected feelings most positively in the triplet comparisons. In response to the Anthony-Bene measure, children in joint custody scored the most positive father relationships in four of the triplets while those children in single custody and intact families each scored highest in two triplets. Children residing solely with the mother reflected the lowest father relationships in four of the eight triplets, while children residing with each parent jointly scored lowest in three of the triplets. One child in an intact family scored lowest in one triplet.

Responding to mother relationships, children from joint custody families reacted the most positively in five of the eight triplets. Children from intact families scored highest in two triplets, while children in single custody scored highest in only one triplet. Children in joint custody and single custody scored lowest of this measure in three triplets each, and children from intact families scored lowest in the two remaining triplets.

Post-Divorce Adjustment

Comparison of the children from the two divorced groups on the post-divorce adjustment measure showed that joint-custody children achieved the more positive scores in six of the eight pairs with the single-custody children scoring more positively in only two comparisons of post-divorce adjustment.

Chi-Square Analyses

Repeated-measures chi-square analyses were employed to determine if differences occurred among most positive/least positive responses by the three groups to the measures of locus of control, self-concept, father relationships, and mother relationships. None of the differences was significant. However, of 32 possible most-positive responses on the four measures by the 24 children, 16 were achieved by the children in joint custody, 6 by the children in single custody, and 10 by children in the intact families. (See Table 3.)

Repeated-measures chi-square analyses utilizing responses of children in joint and single custody to the five measures — locus of control, self-concept, father relationships, mother relationships, and post-divorce adjustment — resulted in no significant differences. However, of 40 possible more-positive responses, 26 were achieved by joint-custody children, and 14 by those in single custody. (See Table 4.)

Table 3.

Frequency of Most Positive and Least Positive Responses of

Children by Custodial Arrangement

| | Most Positive | | | Least Positive | | |
	Joint	Single	Intact	Joint	Single	Intact
Locus of Control	3	2	3	2	4.5	1.5
Self-Concept	4	1	3	2	4.5	1.5
Father Relations	4	2	2	3	4	1
Mother Relations	5	1	2	3	3	2
Total	16	6	10	10	16	6

Table 4.

Frequency of More Positive Responses of Children

in Joint and Single Custody

| | More Positive | |
	Joint	Single
Locus of Control	5	3
Self-Concept	6	2
Father Relations	5	3
Mother Relations	5	3
Divorce Adjustment	6	2
Total	26	14

DISCUSSION

Joint custody has been highly publicized as a potentially more positive parenting arrangement after divorce. Some argue to the contrary. This exploratory study addressed the need to compare the effects on children within joint- and single-custody arrangements that occur as a result of divorce. Comparison of divorced parent-child interactions with intact family members who have not experienced the impact from divorce is necessary although such comparisons have rarely been presented in the literature. Having only eight families in three groups of joint-custody, single-custody, and intact-family children (N = 24) seriously precluded meaningful statistical analysis of the data; nevertheless, compilation of the data for trend comparisons made it possible to draw several tentative conclusions.

Although children in intact families achieved higher mean scores than those from joint- or single-custody arrangements on the measures of locus of control, self-concept, and father relationships, joint-custody children demonstrated higher scores than those in single-custody on measures of self-concept and father relationships. When the eight triplets' responses were compared instead of group mean scores, joint-custody children had more "most-positive" responses than either intact-family or single-custody children in self-concept, father relationships, and mother relationships. These findings reflect the notion that having access to both parents appears to retain positive feelings about self, the father, and especially the mother. Furthermore, children in joint custody had fewer "least-positive" responses than single-custody children on all measures except mother relationships where both groups had the same number "least-positive" responses, while children in intact families had fewer "least-positive" responses than children in either of the other custodial arrangements.

On the evaluation of internality/externality (locus of control), children in joint custody registered a higher degree of externality than either the intact-family or single-custody children, but had more "most-positive" responses and fewer "least-positive" responses than single-custody children.

Like Pojman (1981), who concluded that joint custody was preferable to single custody, divorce adjustment mean scores in the present study revealed joint-custody children to be more positively adjusted to the divorce of their parents than did those in single custody. In fact, children in joint custody had six of eight "more-positive" reactions to the divorce in their families. The joint-custody sample revealed a level of understanding and acceptance of both parents higher than that of the single-custody children — possibly attributable to the continued relationship between those children in joint custody and both parents as a result of the shared living arrangements.

While Freed (1979), who also measured child, mother, and father relationships using the Anthony-Bene Family Relations Test, concluded that children from divorced families were more likely to feel positively or ambivalently toward the mother and positively toward the father, the present study indicated that children in both joint and single custody felt positively toward the mother, yet more ambivalently, and sometimes negatively, toward the father. The highly selected nature of the present study's sample may account for this finding. Further study regarding the child/parent interactions is justified.

Kurdek, Blisk, and Siesky (1981) noted a degree of internality as a good predictor of children's adjustment to parental divorce. Children in the present study revealed a more internal than external orientation and responses concerning post-divorce adjustment indicated that these children were not adversely affected by the divorce of their parents. For the majority of the children, a more internal score was coupled with a more positive score in regard to post-divorce adjustment, thereby corresponding with the conclusion of Kurdek et al. (1981). While the joint-custody children had a higher externality orientation than single-custody children, the higher level of divorce adjustment by joint-custody children seems to show that higher internality may not always predict children's more positive adjustment to parental divorce. In future studies, attention should be paid to this factor in discerning healthful adjustment to divorce.

Future study regarding child custody might investigate the use of joint custody where the living arrangement was both agreed upon by the parties as well as mandated by the courts. In this manner, perhaps a more definitive or standardized view of joint custody and its impact on children of divorce may be obtained. Due to the nature of the current provisions for joint custody in the state of Texas where seven of these children were located, each parent was required to agree to that custodial arrangement before it was ordered by the courts (Smith, 1982). Therefore, this study excluded joint-custody arrangements in which one or neither parent has sought such an arrangement.

Contrary to the opinion of many legal and psychological professionals that the continual shifting of homes created by joint custody is more detrimental to the child than time lost with the non-custodial parent in the single-custody arrangement (Miller, 1979), responses of children in this study indicated that joint custody was, at the very least, no less beneficial to the child than single custody — similar to the conclusions of Steinman (1981) and Abarbanel (1979). In fact, children's responses in this study revealed that children in joint custody often scored as positively or more positively than children in single custody or than those children never having experienced parental divorce. In other words, responses of children in joint custody regarding their self-regard, their feelings of event control, and their relationships with mother and father reflected that the joint-custodial parenting arrangement was at least as beneficial — and possibly more emotionally helpful to the child — as single custody. It may have been that the joint-custody parents maintained healthy attitudes toward parenting as revealed by the election of joint custody and, therefore, a willingness to work and maintain a positive relationship with the child. Or, is it possible that the parenting arrangement promoted the emotional health of both parents and child, resulting in the higher scores in self-concept and father relationships.

This exploratory study contributes to the limited, yet growing volume of literature regarding joint custody. Though the "matched-set" method of obtaining the population for study does not solve the problems inherent in comparison of variables, this study adds to the present understanding of joint custody and its utility as an alternative custody arrangement.

REFERENCES

Abarbanel, A. (1979). Shared parenting after separation and divorce: A study of joint custody. *American Journal of Orthopsychiatry, 49* (2), 320-329.

Anthony, E., & Bene, E. (1957). A technique for the objective assessment of the child's family relationships. *Journal of Mental Science, 103*, 541-555.

Dean, J. (1983). Joint custody: A new kind of family. New Jersey: New Day Films.

Freed, R. (1979). The emotional attitudes experienced by children of divorce in relation to their parents. (Doctoral dissertation, University of Southern California.) *Dissertation Abstracts International, 39* (12-A), 7522-7523.

Goldstein, J., Freud, A., & Solnit, A. (1979). *Beyond the best interest of the child.* New York: Free Press.

Hess, R., & Camara, K. (1979). Post-divorce family relationships as mediating factors in the consequences of divorce for children. *Journal of Social Issues, 35* (1), 79-96.

Kelly, J., & Wallerstein, J. (1976). The effects of parental divorce: Experiences of the child in early latency. *American Journal of Orthopsychiatry, 46* (1), 20-32.

Kurdek, L., Blisk, D., & Siesky, A., Jr. (1981). Correlates of children's long-term adjustment to their parents' divorce. *Developmental Psychology, 17* (5), 565-579.

Kurdek, L., & Siesky, A., Jr. (1980). Children's perceptions of their parents' divorce. *Journal of Divorce, 3* (4), 339-378.

Levy, B., & Chambers, C. (1981). The folly of joint custody. *Illinois Bar Journal, 69* (7), 412-418.

Luepnitz, D. (1982). *Child custody.* Lexington, Mass.: D. C. Heath & Co.

Miller, D., (Ed.). (1979). Joint custody. *Family Law Quarterly, 13* (3), 345-412.

Nowicki, S., Jr., & Strickland, B. (1973). A locus of control scale for children. *Journal of Consulting and Clinical Psychology, 40* (1), 148-154.

Parish, T., & Dostal, J. (1980). Evaluation of self and parent figures by children from intact, divorced, and reconstituted families. *Journal of Youth & Adolescence, 9* (4), 347-351.

Piaget, J., & Inhelder, B. (1969). *Psychology of the child.* New York: Basic Books.

Piers, E., & Harris, D. (1964). Age and other correlates of self-concept in children. *Journal of Educational Psychology, 55* (2), 91-95.

Pojman, E. (1981). *Emotional adjustment of boys in sole custody and joint custody divorces compared with adjustment of boys in happy and unhappy marriages.* Unpublished doctoral dissertation. California Graduate Institute, West Los Angeles, Ca.

Rosen, R. (1979). Some crucial issues concerning children of divorce. *Journal of Divorce, 3,* 19-25.

Santrock, J. (1986). *Life-span development,* 2nd edition. Dubuque, Iowa: Wm. C. Brown Publishers.

Smith, E. (1982). Title 2. Parent and child (Commentary). In F. Posey, et al. (Eds.). *Texas Tech Law Review: The Texas Family Code Symposium* (Vol. 13). Lubbock, Tex.: Texas Tech University School of Law.

Steinman, S. (1981). The experiences of children in a joint custody arrangement: A report of a study. *American Journal of Orthopsychiatry, 51* (3), 403-414.

Trombetta, D. (1980-81). Joint custody: Recent research and overloaded courtrooms inspire new solutions to custody disputes. *Journal of Family Law, 19* (2), 213-234.

Vander Zander, J. (1985). *Human development,* 3rd edition. New York: Alfred A. Knopf, Inc.

Ware, C. (1982). *Sharing parenthood after divorce.* New York: Viking Press.

Siblings' Reactions to Parental Divorce

Lawrence A. Kurdek

SUMMARY. Because previous studies of children and divorce have typically included only one child per family, little is known about how siblings in the same family experience their parents' divorce. Three samples, totalling 49 pairs of white middle-class adolescent and preadolescent first-born and second-born siblings whose parents were separated no more than 24 months, were studied to assess the relation between siblings' divorce adjustment and the relation between siblings' general behavioral adjustment. Siblings' self-reports and custodial mothers' ratings of each sibling were obtained. For both sets of data, siblings' scores were positively related; when differences were found, older siblings were better adjusted than younger siblings. Based on siblings' self-report scores, relative to younger siblings, older siblings had a better understanding of the divorce, fewer problematic beliefs regarding the divorce, a better understanding of conflict resolution, and a more internal locus of control. Relative to boy/boy dyads, girl/girl dyads had a better understanding of both the divorce and conflict resolution. Based on mothers' ratings, older siblings had more positive reactions to the divorce and were less dependent on adults than younger siblings. There was no support for the position that second-born children with older brothers would show enhanced adjustment.

Lawrence A. Kurdek, PhD, is Professor, Department of Psychology, Wright State University, Dayton, OH 45435.

The author would like to thank the children and mothers who participated in these studies; Gene Siesky, Connie Kuhn, Marilyn Baumer, and Nancy Hickey for their assistance in data collection and data entry; and Mike Hennessy, Mark Fine, and Marie Tisak for their critical reading of the paper. Correspondence should be addressed to: Lawrence A. Kurdek, Wright State University, Psychology Department, Dayton, OH 45435.

203

Although children's experiences of parental divorce have received increased empirical attention (see Emery, Hetherington, and DiLalla [1984] for a recent review), little is known about siblings' experiences of parental divorce (Nichols, 1986). The overall neglect of siblings in the divorce literature may be due, in part, to the common practice of either randomly selecting one child per family when siblings exist (e.g., Kurdek, Blisk, & Siesky, 1981) or selecting only one sibling on the basis of age (e.g., Hetherington, Cox, & Cox, 1978) in order to satisfy statistical assumptions of independence of observations (Applebaum & McCall, 1983). However, if siblings' experiences of parental divorce are dissimilar, then findings based on one sibling would not generalize to another sibling.

What little is known about siblings and parental divorce comes from Wallerstein and Kelly (1980) who report that the presence of siblings diluted the degree of exposure to interparent conflict; that many children did not consider their siblings to be helpful in dealing with the divorce; that reactions to older siblings who assumed parental responsibilities were mixed; and that age differences among siblings made it difficult for the noncustodial parent to choose a common activity.

Although parental divorce has been described as a powerful set of events (Coddington, 1984) that might affect all siblings negatively, four findings derived from intact families lead one to doubt that siblings experience parental divorce similarly. First, Scarr and Grajek (1982) report that the amount of variance common to sibling pairs is 35 to 50% for intelligence, and only 15 to 20% for personality variables, interests, attitudes, and psychopathology. Second, adolescents and young adults have reported that they and their siblings differ with regard to social-affective environments, parental treatment, and personality characteristics (Daniels, 1986; Daniels & Plomin, 1985). Third, Baskett (1985) reported that adults have higher expectations for, and more positive ratings of, oldest children as compared to only or youngest children. Finally, there is intriguing evidence that parents as well as siblings themselves have a bias to perceive members of a sibling dyad at opposing ends of global bipolar continua (such as same/different or easy/difficult) (Schachter, 1982, 1985; Schachter, Shore, Feldman-Rotman, Marquis, & Campbell, 1976), and that siblings' scores on these continua are negatively correlated (Schachter & Stone, 1985). Schachter (1982, 1985) indicates that this sibling deidentification effect may occur mainly in the first pair of children in the family, especially if they are of the same gender, and hypothesizes that sibling deidentification mitigates sibling rivalry and maintains family harmony.

On the basis of the above studies, one might predict that siblings would experience parental divorce differently. Indeed, Shapiro and Wallace (in press) report that five single divorced parents indicated differences in siblings' reactions to divorce, but their sample was too small to draw any clear conclusions. The first purpose of this exploratory study was to assess similarities between siblings' divorce adjustment and between their general behavioral adjustment. Because directions to contrast one sibling with another may heighten perceived differences between siblings, such a procedure was not used. Rather, siblings independently completed measures and mothers independently rated siblings, and the resulting pairs of scores were correlated and compared.

Only first- and second-born sibling pairs were studied because the deidentification effect has been most pronounced for them (Schachter & Stone, 1985). In analyses of these pairs, developmental and gender effects were of particular interest. Developmental effects in children's divorce adjustment have been inconsistent (Emery et al., 1984; Furstenberg, 1985), perhaps because of the use of interfamily methodologies which fail to hold divorce-related experiences constant. Because intrafamily comparisons allow one to assume that siblings are exposed to similar divorce-related experiences, they provide a more sensitive test of developmental effects than interfamily comparisons. Differences among sibling dyads of different gender compositions (boy/boy vs. girl/girl vs. boy/girl vs. girl/boy) were of interest in view of consistent findings that boys are more negatively affected by divorce than girls (Emery et al., 1984; Guidubaldi & Perry, 1985).

The second purpose of this study was to explore differences in the divorce adjustment and general behavioral adjustment of children with older male siblings and those with either older female siblings or no siblings. Because children in the custody of their mothers typically experience dramatic decreases in their contact with their fathers, older male siblings have been viewed as potential surrogate male role models. Empirical support for the buffering effect of having older male siblings, however, is scant. Wohlford, Santrock, Beyer, and Liberman (1971) found that economically disadvantaged black preschoolers with older male siblings were more aggressive and less dependent than those with either older female siblings or no siblings. One major problem with this study is that the sample was a generic "father absent" sample, with the reasons for father absence unspecified. Because the sample in the present study was composed of white, middle-class preadolescents and adolescents from mother-custody families, no predictions regarding the effect of having older male siblings were made.

The selection of specific divorce adjustment and general behavior adjustment measures was guided by previous work in the area (Kurdek, in press-a, b; Kurdek & Berg, in press; Kurdek et al., 1981). Self-reports and maternal reports for each sibling were obtained. Self-report divorce adjustment measures included understanding of the divorce and problematic beliefs regarding the divorce, while self-report behavioral adjustment measures included understanding of conflict resolution and internal locus of control. Maternal report divorce adjustment measures included problematic beliefs regarding the divorce and emotional reactions to the divorce, while maternal report behavioral adjustment measures included ratings of dependency, independence, and aggression. Because the sample represents different phases of a larger research program, *n*s fluctuate in the analyses reported below.

In sum, this exploratory study sought preliminary answers to five questions: (a) What is the relation (positive, negative, or nonsignificant) between siblings' self-report divorce adjustment scores and between siblings' self-report general behavioral adjustment scores?; (b) Do these self-report scores differ by relative age of sibling (younger vs. older) or gender composition of sibling dyad (boy/boy vs. girl/girl vs. boy/girl vs. girl/boy)?; (c) What is the relation (positive, negative, or nonsignificant) between custodial mothers' ratings of siblings' divorce adjustment scores and between siblings' general behavioral adjustment scores?; (d) Do mothers' ratings vary according to relative age of sibling or gender composition of sibling dyad?; and (e) Do children with older male siblings differ in divorce adjustment and general behavioral adjustment from children with either older female siblings or no siblings?

METHOD

Subjects

One member of each of the sibling pairs in this study was originally a participant in one of three separate studies (Kurdek et al., 1981; Kurdek & Berg, 1983; Kurdek, in press-a). Siblings and their custodial mothers were recruited from members or friends of members of a local chapter of Parents Without Partners (Sample 1, $n = 16$), from requests for participants published in local newspapers (Sample 2, $n = 20$), or from court records (Sample 3, $n = 13$). Whenever possible, samples were combined when common measures were available. In these instances, preliminary analyses indicated that scores did not vary significantly by source of recruitment. Information regarding the number of boys, number of girls, and age of younger and older siblings is presented for each of the three samples in Table 1. Information regarding the mean age difference between siblings, length of parental separation (which never exceeded 24 months) and mothers' Hollingshead (1977) social status scores is also presented for each sample. Across all samples, the number of boy/boy, girl/girl, boy/girl, and girl/boy first-born/second-born pairs was 12, 20, 12, and 5, respectively. The number of sibling pairs in families with 2, 3, and 4 children was 28, 19, and 2, respectively.

The comparison group of children without siblings included 6 boys and 12 girls, mean age $= 9.20$ years, and their single custodial mothers. All were white and middle-class, mean Hollingshead (1977) social status score $= 40.44$. Mothers were separated from their ex-spouses a mean of 9.56 months.

Child Measures

The child and mother measures were completed in a single session which occurred either at the subjects' homes (Samples 1 and 3, $n = 29$ families) or at an office (Sample 2, $n = 20$ families). Site of testing did not affect scores. Mothers were given directions on

TABLE 1. Descriptive Information for Each Sample

	Sample 1		Sample 2		Sample 3	
	Younger	Older	Younger	Older	Younger	Older
n of boys	5	2	13	9	6	6
n of girls	11	14	7	11	7	7
Mean age	12.25	14.82	9.54	12.49	10.79	14.27
Mean sibling age difference	2.57		2.95		3.47	
Mean months of parental separation	18.44		11.30		9.54	
Mother's social status	31.04		40.33		41.26	

how to complete their measures, and then did so without assistance and out of earshot of the children. While mothers completed their forms, the child measures were group administered to the siblings who sat far enough from each other so that they could not see each other's answers. After each item was read aloud, time was provided for writing a response. Individual assistance was provided when needed. As noted above, because children in each sample did not complete the same measures, *n*s fluctuate in the analyses reported below.

Understanding the divorce (Samples 1, 2, and 3). Children completed an open-ended questionnaire (Kurdek et al., 1981) that covered understanding various aspects of their parents' divorce. Children's responses were given 1 point apiece if they (a) answered the question "What does it mean when two people get divorced?" with a response that indicated incompatibility or loss of love between parents; (b) answered the question "Why don't your Mom and Dad live together anymore?" with a response that indicated incompatibility or loss of love between parents; (c) answered "No" to the question "Do you think your Mom and Dad will ever live together again?"; (d) indicated that the parents would not live together again because of their incompatibility or their current happiness; (e) answered "Yes" to the question "Have you told many friends that your Mom and Dad don't live together?"; and (f) answered "No" to the question "Do you think it matters to your friends that your Mom and Dad no longer live together?" Percent perfect agreement between two independent codings of all protocols was 95%. Here and below, the author resolved all disagreements. Cronbach's alpha for the sum of 0/1 scores across the 6 questions was .54.

Beliefs regarding the divorce (Samples 2 and 3). The Children's Beliefs About Parental Separation Inventory (Kurdek & Berg, in press) requires children to respond Yes or No to 36 items that tap six major problematic beliefs: peer ridicule and avoidance (e.g., "It would upset me if other kids asked a lot of questions about my parents"); fear of abandonment (e.g., "I know there will always be somebody to take care of me"); hope of reconciliation (e.g., " My parents will always live apart"); paternal blame (e.g., "My father tried to stop the breakup of my family"); maternal blame (e.g., "When my family was unhappy it was usually because of my mother"); and self-blame (e.g., "My parents would still be living together if it wasn't for me"). Scores reflected the total number of problematic beliefs. Cronbach's alpha for the summed composite score was .75.

Understanding conflict resolution (Samples 2 and 3). Children were asked four open-ended questions from Selman's (1980) Friendship Domain Interview: "What are some good ways to settle fights or arguments with a friend?", "Can friends have arguments and still be friends?", "What makes a friendship break up or end?", and "If you really broke up with a friend, could you get back together with that friend?" Responses were coded as representing one of Selman's (1980) five levels of interpersonal understanding. Percent perfect agreement between two independent codings of all protocols was 93%. Cronbach's alpha for the summed composite score was .75.

Locus of control (Samples 1 and 2). Children completed the 40-item locus of control scale devised by Nowicki and Strickland (1973). The scale was scored in terms of internality, and Cronbach's alpha for the summed composite score was .83.

Mother Measures

Children's beliefs regarding the divorce (Sample 2). Mothers used a 5-point scale to indicate how much they agreed (1 = Disagree Strongly to 5 = Agree Strongly) each sibling held each of six problematic divorce-related beliefs listed above (peer ridicule and avoidance, fear of abandonment, hope of reunification, paternal blame, maternal blame, and self blame). Cronbach's alpha for the summed composite score was .79.

Children's emotional reactions to the divorce (Sample 2). Based on items derived from Bloom, Hodges, and Caldwell (1983), mothers rated the extent to which (1 = None, 4 = Extreme) each sibling displayed positive feelings (personal growth and self-knowledge, increased happiness, independence and responsibility, relief from conflict) and negative feelings (loneliness, sadness, helplessness, confusion, guilt or self-blame, and nervousness). Scores were keyed for adjustment, and Cronbach's alpha for the summed composite score was .71.

Children's general behavioral adjustment (Sample 1). Mothers indicated how frequently (1 = Very Rarely to 7 = Very Often) each sibling showed dependency on peers (4 items), dependency on adults (4 items), independence (4 items), and aggression (11 items). Items were derived from Hetherington (1966). Cronbach's alpha for the summed composite scores was .74, .79, .70, and .90, respectively.

RESULTS

Preliminary analyses indicated that the four sibling dyad groups were equivalent on length of parental separation, mothers' social status, age differences between siblings, and age of younger and older sibling (see means at top of Table 2). For both the sibling self-report scores and mothers' ratings, siblings' scores were first correlated and then examined for developmental and gender differences.

Siblings' Self-Report Scores

Correlations between siblings' scores. The Pearson correlations between siblings' four self-report scores are presented in the last column of Table 2 with the effects of both siblings' ages partialled out. Three of the four *r*s were statistically significant, and accounted for between 16 to 64% of the total variability.

Age and gender effects. In order to assess age and gender differences in the four self-report scores, they each were submitted to a 2 (Relative Age: younger vs. older) × 4 (Gender Composition of Sibling Dyad: boy/boy vs. girl/girl vs. boy/girl vs. girl/boy) MANOVA. The family was used as the unit of analysis, so relative age was a repeated measures factor. Relevant means are presented in Table 2. As summarized in the columns labelled "Age *F*" and "Gender *F*," a main effect for relative age was obtained for each score, and a main effect for gender composition of sibling dyad was obtained for both the understanding the divorce and the understanding conflict resolution scores. All interaction effects were nonsignificant. On each score, older siblings presented a picture of better adjustment. Compared to younger siblings, they had a more mature understanding of the divorce; held fewer problematic beliefs regard-

TABLE 2. Mean Scores for Younger and Older Siblings Within Each Sibling Dyad, F Ratios for Gender and Age Effects, and Partial (Age) Correlations Between Siblings' Scores

	Boy/Boy		Girl/Girl	
	Younger	Older	Younger	Older
Demographic Scores				
Length of separation	7.75		15.75	
Mother social status	35.50		31.27	
Siblings' age difference	2.42		2.73	
Age	9.95	12.37	11.65	14.39
Child Self Report Scores				
Understanding the divorce	2.42	3.50	4.10	4.40
Problematic beliefs	20.27	16.91	23.00	23.00
Understanding conflict	8.00	10.40	10.50	13.20
Internal locus	24.43	27.28	23.93	26.78
Maternal Report Scores				
Problematic beliefs	23.39	23.14	24.40	24.60
Emotional reactions	25.43	26.86	23.75	23.75
Dependency on adults	5.00	4.00	5.10	4.80
Dependency on peers	5.00	6.00	5.10	4.40
Independence	5.00	6.00	5.30	5.10
Aggression	3.00	3.00	1.90	1.90

* $\underline{P} < .05.$ ** $\underline{P} < .01.$

| Boy/Girl | | Girl/Boy | | | | |
Younger	Older	Younger	Older	Gender F	Age F	r
13.08		16.00		2.10		
35.00		36.00		1.23		
3.58		3.72		1.63		
10.50	14.08	9.74	13.45	0.97		
3.58	4.00	3.80	4.00	2.94*	4.21*	.51**
25.88	17.13	24.25	24.75	0.28	3.37*	.80**
10.83	12.50	9.50	10.00	3.22*	12.59**	.40*
21.30	26.50	22.00	24.00	0.46	5.38*	.10
20.67	21.50	20.00	21.00	0.70	0.46	.86**
25.40	29.00	22.50	27.50	0.65	4.62*	.51*
4.75	4.75	5.00	3.00	0.55	6.87*	.48*
4.75	3.75	5.00	4.00	0.86	1.04	.19
5.25	5.50	6.00	3.00	0.27	0.95	.16
3.25	2.75	2.00	2.00	1.57	0.26	.83**

ing the divorce; had a more mature understanding of conflict resolution; and had a more internal locus of control. Student Newman-Keuls post hoc comparisons (p < .05) indicated that relative to boy/boy sibling dyads, girl/girl sibling dyads had a more mature understanding of the divorce and a more mature understanding of conflict resolution.

Maternal Ratings of Siblings

Correlations between siblings' scores. The Pearson correlations between mothers' six ratings of younger and older siblings are presented at the bottom of Table 2 with the effects of both siblings' ages partialled out. Four of the six *r*s were statistically significant, and accounted for between 23 to 74% of the total variance.

Age and gender effects. Relative age and gender composition of sibling dyad effects on mothers' ratings were assessed by submitting each score to a 2 (Relative Age) × 4 (Gender Composition of Sibling Dyad) MANOVA. The family was once again the unit of analysis, with relative age as a repeated measures factor. As shown in Table 2, age effects were obtained for emotional reactions to the divorce and dependency on adults, with older siblings being better adjusted than younger siblings. All other effects were nonsignificant.

Effects of Having an Older Male Sibling

In order to see if children with older male siblings differed from children with either older female siblings or no siblings on divorce adjustment and general behavioral adjustment, three groups of children were compared on the four self-report scores and the six maternal report scores: children with an older male sibling (12 boys, 4 girls), children with an older female sibling (11 boys, 20 girls), and children with no sibling (6 boys, 12 girls). Preliminary analyses indicated that these three groups were comparable on age and length of parental separation. A series of 3 (Older Sibling Status) × 2 (Gender of Younger Sibling) ANOVAs on the 10 adjustment scores yielded nonsignificant effects.

DISCUSSION

Because most studies of children living with custodial mothers include only one child per family, this study explored the relation between and the comparability of siblings' reactions to parental divorce as well as the effects of having an older male sibling on divorce adjustment and general behavioral adjustment in the first two years after parents' separation. Although the size of the sample is small, and *n*s for different analyses fluctuated, some preliminary answers can be provided to the questions that guided the analyses presented above.

What Is the Relation Between Siblings' Self-Report Scores?

With age effects controlled statistically, siblings' understanding of the divorce, dysfunctional beliefs regarding the divorce, and understanding of conflict resolution scores were significantly positively related. The significant *r*s accounted for between 16 to 64% of the total variance. Thus, for the variables studied, the rank ordering of siblings' scores was similar.

Are There Developmental and Gender Composition Differences in Siblings' Self-Report Scores?

Although, as noted above, the rank ordering of siblings' scores was similar, significant differences between siblings were found for each of the four self-report scores. Compared to younger siblings, older siblings showed a more mature understanding of the divorce, fewer dysfunctional beliefs regarding the divorce, more mature understanding of conflict resolution, and a more internal locus of control. These intrafamily developmental effects provide a solid basis for concluding both that younger and older siblings process and appraise divorce-related events at different levels and that sibling scores are not interchangeable. Future studies could identify what age-related processes (e.g., cognitive development, socialization practices) mediate these developmental effects.

The gender composition effects indicated that boy sibling dyads reasoned about parental divorce and interpersonal conflict in a less complex fashion than did girl sibling dyads. This gender difference suggests the intriguing possibility that boys' greater risk for short- and long-term problems related to parental divorce (Guidubaldi & Perry, 1985) may be due, in part, to limitations in their interpersonal reasoning (cf. Selman, 1980).

What Is the Relation Between Mothers' Ratings of Siblings?

For none of the six maternal ratings were contrast effects (i.e., negative correlations) obtained. Rather, with age effects controlled statistically, mothers' ratings of siblings' adjustment scores were positively correlated, particularly with regard to problematic beliefs regarding the divorce, emotional adjustment, dependency on adults, and aggression. The four significant correlations that were obtained accounted for between 23 to 74% of the total variability. Thus, as with the self-report scores above, the rank ordering of siblings' scores was similar.

Why did mothers in this study perceive siblings as similar while mothers in the Schachter studies (Schachter, 1982, 1985; Schachter & Stone, 1985) and the Shapiro and Wallace (in press) study perceived siblings as contrasting? Three possibilities can be considered.

First, mothers may perceive the divorce process as having pervasively affected both themselves and their children (cf. Wallerstein, 1986). Second, because comparing children to children at large tends to reduce the contrast effect (Schachter & Stone, 1985), mothers may have completed their ratings with a general group of "other children" or "other children from divorced families" as the reference group. Third, the inverse relation between siblings' scores reported by Schachter has been obtained on the basis of global bipolar evaluations of siblings (e.g., alike/different [Schachter, 1985] or easy/difficult/half-and-half temperament [Schachter & Stone, 1985]). Such a methodology pits sibling against sibling and may heighten the contrast bias.

Are There Developmental and Gender Composition Differences in Mothers' Ratings of Siblings?

Consistent with the results based on children's self-report data, mothers rated older siblings as having more positive reactions to the divorce and as being less dependent on adults than younger siblings. However, no gender composition effects were obtained, a surprising finding given the gender effects frequently obtained in studies of children's divorce adjustment (Emery et al., 1984) and general behavioral adjustment (Achenbach & Edelbrock, 1981). These studies, however, are based on interfamily comparisons, leading one to speculate that intrafamily comparisons like those in the present study might reveal less pronounced gender differences.

Do the Adjustment Scores of Children with Older Male Siblings Differ from Those of Children Without Older Male Siblings?

Wohlford et al.'s (1971) finding that children with older male siblings were rated by their mothers as more aggressive and less dependent than children without older male siblings was not replicated. In the current study, children with older brothers were equivalent on self-report and maternal ratings to children with older sisters and to children with no siblings. Further, in no instance was the Older Sibling Status x Gender of Younger Sibling interaction significant; i.e., boys with older brothers were indistinguishable from boys with older sisters and from boys with no siblings. The failure to replicate Wohlford et al.'s (1971) results may be due to differences between the present sample and that of Wohlford et al. (1971). Wohlford et al.'s (1971) sample included economically disadvantaged "father absent" black preschoolers and their mothers, while the present sample included middle-class white preadolescents/adolescents and their custodial mothers. While this difference suggests that older male siblings may function as surrogate male role models for children only at certain socioeconomic and developmental levels, further study with divorced samples is needed. In particular, surrogate effects could be examined for children who have varying degrees of contact with their noncustodial fathers.

REFERENCES

Achenbach, T. M. & Edelbrock, C. S. (1981). Behavioral problems and competencies reported by parents of normal and disturbed children aged four through sixteen. *Monographs of the Society for Research in Child Development, 46* (1, Serial No. 188).

Applebaum, M. I. & McCall, R. B. (1983). Design and analysis in developmental psychology. In W. Kessen (Ed.), *Handbook of child psychology: Vol. 1. History, theory, and methods* (pp. 415-476). New York: Wiley.

Baskett, L. M. (1985). Sibling status effects: Adult expectations. *Developmental Psychology, 21,* 441-445.

Bloom, B. L., Hodges, W. F., & Caldwell, R. A. (1983). Marital separation: The first eight months. In E. J. Callahan & K. A. McCluskey (Eds.), *Lifespan developmental psychology: Nonnormative life events* (pp. 217-239). New York: Academic Press.

Coddington, R. D. (1984). Measuring the stressfulness of a child's environment. In J. H. Humphrey (Ed.), *Stress in childhood* (pp. 97-126). New York: AMS Press.

Daniels, D. (1986). Differential experiences of siblings in the same family as predictors of adolescent sibling personality differences. *Journal of Personality and Social Psychology, 51,* 339-346.

Daniels, D. & Plomin, R. (1985). Differential experience of siblings in the same family. *Developmental Psychology, 21,* 747-760.

Emery, R. E., Hetherington, E. M., & DiLalla, L. (1984). Divorce, children, and social policy. In H. W. Stevenson & A. E. Siegel (Eds.), *Child development research and social policy* (pp. 189-266). Chicago: University of Chicago Press.

Furstenberg, F. F. (1985, April). *Effects of divorce on children.* Paper presented at the meeting of the Society for Research in Child Development, Toronto.

Guidubaldi, J. & Perry, J. D. (1985). Divorce and mental health sequelae for children: A two-year follow up of a nationwide sample. *Journal of the American Academy of Child Psychiatry, 24,* 531-537.

Hetherington, E. M. (1966). Effects of paternal absence on sex-typed behaviors in Negro and white preadolescent males. *Journal of Personality and Social Psychology, 4,* 87-91.

Hetherington, E. M., Cox, M., & Cox, R. (1978). The aftermath of divorce. In J. H. Stevens, Jr. & M. Mathews (Eds.), *Mother-child, father-child relations* (pp. 149-176). Washington, DC: National Association for the Education of Young Children.

Hollingshead, A. B. (1977). *Four factor index of social status.* Unpublished manuscript, Yale University.

Kurdek, L. A. (in press-a). Children's adjustment to parental divorce: An ecological perspective. In J. P. Vincent (Ed.), *Advances in family intervention, assessment and theory* (Vol. 4). Greenwich, CT: JAI Press, Inc.

Kurdek, L. A. (in press-b). Cognitive mediators of children's adjustment to divorce. In S. Wolchik & P. Karoly (Eds.), *Children of divorce: Perspectives on adjustment*. New York: Gardner Press.

Kurdek, L. A. & Berg, B. (1983). Correlates of children's adjustment to their parents' divorces. In L. A. Kurdek (Ed.), *Children and divorce* (pp. 47-60). San Francisco: Jossey-Bass.

Kurdek, L. A. & Berg, B. (in press). The Children's Beliefs About Parental Separation Inventory: Psychometric characteristics and concurrent validity. *Journal of Consulting and Clinical Psychology*.

Kurdek, L. A., Blisk, D., & Siesky, A. E. (1981). Correlates of children's long-term adjustment to their parents' divorce. *Developmental Psychology, 17*, 565-579.

Nichols, W. C. (1986). Sibling subsystem therapy in family systems reorganization. *Journal of Divorce, 9*, 13-31.

Nowicki, S. & Strickland, B. R. A locus of control scale for children. *Journal of Consulting and Clinical Psychology, 40*, 148-155.

Scarr, S. & Grajek, S. (1982). Similarities and differences among siblings. In M. E. Lamb & B. Sutton-Smith (Eds.), *Sibling relationships: Their nature and significance across the lifespan* (pp. 357-381). Hillsdale, NJ: Erlbaum.

Schachter, F. F. (1982). Sibling deidentification and split parent identification: A family tetrad. In M. E. Lamb & B. Sutton-Smith (Eds.), *Sibling relationships: Their nature and significance across the lifespan* (pp. 123-151). Hillsdale, NJ: Erlbaum.

Schachter, F. F. (1985). Sibling deidentification in the clinic: Devil vs. angel. *Family Process, 24*, 415-427.

Schachter, F. F., Shore, E., Feldman-Rotman, S., Marquis, R. E., & Campbell, S. (1976). Sibling deidentification. *Developmental Psychology, 12*, 418-427.

Schachter, F. F. & Stone, R. K. (1985). Difficult sibling, easy sibling: Temperament and the within-family environment. *Child Development, 56*, 1335-1344.

Selman, R. L. (1980). *The development of interpersonal understanding*. New York: Academic Press.

Shapiro, E. K. & Wallace, D. B. (in press). Siblings and parents in one-parent families. In F. F. Schachter & R. K. Stone (Eds.), *Sibling problems: Bridging the research-practice gap*. Pittsburgh: Haworth Press.

Wallerstein, J. S. (1986). Women after divorce: Preliminary report from a ten-year follow-up. *American Journal of Orthopsychiatry, 56*, 65-77.

Wallerstein, J. S. & Kelly, J. B. (1980). *Surviving the breakup*. New York: Basic Books.

Wohlford, P., Santrock, J. W., Berger, S. E., & Liberman, D. (1971). Older brothers' influence on sex-typed, aggressive, and dependent behavior in father-absent children. *Developmental Psychology, 4*, 124-134.

Sibling Interactions in Married and Divorced Families: Influence of Ordinal Position, Socioeconomic Status, and Play Context

Carol E. MacKinnon

SUMMARY. One hundred twenty-eight sibling dyads, 64 from married families, and 64 from divorced, were observed on two separate occasions while playing a structured and an unstructured game. Half of the sibling dyads within each family form were from higher socioeconomic status (SES) families and half from lower SES families. The frequency of caretaking (e.g., directing, teaching, helping), negative, and positive behaviors were coded. Results revealed that sibling interactions in divorced families are both more negative and less positive than in married families. Siblings in divorced families also engage in more caretaking behavior. Similar differences were detected between lower and higher SES families, yet differences in sibling interactions in married and divorced families were not exacerbated by socioeconomic status. Younger siblings were more likely to be the recipient of caregiving behavior and to be more positive in their interactions. However, both older and younger siblings' behavior was influenced by the game context.

During the last decade researchers have begun to systematically examine how family structure and interaction among family members contribute toward developmental outcomes for children. A shift in focus from parents, particularly mothers, as the primary agent of children's socialization to an incluson of other family members and subsystems has revealed that children contribute sig-

---

Carol E. MacKinnon, PhD, is Assistant Professor, Department of Child Development and Family Relations, School of Human Environmental Sciences, University of North Carolina-Greensboro, Greensboro, NC 27412.

nificantly to each other's development. Through their interactions, siblings assume roles that facilitate the acquisition of skills central to cognitive and social developmental outcomes for children. Older siblings assume the more dominant roles of manager, teacher, and helper; younger siblings less dominant roles of managee, learner, and helpee. Older siblings benefit from assuming dominant roles that require the acquisition and organization of knowledge (Bargh & Shul, 1980) while younger siblings reap the benefits of stimulation and instruction provided by the older sibling.

Though numerous studies have documented the potential influence of siblings on development, these investigations have been conducted with siblings in intact families with two parents. This acknowledgement is not intended to understate the significance of sibling contributions, but rather to suggest that in families where one parent is absent, siblings may play an even greater role in each other's development. Yet, we know very little about sibling relations in those families (Hetherington, 1987).

An examination of the home environments of children from single-parent, mother-headed families revealed that the quantity and quality of cognitive and social stimulation was less than in married families (MacKinnon, Brody, & Stoneman, 1982). Two years later, the home environments of children from divorced families were still significantly different from those of children from married families (MacKinnon, Brody, & Stoneman, 1986). MacKinnon et al. (1982) suggested that in the absence of one parent, the remaining parent must simultaneously attend to multiple responsibilities that compete with their parenting roles. The high level of discord that characterizes recently divorced families coupled with stress associated with downward economic mobility, child care demands, and employment demands contribute toward the negative effects of divorce increasing multiplicatively (Hetherington, 1981). Under such conditions, children stand to suffer consequences that may have significant impact on their cognitive and social development.

However, siblings may assume more dominant roles in divorced families than in married in response to situational demands. A lack of maternal responsiveness has been found to serve as a cue for older siblings to engage in more caretaking behavior (e.g., managing, teaching, helping) with their younger siblings. Younger siblings were not as likely to be as responsive to their older siblings' needs (Cicirelli, 1976). Moreover, younger siblings respond to their older siblings' caretaking differently than to their mothers'. They are more likely to engage in more independence-seeking behaviors and fewer help-seeking behaviors with their siblings (Cicirelli, 1976). Older children are also more likely to offer nurturance and support than their younger siblings (Bryant & Crockenberg, 1980), behaviors associated with positive social developmental outcomes in younger siblings (Bryant, 1982). Whiting and Whiting (1975) found that assuming responsibility for younger siblings fosters prosocial development.

It appears that prosocial interaction between siblings is stimulated when mothers ignore requests for attention (Bryant & Crockenberg, 1980). In divorced families, where mothers must attend to responsibilities that are typically managed by two parents in married families, older siblings may assume roles typically held by parents. In these families, sibling relationships may be particularly salient in predicting cognitive and social development.

Not only may siblings' roles in divorced families be different than in married families, but the affective tone of the relationship may be different as well. Children experiencing marital dissolution may exhibit more aggression and hostility with their siblings following divorce. Current evidence suggests that stress associated with divorce is related to behavior problems in children, particularly boys (Hetherington, Cox, & Cox, 1978, 1979), who are more noncompliant and aggressive. Moreover, when compared to mothers in married families, divorced mothers are less affectionate, more punitive, more inconsistent in their discipline, and communicate less well. These problems are more likely to be evidenced by divorced families who experience a high degree of conflict. Thus, siblings may become more hostile as they compete for attention and affection in a climate of diminished parenting characterized by punitiveness and irritability (Hetherington, 1987).

Alternatively, though less likely, children's reactions with their siblings may be enhanced following divorce. In families where one parent is absent due to divorce and relations with the remaining parent are unstable and tense, children may turn to each other for support and solace. Bank and Kahn (1982) suggest that unavailability of parents can promote sibling loyalty, especially if previous sibling relations were harmonious and the siblings had at least one nurturant parent.

A pattern supportive of both hypotheses emerged in Hetherington's (1987) six-year follow-up of divorced, married, and blended families. Boys and girls in divorced families were warmer and more involved with their siblings than children in stepfamilies. However, male siblings from divorced families were more coercive, agonistic, and less supportive than males in nondivorced families. Similar results emerged in a study by MacKinnon (1988) that compared male and female sibling dyads from married and divorced families. Male sibling dyads in divorced families emitted more negative physicals, verbals, and affects than male dyads in married families or female dyads in married or divorced families.

Taken together, it appears that sibling relations may be different in married and divorced families. However, the extent to which children exhibit behaviors associated with positive cognitive and social outcomes for children has not been addressed; this is the first purpose of this study. Extrapolating from previously cited evidence, older siblings were expected to engage in more managing, teaching, and helping behaviors; however, no predictions were made concerning differences among the different family structures.

It was further hypothesized that siblings from high socioeconomic status (SES) families would engage in more positive, managing, teaching, and helping behaviors than siblings in lower SES families. Parents who are punitive, restrictive, unresponsive, and erratic in discipline, produce children who have more hostile and unaffectionate sibling interactions (Hetherington, 1987). These are parenting behaviors more characteristic of lower than higher SES families. Not only are parents from lower SES families more punitive and restrictive, but so are mothers from divorced families (Hetherington et al., 1978, 1979). Thus, it could be expected that sibling interactions would be most negative in lower SES divorced families. Children from divorced families are exposed to parenting styles that are more negative than in married families, a situation that would likely be exacerbated by lower SES status of the family. Thus, the second purpose of the present study was to examine sibling relations in upper and lower SES married and divorced families.

Older and younger siblings' behavior was expected to vary as a function of marital status and socioeconomic status of the family. However, it was also predicted that play contact may mediate the behaviors that siblings exhibit with one another (Brody, Stoneman, & MacKinnon, 1986). Bronfembrenner's (1977) contention that context alters behavior has been supported in previous studies. Brody et al. (1986) found the role asymmetries (teacher/learner, manager/managee) documented in previous studies of siblings (Brody et al., 1982; Stoneman, Brody, & MacKinnon, 1984) to be most pronounced during a more structured board game than in a less structured construction task. They concluded that sibling interactions are influenced by not only the competence of each child, but the demands of the context. In less structured, disorganized households that are characteristic of many divorced families following divorce (Hetherington, 1981; Hetherington et al., 1978), the demands of the context may alter sibling relationships. Thus, children were observed in two games, a structured and unstructured one, in order to examine how play context mediates the interactional patterns of siblings.

METHOD

Subjects

One hundred twenty-eight siblings dyads, 64 from married families and 64 from divorced, were observed in a laboratory setting. Subjects were from a metropolitan Southeastern city and were recruited through local schools, court records, and referrals from participating families. Half of the sibling dyads within each family form were from lower SES families and half from lower SES families, as determined by mothers' education level. Mothers of the lower SES families had a high school education or less. Mothers of the higher SES families had college education or more. The younger siblings ranged in age from 4.5 to 8 years and the older siblings 6.5 to 10 years. The sibling pairs were separated in age by at least two years, but not more than four years. All families were Caucasian, with mothers who worked outside the home. Families were matched on number of children in the family. In the divorced families, mothers were the primary caretaker of their children and were separated from their spouses for at least one year. Time of separation was the critical point used in identifying families (Hetherington et al., 1978); however, all families were divorced.

Procedure

The sibling pairs were observed on two separate occasions in two game situations, a board game (Trouble, Gilbert Industries) and card tossing game. These games were included because Trouble is structured with specific rules and the card toss game is more unstructured, with few rules. The observational sessions were 1 to 2 weeks apart. The laboratory setting was selected for the observations instead of the home because the coders could observe the children unobtrusively from behind a one-way mirror. In addition, it was felt that the games were intriguing enough that the children would become engrossed, making the unfamiliar setting less problematic. The order of presentation of the games was counterbalanced in order to minimize a possible confound due to an order artifact. The children were observed for a total of 30 minutes each session, 15 minutes in each game. However, the actual data collection did not begin until the children had played for 5 minutes to allow them to become engrossed in the game.

Two observers coded the behaviors of the sibling pairs. One coded the sequences of behaviors, attending to specific initiating behaviors by one child as well as the response emitted by the other. A sequence was terminated in one of the following ways: (a) a new initiating behavior was emitted, (b) the emission of a response, or (c) a 10-second lapse of time wherein no response was emitted. Initiating behaviors (e.g., explicit directive, teaching, helping, help seeking) and responses (e.g., compliance, resistance, ignore) were selected because differences have been found previously among siblings on these measures. A description of the initiating behaviors and responses that constituted the sequence codes may be found in Table 1. The sequence data were converted to proportions in order to standardize the unit of analysis. This was accomplished by dividing the number of times an initiating behavior led to a particular response by the total number of occurrences of the initiating behavior. Thus, the scores represent the percentage of times a particular response follows a behavior, given that the behavior occurred.

A second observer coded the frequency of positive and negative behaviors emitted according to a time-sampling quantification procedure. Within each session, the 15-minute observation session for each ·game was divided into 180 5-second scoring intervals. The occurrence of specific positive and negative behaviors was recorded

TABLE 1. Operational Definitions of Sequence and Frequency Codes

Sequence Codes

Initiating Behaviors	Definition
Explicit Directive in	A direct, clearly stated order or direction in declarative form
Teaching	Any verbal instructions on how to play the game or physically demonstrating how to play the game
Helping	Any physical assistance given
Help Seeking	Any request for physical assistance from another

Responses	Definition
Compliance	A cooperative response to an initiating behavior
Resistance/Noncompliance	An uncooperative response to an initiating behavior
Ignore/No response	Failure to respond to an initiating behavior

TABLE 1 (continued)

Frequency Codes

Behaviors	Definition

Positives:

  Verbal   Any positive verbal expression that praises, reinforces, shows excitement or affection

  Physical   Any positive physical contact such as touching affectionately, kissing, hugging

  Affect   Any facial expression denoting positive emotions such as smiling, laughing, giggling, nodding in approval

Negatives:

  Verbal   Any negative verbal expression such as threatening, quarreling, sarcasm, name-calling, teasing, insulting, whining, demeaning remarks

  Physical   Any negative physical contact such as grabbing, hitting, slapping, pushing, attacking

  Affect   Any facial expression denoting negative emotions such as frowning, crying, anger, disgust, making faces

All of these behaviors should be directed toward the other person in order to be coded.

for each child during alternating 5-second observe-record periods. Operational definitions of the frequency codes may be found in Table 1. The frequency data were converted to proportions by dividing the frequency of a particular behavior by 90, i.e., the total number of intervals the behavior could have occurred per child, per session.

RESULTS

A 2 (marital status: married, divorced) × 2 (SES: higher, lower) × 2 (actor: older, younger) × 2 (game: structured, unstructured) × 2 (session: time 1, time 2) multivariate analysis of variance (MANOVA) with repeated measures on the last two factors was performed. Independent variables producing a significant multivariate effect were analyzed for their influence on each separate dependent measure by univariate F-tests. Post hoc comparisons were made via Duncan's multiple range tests.

The MANOVA revealed significant main effects for marital status, F mult $(21,100) = 1.71$, $p < .05$, SES, F mult $(21,100) = 2.92$, $p < .0001$ actor, F mult $(21,100) = 12.75$, $p < .001$, and game, F mult $(21,100) = 21.42$, $p < .0001$; however, the actor and game main effects were qualified by a significant actor × game interaction, F mult $(21,100) = 3.54$, $p < .0001$. No other main effects or interactions attained significance.

The significant MANOVA main effect for marital status was followed up with 2 (marital status) × 2 (SES) × 2 (actor) × 2 (times) × 2 (game) repeated-measures analyses of variance. The significant F values, as well as the mean proportions of occurrence of each sequence and behavior are presented in Table 2. It can be seen that sibling interactions are more negative and less positive in divorced families than in married. They are also more resistant to direct commands than siblings in married families. However, they are more likely to comply to teaching and requests for help.

The significant main effect for SES was also further examined through separate repeated-measures univariate analyses. The significant F values, as well as mean proportions of behaviors emitted, may be found in Table 2. SES effects were found for the proportion of positives emitted. Differences were also found between higher and lower SES families in the proportion of time siblings resist direct commands and comply to teaching and help-seeking re-

TABLE 2. F Ratios and Mean Proportions of Behaviors Emitted By Family Form, Socioeconomic Status, and Actor X Game Effects

	Marital status			SES			Actor x Game				
	F	Married	Divorced	F	Higher	Lower	F	Older Sib Trouble	Older Sib Card Toss	Younger Sib Trouble	Younger Sib Card Toss
ED → C							5.04*	.887	.862	.426	.548
ED → R	11.94***	.065	.132	3.93*	.073	.131					
ED → I					.046	.083					
T → C	3.85*	.019	.043	5.94*	.090	.044	25.64***	.804	.360	.257	.147
H → C							46.18***	.691	.317	.115	.016
HS → C	4.31*	.360	.461	3.75*	.363	.458					
Positives	5.05*	.064	.031	13.07***	.049	.022	4.15*	.014	.038	.023	.068
Negatives	3.88*	.026	.048				5.03*	.663	.431	.486	.324

* p < .05
** p < .01
*** p < .001

quests. Siblings from lower SES families emitted fewer positive affects, verbals, and physicals than siblings from higher SES families. Siblings in lower SES families are more likely to resist and ignore direct commands and are less likely to be responsible to teaching. However, they are more likely to comply to help-seeking requests than siblings in higher SES families.

The significant actor × game interaction was further examined through separate repeated measures univariate analyses (Table 2). Significant univariate effects were found for compliance to explicit directives, teaching, and helping behaviors and the frequency of negatives and positives emitted. The structured game elicited more negatives from the siblings than did the unstructured game, with the older sibling being the most negative. The card toss game elicited more positives. Younger siblings were more positive during the card toss game than in Trouble or than older siblings, regardless of game. However, older siblings were more positive when playing the card toss game than they were when playing Trouble.

Younger siblings were more likely to be compliant to directives and responsive to teaching than were older siblings, regardless of game. However, they were especially more likely to comply while playing Trouble than card toss. Younger siblings were also more likely to accept help from their older siblings while playing Trouble than card toss or than older children were to accept help from their younger siblings in either game.

DISCUSSION

The results of the present study suggest that sibling interactions in divorced families are both more negative and less positive than in married families. Siblings from divorced families emitted more negative affects, physicals, and verbals and fewer positive affects, physicals, and verbals. They were also more noncompliant with one another. These findings on sibling relations resemble those of Hetherington et al. (1978, 1979) where children from divorced families were found to be more negative and noncompliant in their interactions with their mothers, peers, and teachers. However, despite the higher frequency of negative behaviors emitted, it appears that following divorce siblings also engage in more caretaking behaviors than siblings in married families. They are more likely to comply to help-seeking requests and teach one another. Thus, as Bank and Kahn (1982) suggest, the unavailability of parents may promote feelings of loyalty among siblings which would likely result in more caretaking behavior. Moreover, they note that this dimension of sibling relationships may coexist with conflict and negativity (Bank & Kahn, 1982), which was the case in the present investigation. Although these behaviors were more evident in sibling dyads in divorced families, older siblings were no more likely to engage in caretaking behavior than were older siblings in married families.

It is important to note that differences in sibling interactions in married and divorced families were not exacerbated by socioeconomic status. It may be that if socioeconomic status had been measured by income, rather than mothers' education, an interaction would have emerged. The stress associated with divorce and low income would likely be reflected in more strained interactions among family members, including siblings. Because mothers' education level is associated with her teaching and managing styles, and, presumably would be with her children's, it was deemed necessary to measure socioeconomic status using mothers' educational level. Differences did emerge in sibling interactions as a function of socioeconomic status as defined.

Irrespective of family form, sibling interactions in higher SES families were more positive than in lower SES families. Children in higher SES families have an opportunity to model more positive styles of interaction since their parents tend to exhibit more warmth and affection than lower SES parents (Maccoby, 1980). Siblings from higher SES families were also more likely to teach, while siblings from lower SES families were more likely to resist and ignore directives. This is not surprising since higher SES parents tend to adopt an authoritative parenting style and lower SES parents, an authoritarian parenting style (Maccoby, 1980). An authoritative parenting style is more likely to produce children who are more cooperative (Baumrind, 1971). As with siblings in the divorced families, children from lower SES families, though more resistant to directives, responded more positively to being asked for help than siblings from higher SES families. It may be that an authoritarian parenting style that is more prevalent in divorced (Hetherington et al., 1978) and lower SES families (Maccoby,

1980) produces children who are particularly sensitive to the use of control.

The tendency for younger siblings to be more compliant to control techniques than older siblings is supported in the literature (Brody et al., 1982; Stoneman et al., 1984). However, differences in actor effects as a function of activity are not as well documented. Younger siblings were more likely to comply to directives, or be taught and helped than were their older siblings, regardless of game. However, both siblings were more likely to be taught and helped while playing the structured game than during the unstructured game. The younger siblings were more positive while playing card toss than Trouble, or than their older siblings during either game. Even the older siblings emitted more positive behavior during the card toss game than either of the two siblings during the Trouble game. The most negative behavior during any of the interactions was emitted by older siblings while playing Trouble.

These findings have important implications for parents and caregivers planning activities for children. If the goal is one of encouraging interactions associated with cognitive outcomes for older and younger siblings such as a tutor/tutee relationship, then a more structured game such as a board game may be more desirable. Such an activity seems to better provide younger children an opportunity to be helped, taught, and directed by an older, more competent child. However, more unstructured games appear to elicit more positive behaviors in siblings, particularly in the younger. It may be that in games with fewer rules, younger children can assume more equalitarian, symmetrical roles (Brody et al., 1986). At the very least, the findings support Bronfenbrenner's (1977) contention that context interacts with the characteristics of children to alter their behavior.

REFERENCES

Bank, S., & Kahn, M. D. (1982). *The sibling bond*. New York: Basic Books.

Bargh, J. A., & Shul, Y. (1980). On the cognitive benefits of teaching. *Journal of Educational Psychology, 72*, 593-604.

Baumrind, D. (1971). Current patterns of parental authority. *Developmental Psychology Monographs*, *4*, (1, Part 2).

Brody, G. H., Stoneman, Z., & MacKinnon, C. E. (1982). Role asymmetries in interaction among school age children, their younger siblings, and their friends. *Child Development, 53*, 1364-1370.

Brody, G. H., Stoneman, Z., & MacKinnon, C. E. (1986). Contributions of maternal child-rearing practices and play contexts to sibling interactions. *Journal of Applied Developmental Psychology, 7*, 225-236.

Bronfenbrenner, V. (1977). Toward an experimental ecology of human development. *American Psychologist, 32*, 513-531.

Bryant, B. K. (1982). Sibling relationships in middle childhood. In M. Lamb and B. Sutton-Smith (Eds.), *Sibling relationships*. Hillsdale, NJ: Erlbaum.

Bryant, B., & Crockenberg, S. (1980). Correlates and dimensions of prosocial behavior: A study of female siblings with their mothers. *Child Development, 51*, 529-544.

Cicirelli, V. G. (1976). Mother-child and sibling-sibling interactions on a problem-solving task. *Child Development, 47*, 588-596.

Hetherington, E. M. (1981). Children and divorce. In R. W. Henderson (Ed.), *Parent-child interaction: Theory, research, and prospects*. New York: Academic Press.

Hetherington, E. M. (1987). Parents, children and siblings, six years after divorce. In R. Hind and J. Stephenson (Eds,), *Toward understanding families*. New York: Oxford Press.

Hetherington, E. M., Cox, M., & Cox, R. (1978). The aftermath of divorce. In J. H. Stevens and M. M. Matthews (Eds.), *Mother-child, father-child relations*. Washington, DC: NAEYC.

Hetherington, E. M., Cox, M., & Cox, R. (1979). Play and social interaction of children following divorce. *Journal of Social Issues, 35*, 26-49.

Maccoby, E. E. (1980). *Social development*. New York: Harcourt Brace Jovanovich.

MacKinnon, C. E. (1988). *An observational investigation of sibling interactions in married and divorced families*. Manuscript submitted for publication.

MacKinnon, C. E., Brody, G. H., & Stoneman, Z. (1982). The effects of divorce and maternal employment on the home environments of preschool children. *Child Development, 53*, 1392-1399.

MacKinnon, C. E., Brody, G. H., & Stoneman, Z. (1986). The longitudinal effects of divorce and maternal employment on the home environments of preschool children. *Journal of Divorce, 9*, 65-78.

Stoneman, Z., Brody, G. H., & MacKinnon, C. E. (1984). Naturalistic observations of children's activities and roles while playing with their younger siblings and friends. *Child Development, 55*, 617-627.

Whiting, B., & Whiting, J. (1975). *Children of six cultures: A psycho-cultural analysis*. Cambridge, MA: Harvard University Press.

Mothers' Behavior
and Sons' Adjustment
Following Divorce

Robert M. Greene
Leigh A. Leslie

SUMMARY. Research on children's adjustment to divorce has repeatedly found that sons fare more poorly than daughters. In an effort to better understand the post-divorce adjustment of boys, this study focuses on two aspects of the mother-son relationship; maternal support and coercion, as reported by the son. In addition, we examine the extent to which the mother's attitude toward her ex-spouse might be affecting her interactions with her son. The results of a path analysis suggest that 18 to 39 months after parental separation, a mother's attitude toward her former mate is related to how supportive and coercive her son reports her to be in their relationship. Likewise, how coercive the mother is perceived to be is related to the son's level of aggression in school. These findings are discussed in light of the larger context in which the mother-son relationship exists. Expansion of the proposed path model is suggested in order to incorporate other family relationships and critical external factors such as financial circumstance.

The rising divorce rate has been accompanied by a host of questions concerning its impact on the children who experience it. A growing body of literature has begun to identify some of the apparent patterns of adjustment for specific groups. Most notable is the finding that, regardless of age, divorce seems to have a greater af-

Robert M. Greene, PhD, is on the staff of the South Beach Psychiatric Center, Brooklyn, NY. Leigh A. Leslie, PhD, is on the faculty of the Department of Family and Community Development, University of Maryland, College Park, MD 20742.

235

fect on boys than girls (e.g., Guidubaldi, Clemishaw, Perry, & McLaughlin, 1983; Hetherington, Cox, & Cox, 1979). In studies of nursery school-age children, Hetherington, Cox and Cox, (1978 found that two years following the divorce of their parents, girls appear to be adjusting well. Boys, on the other hand, though showing improvement, may still demonstrate increased aggressive or noncompliant behavior. Similarly, Hess and Camara (1979) have found that six months to two years following parental separation, 9- to 11-year-old boys have more difficulty with their schoolwork, and exhibit greater stress and a higher level of aggression than boys from intact families. Girls, however did not demonstrate the same level of difficulty in these areas following their parents' separation. It also appears that in addition to better behavioral functioning, 8- to 12-year-old girls from divorced homes exhibit better cognitive functioning than do same age boys from divorced homes (Krantz, Clark, Pruyn, & Usher, 1985).

Various explanations have been offered as to why boys have a more difficult time than do girls in adjusting to divorce. The "father absence" explanation (e.g., Tuckman & Regan, 1966) which was popular in early work on divorce has been called into question by more recent research (Herzog & Sudia, 1973; Raschke & Raschke, 1979).

An alternative to looking at the role of the "absent" parent in boys' adjustment is to focus on the son's relationship with the custodial parent. Hetherington et al. (1979) suggest that a frequently found situation following divorce is the child or children living alone with a single mother and having little or no contact with the father. They conclude that by the second year after divorce the custodial mother has become more influential than the non-custodial father in the cognitive, social, and emotional development of her children. Yet, relatively little research has been attempted to identify those aspects of the mother-child relationship that are associated with a child's adjustment in the single-parent family. The work which has focused particularly on the quality of the mother-child relationship suggests that maternal warmth appears to be an important factor in the child's adjustment (Hodges, Buchsbaum, & Tierney, 1983; Santrock & Warshak, 1979).

Further insight may be gained into the critical variables in the mother-child relationship by looking at studies involving intact families. Two factors that have repeatedly been found to be related to healthy adjustment of both boys and girls in such families are the parents' supportiveness of the children and approach to discipline. In their review of research on parent-child interaction, Rollins and Thomas (1979) conclude that in intact families the more supportive the parents, the less likely it is that their children will demonstrate antisocial, aggressive behaviors. Support refers here to the parents' communication to the child, that he or she is accepted and approved of. It seems reasonable to expect that the relationship between parental support and the child's non-aggressive behavior will hold true not only for intact families but also for mother-child relationships in divorced families. In fact, one might argue that the connection should be even stronger. In two-parent families children may experience support without the same parent always being supportive. If one parent has a bad day (or week), or is generally not supportive, the other parent can mediate the effects. In the single-parent family, however, the day-to-day reactions of the custodial parent to the child may have a more direct effect on the child.

In the same review, Rollins and Thomas (1979) also conclude that aggressive behavior in children is related to the way in which they are disciplined. Categorizing parental discipline techniques as being either coercive or inductive, these authors identify coercive techniques as those which pressure the child to follow the parents' commands or desires. An example of coercive discipline would be a father trying to modify his child's behavior by regularly complaining about what the child does or does not do. Inductive techniques, on the other hand, are intended to obtain "Voluntary compliance to parental desires, thereby avoiding a direct conflict of wills with the child" (p. 332). An example of this kind of discipline would be a father telling his child how much it helps when the child follows through on what he or she is asked to do. It is the coercive approach to discipline which appears to be associated with aggressive behavior for both boys and girls. Such punitive practices by the parents are thought to result in aggression in the child because they serve as models of aggression and are a source of frustration for the child (Becker, 1964; Martin, 1975).

These findings seem particularly relevant to the issue of aggressive behavior in boys following divorce in light of research by Hetherington, Cox and Cox (1976) which suggests that in the months following divorce, mothers of preschoolers use more negative commands and negative sanctions with sons than with daughters. One purpose of this study, then, is to examine if the relationships between parental support and coercion and a child's aggression holds for mothers and sons following divorce.

A second purpose of the study is to begin to examine factors which may contribute to such a relationship. Studies have suggested that in both two-parent and single-parent families, the extent to which the mother feels supported by friends and family and her income level (e.g., Colletta, 1983) affects how she functions as a parent. A factor which may be unique to the single mother, however, is her attitude toward her former husband. Support for examining the importance of a mother's perception of her ex-spouse is based on two lines of research. First the level of arguing and hostility between mothers and their ex-spouses has been found to be related to post-divorce adjustment in children (Kurdek & Blisk, 1983). Second, Hetherington (1980) found that mothers are more likely to see their sons than their daughters as being like the child's father in a negative way. Based on their interviews with parents, Wallerstein and Kelly (1980) have similarly suggested that a mother or a father may "perceive all children of the opposite sex as representative of the rejected spouse" (p. 101). It seems quite possible then that mothers who have a negative attitude toward their former spouse may be more likely to perceive their sons negatively than would mothers whose experience with and attitude towards the child's father is more positive. Thus, we will examine the relationship between a mother's attitude toward her former husband and the degree to which she is reported to be emotionally supportive and coercive with her son following divorce.

In integrating the two foci of this study, a model of maternal influence on son's behavior following divorce is proposed (see Figure 1). First, it is predicted that a mother's attitude toward her ex-spouse will be related to how she deals with her son, with mothers who have a more positive attitude toward their former spouses being more supportive and less coercive with their sons. It is then predicted that both the level of support and coercion experienced by

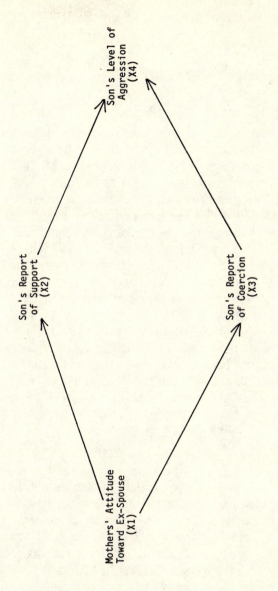

Figure 1. Proposed Path Model

239

the son will be related to his level of aggression following divorce, with sons whose mothers are supportive and use low levels of coercion being the least aggressive.

METHODS

Participants

The participants in this study were 51 white middle-class boys and their divorced mothers. The children were between 9 and 12 years old with a mean age of 10.3. The sample was limited to later school-age, or preadolescent boys based on findings which suggest that this is the age group in which increased aggression is more apparent and sustained (Wallerstein & Kelley, 1976). All of the children attended public school in one of three school districts in a suburb of New York City. Only those families in which the mother had been separated for between 18 and 39 months were used in this study. This time frame was selected in order that the family dynamics operating after the initial period of crisis could be examined (Kurdek, Blisk, & Siesky, 1981).

The 51 mothers who took part in this study ranged in age from 29 to 50 years old with a mean age of 35.6. The average income in the single-parent families headed by these women was $19,000, with a range from $5,000 to $60,000. Forty-three percent of these women (N = 22) had graduated from high school, 29% (N = 15) had some college or technical school training, 10% (N = 5) had completed college, and 16% (N = 8) held a graduate degree.

Procedure

The superintendents of approximately 40 school districts in the New York City area were contacted and asked if they would allow canvas letters to be sent home to the parents of students in their schools. In those schools in which both the superintendent and principal gave their endorsement, an introductory letter was sent home to the parent(s) of all the boys in the fourth, fifth, and sixth grades. This letter explained the nature of the study and requested the participation of those mothers who had been recently divorced. Interested parents were invited to contact the investigator by phone for additional information and to determine their appropriateness for the sample. Approximately 75 mothers called to inquire about the study. Of those, 51 fit all criteria and were included in the study.

Interviews were conducted in the homes of the participants. During this home visit, mothers provided marital history and demographic information and completed the Mother's Evaluation of Father Rating Scale (Miller, 1961) and the mother's form of the parental support and coercion scales (Peterson, 1978). Sons completed the children's form of the parental support and coercion scales (Peterson, 1978) in a separate room at the same time the mother completed her questionnaire.

It is important to note that when studying maternal behavior, several methods of obtaining information are available, each with its own advantages and disadvantages. Though the mother's reports have typically been used, some support exists for a possible bias in mothers' reports (i.e., mothers' ratings of child behavior, as compared to teachers' ratings of child behavior, are more highly correlated with mothers' ratings of the quality of their parenting) (Hodges et al., 1983). While there is also evidence to suggest that sons' and mothers' perceptions of maternal behavior are similar (Brook, Whiteman, Gordon, Brenden, & Jinishian, 1980), reports of maternal behavior were obtained from mothers as well as from sons in order that the relationship between the scores could be tested.

Teachers of those boys who participated in the study were asked to complete the School Behavior Checklist (Miller, 1981). While teachers were told that this project was part of a study on "family relationships," they were not aware of the specific purpose of the study.

Measures

Evaluation of Father

A woman's attitude toward her former husband was assessed, using the Mother's Evaluation of Father Rating Scale. This 50-word, five-point adjective rating scale was devised by Miller (1961) and is based on Gough's Adjective Checklist. Some examples of adjectives used to describe the ex-spouse are "affectionate," "alert," "moody" and "rude." The mother was asked to indicate whether each item described her ex-husband "seldom, occasionally, half the time, frequently, or most of the time." The score is the sum of the difference scores on each of the 50 words between the rating given to the ex-husband and that given to an ideal male. Thus, the higher the score, the more negative a woman's attitude towards her ex-spouse.

Maternal Behavior

The degree to which a mother was supportive and coercive in her interactions with her son was assessed using measures designed by Peterson (1978). The parental support scale consists of nine items and is designed to measure those parent-child interactions characterized by acceptance, approval, and general positive sentiments (Ellis, Thomas, & Rollins, 1976). An example of a question on the support scale is "Over the past several months, whenever my son had any kind of problem he could count on me." The parental coercion scale is an eight-item measure that is designed to assess parental behaviors intended to pressure the child into complying with the parent's wishes (Rollins & Thomas, 1979, p. 321). An example of a question on the coercion scale is "I often complain about what my son does."

Equivalent versions of the questionnaire were given to the mothers and their sons. The two forms contained the same items with only slightly different wordings (i.e., Son's form: ". . . my mother seemed to trust me" Mother's form: ". . . I seemed to trust my son").

Son's Behavior

The son's level of aggressive behavior was assessed using the aggression Scale of the School Behavior Checklist (Miller, 1981). The checklist was completed by the child's teacher and is composed of 96 items of prosocial and deviant behaviors which can be answered either true or false. The aggression scale consists of 36 items which are designed to measure both active aggression, such as hitting, teasing, pushing and arguing, as well as passive aggression items such as refusing to speak and stubbornness.

RESULTS

Prior to testing the model proposed in the present study, the question concerning the similarity of mothers' and sons' reports of support and coercion was addressed. Results of matched pair t-tests suggests that mothers and sons do not differ in the perception of how coercive the mother is in dealing with her sons $t(50) = .07$, $p = .94$. They do, however, seem to differ in their reports of how supportive she is, $t(50) = 2.48$, $p < .05$, with mothers seeing themselves as being more supportive than their sons perceive them to be.

An attempt was made to explain why the sons' might have seen their mothers as less supportive than the mothers themselves did. A stepwise multiple regression was performed to determine if one or more of the following factors might be related to the sons ' reports of maternal support; (a) changes in the amount of time the mother is available as a result of her having to work since the divorce; (b) changes in the family income since the parents' divorce; (c) the number of friends the son had whose parents were also divorced; and (d) whether or not the child had to move and make new friends as a result of his parents' divorce. The results of the stepwise multiple regression revealed that none of the four factors examined were significantly related to the son's reports of maternal supportive behavior (Overall $F[3,47] = .35$). Furthermore, when taken as a group, the four variables entered into the equation accounted for less than three percent of the variance in the sons' reports of how supportive the mothers were. Thus, it appears that differences between the mothers' and sons' reports cannot be explained by these additional life changes which often accompany divorce. Future work will need to consider the role of other individuals, particularly the father in understanding a son's perception of how supportive his mother is. It is quite possible that communication from the father to the son will affect how the son sees his mother.

Despite the differences between mothers' and sons' reports of maternal support, only the sons' reports were used in the subsequent analyses. This decision was based on findings suggesting that a child's perceptions of parental behavior have a greater impact on the child's development than does the parents' actual behavior (Serot & Teevan, 1961).

With regard to the primary purpose of this investigation, a path analysis was performed to test the proposed model. The mother's attitude towards her ex-spouse (X1) is considered, for purposes of the path analysis, to be an exogenous variable since it is presumed to be affected by factors outside the proposed model. However, the son's report of maternal support (X2) and maternal coercion (X3) are endogenous variables as they are believed to be directly affected by a factor included in the model, namely, the mother's attitude towards her ex-spouse (X1). Similarly, the son's level of aggression (X4) is also an endogenous variable as it is presumed to be directly affected by the son's perception of maternal support (X2) and coercion (X3). The specific model employed in this study is recursive; thus the adequacy of a unidirectional explanation will be tested. It is noted that while the model presented is compatible with existing theory and data, other models are plausible. For example, it is quite possible that the relationship is bidirectional with the son's level of aggression affecting the mother's behavior as well as her attitude towards her ex-spouse.

The first step in path analysis is to calculate the path coefficients indicating the effect of one variable upon another. Since the model considers only the effect of one factor, namely the mother's attitude towards her ex-husband, on reports of maternal support and coercion, the path coefficient is equal to the correlation coefficient (see Figure 2). Thus, the path coefficient between attitude toward ex-spouse and maternal support $p31$ is $-.32$, while the path coefficient for maternal coercion is .26.

The son's level of aggression is proposed to be affected by two variables; maternal support and coercion, which are not independent of one another ($r = -.61$; $p < .01$). As a result of this strong correlation, maternal support and maternal coercion, have both a direct, as well as an indirect, effect on the son's behavior.[1] Prior to dealing with the direct and indirect effects, it is first necessary to

1. It should be noted that with this high level of correlation between coercion and support, the error variance may be unstable and the coefficients unreliable. Since there is no clear indication of the level at which multicolinearity becomes a problem, caution should be taken in interpreting these results.

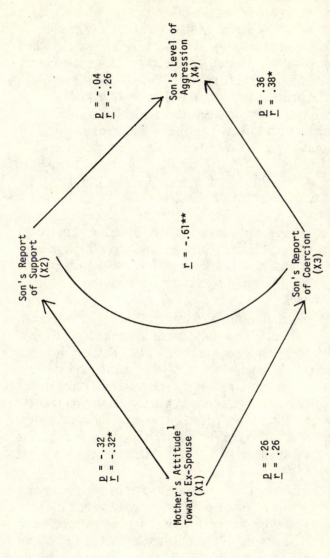

Figure 2. Proposed Path Model Including Path Coefficients (p) and Correlations Coefficients (r)

[1]Note: This score is a discrepancy score. Thus, the higher the score, the more negative a woman's attitude toward her ex-spouse

* p <.05
** p <.01

245

perform a regression analysis to calculate the path coefficient between maternal support, maternal coercive behavior and the son's level of aggression. The resulting standardized regression coefficients or Beta values are equal to the path coefficient (Kerlinger & Pedhazur, 1973; Nie et al., 1975). As indicated in Figure 2 when son's aggression (X4) is regressed on perceived maternal support (X2) and coercion (X3), one obtains $p_42 = -.037$ and $p_43 = .358$. Having derived the path coefficients, it is then possible to determine what part of the correlation between two variables is due to the direct effect and indirect effects. Kerlinger and Pedhazur (1973) suggest that by breaking down a correlation into a direct effect and "Total Indirect Effects" (TIE), one is better able to determine the role played by each variable in the model. The TIE can be determined by subtracting the path coefficient from the correlation coefficient between two variables. Thus while the path coefficient of maternal coercion on the son's aggression is .358, the indirect effect is .023. As the direct effect is considerably larger than the indirect effect, it appears that maternal coercion has a very strong direct effect on the son's level of aggression thereby supporting this aspect of the proposed model.

With regard to the relationship between maternal support and the son's level of aggression, it is noted that while the path coefficient is .027, the total of the indirect effects is .219. The fact that the direct effect is relatively small when compared to the total indirect effects suggests that the correlation between maternal support and the son's level of aggressive behavior is mainly due to indirect effects. It appears then that supportive behavior by the mother has practically no direct effect on the son's level of aggressive behavior and only affects the son's level of aggression through its correlation with maternal coercion.

Furthermore, the finding that maternal support has practically no direct effect on the son's aggressive behavior suggests that the proposed model is not entirely supported and that the path between maternal supportive behavior (X2) and the son's level of aggressive behavior (X4) should be eliminated from the model. The resulting model suggests that a mother's attitude toward her ex-husband has a direct effect on the degree to which she is perceived to be supportive and coercive in her relationship with her son following divorce and that the mother's perceived level of coercion has a direct effect on the level of aggression demonstrated by the son.

DISCUSSION

This investigation examined the relationship between a mother's attitude towards her ex-spouse, her interactions with her 9- to 12-year-old son, and the son's level of aggressive behavior 18 to 39 months following the breakup of the parents' marriage. A model was tested which suggests that a relationship exists between a mother's attitude toward her ex-husband and how supportive and coercive she is in her interactions with her 9- to 12-year-old son. These levels of support and coercion are then proposed to be associated with the son's level of aggression.

The results of the path analysis suggest partial support for the model. Mother's attitude towards her ex-husband was found to have a direct effect on how emotionally supportive and coercive her son perceives her to be one and one-half to three years following the parents' separation. A mother who is particularly negative in her evaluation of the child's father is more likely to be seen as both less supportive and more coercive of her son than a mother who evaluates the child's father in a more neutral or positive way. Empirical support was also found for a connection between a son's perception of his mother's attempts to coerce him and his level of aggression in school. The more coercive the mother is thought to be, the more overt and passive aggression the son displays. How emotionally supportive the mother is in her interactions, however, does not seem to be directly related to the son's level of aggression.

Several points from the testing of the path model are noteworthy. First, the level of supportive, positive interaction in the mother-son relationship does not appear to be as important as the absence of coercion in explaining the son's level of aggression. This initially may seem surprising given previous findings of a negative relationship between parental support and sons' aggressiveness in intact families (Rollins & Thomas, 1979). It may be, however, that in relationships between single mothers and their sons the absence of negative interaction is more significant in determining the level of distress than is actual positive interaction. Such a pattern has certainly been documented for other family relationships, particularly husband-wife (e.g., Wills, Weiss, & Patterson, 1974). The importance of absence of negative interaction may be especially relevant for the age group considered in the present study, preadolescents. This is a time when most parent-child relationships, regardless of whether in a single- or two-parent family, are characterized by some level of struggle or tension as the preadolescent child becomes increasingly egocentric and less cooperative in their dealings with parents. The single mother may be particularly stressed as she tries to handle the onset of adolescence if she is still wrestling with unresolved negative emotions about the boy's father.

An alternative explanation to the seeming lack of influence of mothers' level of support on their sons' behavior is that, in these analyses, the sons' reports of support and coercion were utilized. It is possible that for many preadolescent children a parent's attempts to gain compliance or have the child obey, are, by definition, not supportive. That is, though adults may not define support by the discipline methods used (i.e., the two are relatively independent), a preadolescent is much more likely to interpret support or lack of support based on discipline and the amount of control the parent exercises over the child. Such an explanation may account for both the high correlation between the two variables and the primary of coercion in explaining the son's behavior.

A second noteworthy point is that the data for the present study were collected between one and one-half and three years after the parent's separation and suggest that perceptual or attitudinal factors may still be affecting the behavior of the sons' after the initial crisis period has passed. This finding is particularly interesting when one considers that only 12 months after the breakup of their parents' marriage, no relationship was found between overt hostility between the parents during their marriage and the child's level of adjustment (Jacobson, 1978). It would seem that if we are to achieve a better understanding of those factors that affect a child's adjustment to divorce, we will need to consider not only the overt behaviors and quantitative characteristics of the parent-child interaction, such as amount of time spent with non-custodial parent, but also the less obvious, attitudinal aspects of intrafamily relationships, such as the mother's attitude toward her former partner.

Though this research tested one possible model of the association between attitudes, behavior, and sons' adjustment following divorce, great care should be used in interpreting these results. First of all, the family, whether pre- or post-divorce is a dynamic system of multidirectional influence. The use of a method of analysis such as path analysis forces arbitrary decisions to be made concerning the testing of linear paths of influence. Thus, though the model which was tested may suggest one piece of the larger reciprocal interaction picture, it is important not to be lulled into thinking it proves causation. Additional factors which must be integrated into future models include, at a minimum, the behavior of the son. Research has shown that, in general, boys are more aggressive than girls (Miller, 1972), and in single-parent homes, boys present more behavior management problems for mothers than do girls (Heatherington, 1979). Thus, it is naive to focus only on the impact of mothers' behavior on the sons without considering the reciprocal impact that the son's behavior has on the mother. Such a reciprocal process has been the focus of Patterson's work on coercive family systems (e.g., Patterson, 1976).

In creating a more systemically accurate model, attention will also need to be given to the role the father plays in his son's life and his attitude toward the mother. Unresolved negative feelings on the parts of either parent for the other can produce a painful double bind for any child. Further, attention should be focused on the social and economic context in which the mother-son relationship exists. Single mothers are often struggling with financially supporting the family and reestablishing themselves in relationships. Thus, it is critical to address the impact of societal factors impinging upon the family (e.g., women's wages, child care options) and constraining or facilitating the patterns of family interaction which develop.

REFERENCES

Brook, J., Whiteman, M., Gordon, A., Brenden, C., & Jinishian, A.(1980). Relationship of maternal and adolescent perceptions of maternal child-rearing practices. *Perceptual and Motor Skills, 51,* 1043-1046.

Colletta, N.D. (1983). Stressful lives: The situation of divorced mothers and their children. *Journal of Divorce, 6,* 19-31.

Ellis, G.J., Thomas, D.L., & Rollins, B.C. (1976). Measuring parental support: The interrelationship of three measures. *Journal of Marriage and the Family, 38.* 713-722.

Guidubaldi, J., Cleminshaw, H.K., Perry, J.D., & Mclaughlin, C.S. (1983). The impact of parental divorce on children: Report of the nationwide NASP study. *School Psychology Review, 12,* 300-323.

Herzog, E., & Sudia, C.E. (1973). Children in fatherless families. In B.M. Caldwell & H.N. Ricciuti (Eds.), *Review of child development research* (Vol. 3). Chicago: University of Chicago Press.

Hess , R.D., & Camara, K.A. (1979). Post-divorce family relationships as mediating factors in the consequences of divorce in children. *Journal of Social Issues. 35,* 79-96.

Hetherington, E.M. (1980). Children and divorce. In R. Henderson (Ed.), *Parent-child interaction: Theory, research, and prospect.* New York: Academic Press.

Hetherington, E.M., Cox, M., & Cox, R. (1978). The aftermath of divorce. In J.H. Stevens, Jr. & M. Matthews (Eds.), *Mother- child, father-child relations.* Washington, D.C.: National Associations for the Education of Young Children.

Hetherington, E.M., Cox, M., & Cox, R. (1979). Stress and coping in divorce: A focus on women. In J. Gullahorn (Ed.), *Psychology and women in transition.* New York: Halsted Press.

Hodges, W.F., Birchsbaum, H.K., & Tierney, C.W. (1983). Parent-child relationships and adjustment in preschool children in divorced and intact families. *Journal of Divorce, 1,* 43-53.

Krantz, S.E., Clark, J., Pruyn, J.P., & Usher, M. (1985) Cognition and adjustment among children of separated or divorced parents. *Cognitive Therapy and Research, 9,* 61-77.

Kurdek, L.A., & Blisk, D. (1983). Dimensions and correlates of mothers' divorce experiences. *Journal of Divorce, 6,* 1-21.

Kurdek, L.A., Blisk, D., & Siesky, A.E. (1981). Correlates of children's long-term adjustment to their parents' divorce. *Development Psychology, 17,* 565-579.

Martin, B. (1975). Parent-child relations. In F.D. Horowitz (Ed.), Review of child development research. Chicago: University of Chicago Press.

Miller, B.A. (1961). Effects of father absence and mothers' evaluation of father on the socialization of adolescent boys. *Dissertation Abstracts International, 22,* 1257-1258. (University Microfilms No. 61-3456)

Miller, L.C. (1981). *School Behavior Checklist.* Los Angeles: Western Psychological Services.

Patterson, G.R. (1976). The aggressive child: Victim and architect of a coercive system. In E. Mash, L. Hamerlynck, & L. Hardy (Eds.), *Behavior modification and families.* New York: Brunner/Mazel.

Peterson, G.W. (1978). The nature and antecedents of adolescent conformity (Doctoral dissertation , Brigham Young University, 1978). *Dissertation Abstracts International, 39,* 3167A.

Raschke, H.J., & Raschke, V.J. (1979). Family conflict and children's self-concepts: A comparison of intact and single-parent families. *Journal of Marriage and the Family, 41,* 367-373.

Rollins, B.C., & Thomas, D.L. (1979). Parental support, power, and control techniques in the socialization of children. In W.R. Burr , R. Hill, I. Nye, & I. Reiss (Eds.), *Contemporary theories about the family* (Vol. 1). New York: Free Press.

Santrock, J.W., & Warshak, R.A. (1979). Father custody and social development in boys and girls. *Journal of Social Issues, 35,* 112-125.

Serot, N.M., & Teevan, R.C. (1961). Perception of the parent-child relationship and its relation to child adjustment. *Child Development, 32,* 373-378.

Tuckman, J., & Regan, R.A. (1966). Intactness of the home and behavioral problems in children. *Journal of Child Psychology and Psychiatry. 7,* 225-233.

Wallerstein, J.S., & Kelly, J.B. (1980). *Surviving the breakup: How children and parents cope with divorce*. New York: Basic Books.

Wills, T.A., Weiss, R.L., & Patterson, G.R. (1974). A behavioral analysis of the determinants of marital satisfaction. *Journal of Consulting and Clinical Psychology, 42,* 802-811.

Intimacy in Young Adult Males' Relationships as a Function of Divorced and Non-Divorced Family of Origin Structure

Joseph Guttmann

SUMMARY. This study investigates the long-term effect that parental divorce may have on the levels of intimacy in the relationships of young men with their girlfriends, their willingness to make up and readiness to break up relationships, and their expectancies regarding marriage. The sample contained 40 male soldiers, serving duty in the Israeli army. Twenty were from intact families, and twenty were from divorced families. The results show no differences between the groups on any of the measured variables. These results are discussed in the context of the reasons given for the intergenerational transmission of divorce.

Some researchers suggest that the effect of parental divorce on children may result in certain negative consequences, which con-

Joseph Guttmann, PhD, is on the faculty of the School of Education, Haifa University, Mt. Carmel, Haifa, Israel.

253

tinue into adolescence and adulthood (Stuart & Abt, 1981), while other researchers expect these consequences to disappear after some time (Shinn, 1978). Still others suggest that while no initial detrimental effects may be found among young children (Ferri, 1976; Hess, Shipman, Brophy & Bear, 1968; Rees & Palmer, 1970), nevertheless, significant negative effects can emerge later in their lives (Shinn, 1978). Increased impulse control problems and antisocial, aggressive behaviors have been reported for adolescents and young children who experienced parental divorce (Kalter, 1977; Offord, Abrams, Allen & Pouchinsky, 1979; Offord, Allen & Abrams, 1978). Chapman (1977) found that on the field independence dimension, which is associated with a number of important dimensions of effective interpersonal behavior (Witkin & Goodenough, 1977), boys from divorced families had lower scores than boys from intact families.

In a critical review of social support research Gottlieb (1983) noted that "parents' separation is likely to affect [the children's] attitudes toward close interpersonal ties. What they witness at home is likely to challenge their assumptions about the meaning of loyalty in relationships [and] the permanency of affectional bonds" (p. 285). In their longitudinal studies, Hetherington (1972), and Young and Parish (1977), found parental divorce to be associated with lower self-esteem and greater difficulties in young women's interpersonal relationships with members of the opposite sex. Later studies (Hainline & Feig, 1978; Berg & Kelly, 1979; Vess, Schwebel & Moreland, 1983), however, failed to find such self-concept or sex-role difficulties. Wallerstein and Kelly (1980) examined 21 adolescents and described a distinct polarization of their responses to their parents' divorce. While most adolescents were described as angry and grieving, one-third were viewed as catalyzed into psychological independence which was reflected in their ability to detach from the family conflict and to show a high degree of understanding of interpersonal relationships. The others, however, were less prepared for a premature push into autonomy. Eighteen months after the separation, those who had achieved a "strategic withdrawal" from the family, as well as the majority of the adolescents who had temporarily regressed, were functioning well socially. Wallerstein and Kelly also reported that adolescent boys often dealt with divorce-related stress by seeking refuge in their friends' social network.

Divorce was also found not to relate to college students' adjustment, grades, aspirations, self-confidence, levels of ego development, and ego-identity achievement (Grossman, Shea & Adams, 1980; Flescher, 1986; Gurin & Epps, 1975). Indeed Grossman, Shea and Adams suggested that their study's results indicated that divorce may have "positive consequences on ego functioning [and] identity formation" (p. 268). Kulka and Weingarten (1979) examined the long-term consequences of experiencing a parental divorce from data derived from two large surveys conducted over 25 years; they too concluded that,

> based on our multivariate analyses controlling for contemporary life circumstances and social factors other than parental divorce, one could argue that there is little evidence here for the existence of *any* long-term effects of coming from a home broken by parental divorce or separation. (p. 73)

Only within the last decade have researchers begun to investigate the long-term effect of parental divorce as a question of "heritability of divorce" or "intergenerational transmission" of divorce. These terms refer to the hypothesis that those who experience parental divorce or separation during childhood or adolescence are more prone to divorce or separate themselves (Glenn & Shelton, 1983; Korbin & Waite, 1984; Mott & Moore, 1979; Mueller & Pope, 1977; Pope & Mueller, 1976). The most common reason given by researchers to support the transmission hypothesis is the role model extracted from the social learning theory (Bandura, 1969). Because children learn from their parents by interacting with them and observing them, the learned appropriate sex and marital roles determined to a large extent his or her success of marriage. The child of an unhappy or broken home does not learn marital roles that enhance the chances for a happy marriage. To test this hypothesis Pope and Mueller (1976) analyzed data from five sociological surveys, four of which were comprised of national samples. They concluded that economic, social, and parenting style factors may account more adequately than parental divorce (hence, role model) for the transmission effects found in the surveys. Kulka and Weingarten (1979) also concluded that "contrary to much of the literature and popular thought," experiencing parental divorce has "at most, a modest effect," in comparison to other external variables, on the patterns of an individual's adjustment to his or her role as a spouse.

If external variables rather than parental divorce account for the higher divorce rate among adults of divorced parents, these variables are less likely to intervene in premarriage datings. Personality variables plus past learning and experiences play a more significant role in determining the duration and quality of these relationships. Hence, a more adequate test of the long-term effect of parental divorce on young adults' quality of interpersonal relationships is their premarriage dating. The present study investigates the long-term effect that parental divorce may have on the levels of intimacy in the relationships of young men with their girlfriends, their willingness to make up and readiness to break up relationships, and their expectancies regarding marriage. Because intimacy reflects one's openness, trust and involvement in a relationship (Delega & Chaikin, 1975), it is a good measure of a relationship's quality and potential duration (Erikson, 1974; Sullivan, 1953). It is hypothesized here that no differences are to be found between subjects whose parents were divorced and those who parents were not divorced in: (I) their reported levels of intimacy in their relationship with their girlfriends, (II) their initiation of making up and breaking up the relationships, and (III) their expectations regarding getting and staying married.

METHOD

Subjects

Forty male soldiers, serving duty in a nonvoluntary field unit in the Israeli army volunteered to participate. The soldiers served between 9 to 24 months ($M = 11.2$). The subjects' age ranged from 19 to 21 years ($M = 20.5$); 87% were high school graduates and their socioeconomic background was as diverse as the whole of Israeli society. Twenty were of intact families, and twenty from divorced families. The parents of the latter group divorced between 5 to 12 years ($M = 7.1$) prior to the study. Each of the subjects reported to have had in the past at least one girlfriend; the number of girlfriends in each group ranged from 1 to 5.

Material and Procedure

The stimulus material consisted of written instructions and a questionnaire, which was individually administered and introduced as dealing with young adults' male-female relationships. The subjects were asked to "think, while responding to the questionnaire, of their current or most recent girlfriend, unless otherwise specified." Except for the background questions, the questionnaire included 16 incomplete sentences and 5 questions. Seventeen of the total items were extracted from Sharabany's (1974) Intimate Friendship Test; and 4 were specifically composed for the present study.

In the written instructions, the subjects were asked to "answer the questions and fill-in or complete the following sentences, using one of the three given options below each question or sentence." Each of the options represented a different level of intimacy. For instance, "In my relationship with my girlfriend I _____" (1) trust her completely, (2) trust her, but with reservations, (3) don't trust her; "When my girlfriend is in a bad mood I _____" (1) almost always notice, (2) sometimes notice, (3) rarely notice; "Me and my girlfriend can talk _____" (1) about all our personal problems, (2) about only some personal problems, (3) about everything but our personal problems. The four added questions were, "Following a fight or a heated argument with your girlfriend, who is the one to initiate making up?" (1) me, most of the times, (2) sometimes me and sometimes my girlfriend, (3) my girlfriend, most of the times; "The initiation to break up previous relationships were _____" (1) mostly mine, (2) sometimes mine and sometimes my girlfriend's, (3) mostly my girlfriend's; "Would you like sometime in the future to get married?" (1) yes, (2) not sure, (3) no; "Assuming you do get married, do you expect this marriage to last a lifetime?" (1) yes, (2) not sure, (3) no.

RESULTS AND DISCUSSION

Given the ordinal nature of the obtained data, Pearson's X2 tests of independence were performed to assess the associations between the independent (divorce/intact families) and dependent (intimacy) variables. In order to carry out the analysis on the Intimate Friendship Test, the number of responses indicating, High, Medium, and Low levels of intimacy for each group were calculated (see Table 1). The analysis yielded no significant result, that is, the distribution of the three levels of Intimacy responses was similar for the divorced and intact groups, indicating no association between family structure and the reported level of intimacy in the subjects' relationships with their girlfriends. Parental divorce was also found to be unrelated to the subject's frequency of making up and breaking up the relationship, or to the expectancy of getting and staying married.

Several rationales, in addition to the "role model" mentioned earlier, have been offered to explain the "transmission of divorce" effect. The "social control" rationale, for instance, argues that parents' divorce reduces the size and integration of the child's kin network and thus reduces its effectiveness as a social-control mechanism (Pope & Mueller, 1976). The "withdrawal threshold" rationale argues that children learned from their parents' divorce a particular problem-solving strategy (i.e., when confronted with difficulties and frustration they resolve them by disengagement) (Guttmann, Amir & Katz, 1986). Other psychologically oriented explanations relate to "personality" and "permissive attitudes" and, if valid, should therefore affect children of divorced parents' premarriage dating more than their marriage. That is because many more factors other than the psychological ones contribute to a successful marriage, while such variables play a more dominant role in premarriage dating. The present data indicates that, at least as far as the reported levels of intimacy in a relationship, and the frequencies of "making up" and "breaking up" relationships are concerned, young adults of divorced parents are not different from those of intact families. These two groups are similar in the psychological variables affecting the dependent variables tested here.

The results also lend support to the notion that although parental divorce has been shown to have immediate negative consequences,

Table 1
Frequencies of Responses to Intimate Friendship Test's Items
by Three Levels of Intimacy and Subjects' Family Type.

	Family Type					
	Divorced			Intact		
	Intimacy			Intimacy		
I	H.	M.	L.	H.	M.	L.
Feel close to each other	11	8	1	10	9	1
Trust her	9	9	2	14	4	2
Share secrets	11	7	2	8	9	3
Notice her bad mood	0	6	14	1	7	12
Share personal problems	8	5	7	8	8	4
Can talk about everything	10	6	4	12	7	1
Tell what I think of her	12	8	0	11	8	2
When feel bad, wants her	7	8	5	8	8	4
Want her to know my feelings and thoughts	11	7	1	6	11	4
Like her sharing things with me	16	4	0	19	1	0
Tell her my complaints	12	6	2	13	7	0
Like to consult with her	11	5	4	6	4	10
Free to take her things	7	9	4	8	12	0
Can predict the movies, books and music she likes	7	9	4	2	18	0
Feel loyal to her	11	7	2	10	9	1
Can rely on her support	14	5	1	18	1	1
Talk honestly about our relationship	14	6	0	16	4	0

II	Me	Both	Her	Me	Both	Her
Initiate making-up	7	8	5	9	5	6
Initiate breaking-up	11	4	5	12	6	2

III	Yes	Not Sure	No	Yes	Not Sure	No
Expect to marry	15	3	2	17	3	0
Expect the marriage to last	12	4	4	14	4	2

the severity tends to diminish in time and eventually may altogether disappear (Adams, Miller & Schrepf, 1984; Kurdek, 1986). With regard to degree of intimacy experienced in interpersonal relationships, research shows that even in preadolescence, parental divorce does not have a negative consequence (Hertz-Lazarowitz, Rosenberg & Guttmann, 1986). It is for future research to determine if and what psychological variables, in addition to the external ones, contribute to the transmission of divorce effects.

REFERENCES

Adams, P.L., Miller, J.R., & Schrepf, N.A. (1984). *Fatherless children*. New York: John Wiley & Sons.

Bandura, A. (1969). Social-learning theory of identificatory process. In D.A. Goslin (Ed.) *Handbook of socialization theory and research*. Chicago: Rand McNally.

Berg, B., & Kelly, R. (1979). Measured self-esteem of children from broken, rejected and accepted families. *Journal of Divorce, 2*, 363-370.

Chapman, M. (1977). Father absence, stepfathers and the cognitive performance of college students. *Child Development, 48*, 1155-1158.

Delega, V.J., & Chaikin, A.L. (1975). *Sharing intimacy*. New Jersey: Prentice-Hall Inc.

Erikson, E.H. (1968). *Identity, youth and crisis*. New York: W.W. Norton & Co.

Ferri, E. (1976). *Growing up in one-parent family: A long-term study of child development*. London: National Foundation for Educational Research.

Flescher, M. (1986, August). *Social networks and student adjustment following parental divorce and remarriage*. Paper presented at the 94th APA meeting, Washington, D.C.

Glenn, N.D., & Shelton, B.A. (1983). Per-adult background and divorce: A note of caution about overreliance on explained variance. *Journal of Marriage and the Family, 45*, 405-410.

Gottlieb, B.H. (1983). Social support as a focus for integrative research in psychology. *American Psychologist, 38*, 278-287.

Grosman, S.M., Shea, J.A., & Adams, G.R. (1980). Effect of parental divorce during early childhood on ego development and identity formation of college students. *Journal of Divorce, 3*, 263-277.

Gurin, P., & Epps, E.G. (1975). *Black consciousness, identity, and achievement*. New York: John Wiley.

Guttmann, J., Amir, T., & Katz, M. (1986). Threshold of withdrawal in school work of children of divorced parents. Unpublished manuscript, University of Haifa, Israel.

Hainline, L., & Feig, E. (1978). The correlates of childhood father absence in college-aged women. *Child Development, 49*, 37-42.

Hertz-Lazarowitz, R., Rosenberg, M., & Guttmann, J. (1986). *Children of divorce and their intimate relationship with parents and peers*. Unpublished manuscript, University of Haifa, Israel.

Hess, R.D., Shipman, V.C., Brophy, J.E., & Bear, R.M. (1968). *The cognitive environments of urban preschool children*. Chicago: University of Chicago Press.

Hetherington, E.M. (1972). Effect of father absence on personality development in adolescent daughters. *Developmental Psychology*, *7*(3), 313-326.

Kalter, N. (1977). Children of divorce in an outpatient psychiatric population. *American Journal of Orthopsychiatry*, *47*(1), 40-51.

Kobrin, F.E., & Waite, L.J. (1984). Effects of childhood family structure on the transmission of marriage. *Journal of Marriage and the Family*, *46*, 807-816.

Kulka, R.A., & Weingarter, H. (1979). The long-term effect of parental divorce in childhood and adult adjustment. *Journal of Social Issues*, *35*(4), 50-78.

Kurdek, L.A. (in press). Children's adjustment to parental divorce. In J.P. Vincent (Ed.), *Advances in family intervention, assessment and theory* (Vol. 4). Greenwich, CT: JAI.

Mott, F.L., & Moore, S.F. (1979). The causes of marital disruption among young American women: An interdisciplinary perspective. *Journal of Marriage and the Family*, *41*(2), 355-365

Mueller, C.W. & Pope, H. (1977). Marital instability: A study of its transmission between generations. *Journal of Marriage and the Family*, *39*(1), 83-94.

Nye, F.I. & Berardo, F.M. (1973). *The family: Its structure and interaction*. New York: Macmillan.

Offord, D.R., Abrams, N., Alen, N., & Pouchinsky, M. (1979). Broken homes, parental psychiatric illness and female delinquency. *American Journal of Orthopsychiatry*, *49*, 252-264.

Offord, D.R., Allen, N., & Abrams, N. (1978). Parental psychiatric illness, broken homes and delinquency. *Journal of American Academy of Child Psychiatry*, *17*, 224-237.

Pope, H., & Mueller, C.W. (1976). The intergenerational transmission of marital instability: Comparisons by age and sex. *Journal of Social Issues*, *32*(1), 49-66.

Rees, A.H., & Palmer, R.F. (1970). Factors related to mental test performance. *Developmental Psychology Monograph*, *3*, (2, Pt.2).

Shinn, M.B. (1978). Father absence and children's cognitive development. *Psychological Bulletin*, *85*(2), 295-324.

Stuart, I.R., & Abt, L.E. (1981). *Children of separation and divorce*. New York: Van Nostrand Reinhold Co.

Sullivan, H.S. (1953). *The interpersonal theory of psychiatry*. New York: W.W. Norton & Co.

Vess, J.D., Schwebel, A.I., & Moreland, J. (1983). The effect of early parental divorce on the sex role development of college students. *Journal of Divorce*, *7*(1), 83-95.

Wallerstein, J.S., & Kelly, J.B. (1980). *Surviving the breakup: How children and parents cope with divorce*. New York: Basic Books.

Witkin, H.A., & Goodenough, D.R. (1977). Field dependence and interpersonal behavior. *Psychological Bulletin*, *84*, 74-88.

Young, E.R., & Parish, T.S. (1977). Impact of father absence during childhood on the psychological adjustment of college families. *Sex Roles*, *3*, 217-227.

DETERMINANTS
OF CHILDREN'S
ADJUSTMENT TO DIVORCE

Parental and Environmental Determinants of Children's Behavioral, Affective and Cognitive Adjustment to Divorce

Patricia E. Walsh
Arnold L. Stolberg

SUMMARY. Children's adjustment to their parents' divorce was studied in relationship to interspousal hostility, single parenting skills, child-reported good and bad environmental events and time since separation using a sample of 23 boys and 16 girls between 6 and 11 years of age. Families were recruited through newspaper ads, schools and other community organizations. Their middle income parents were separated for between 5 and 60 months, were divorced and were not remarried. Adjustment was broadly defined to include the child's beliefs about divorce, parent-reported behavioral adjustment and child-reported emotional labeling/reactivity. All four independent variables were found to be significantly correlated with adjustment. The potency of hostility and bad events changed over time since separation. Single parenting skills remained associated with child outcome for families across the time period tapped. Some sex differences in the effects of good events emerged.

A multidimensional definition of children's post-divorce adjustment is suggested by children's display of maladaptation in the cognitive, behavioral and affective domains (Hetherington, Cox and

---

Patricia E. Walsh, MS, was a graduate student and Arnold L. Stolberg, PhD, is on the faculty of the Department of Psychology, Virginia Commonwealth University, Box 2018, Richmond, VA 23284.

This project was a Master's of Science thesis completed by the first author under the supervision of the second author.

Cox, 1978; Wallerstein and Kelly, 1980; Kurdek, 1981; Stolberg and Bush, 1985). Undeserved self-blame and inaccurate perceptions of rejection exemplify maladaptive cognitive responses (Neal, 1983; Wallerstein and Kelly, 1980; Young, 1983). Aggression, diminished social skills, academic failure and regressive behavior are some of the maladaptive behavioral responses (Guidubaldi, Perry and Cleminshaw, 1983; Stolberg and Bush, 1985; Wallerstein and Kelly, 1980). Children's affective and cognitive responses include anger, feelings of loss, fear of exposure, and lowered self-esteem (Stolberg and Anker, 1983; Wallerstein and Kelly, 1980).

Individual, parental/familial and environmental variables have been found to predict adjustment in the described domains (Stolberg and Bush, 1985). These spheres of influence must be considered together in order to avoid misconceptions about the importance (or unimportance) of any one predictor (Kurdek, 1981; Stolberg and Bush, 1985). For example, if only sex of child is studied without sex of the custodial parent, researchers may come to believe boys are more prone to adjustment problems subsequent to divorce. Studies using boys in both mother and father custody suggest that the sex match with custodian may be more important (Warshak and Santrock, 1983). Important interactions may also be missed. For example, environmental events that have high demands for child self-control may be more problematic for younger children.

Individual factors found to be related to divorce in studies tapping one dimension include age and sex of child (Hetherington, 1979; Wallerstein and Kelly, 1980), interpersonal understanding and locus of control (Kurdek, Blisk and Siesky, 1981). Specifically, younger children have been found to show more behavioral problems and more misunderstanding of divorce, presumably due to lower levels of interpersonal understanding. Boys, particularly those in mother custody, have been found to be more aggressive and to copy fathers' hostile conflict resolution techniques (Emery, 1982). Boys may also show more fear of abandonment and be more likely to place blame (Kurdek and Berg, 1983).

Divorce-related parental/familial factors include hostility between parents (Emery, 1982; Stolberg and Bush, 1985; Wallerstein and Kelly, 1980), parent adjustment (Hetherington, 1979), single parenting skills (Stolberg and Bush, 1985; Wallerstein and Kelly, 1980), same sex versus opposite sex custody and contact with the non-custodial parent (Warshak and Santrock, 1983). Children who observe high levels of interspousal hostility show social, emotional and behavioral problems, including lower levels of pro-social behavior, more aggressive behavior, more internalized behavior pathology and more fear (Emery, 1982; Stolberg and Bush, 1985). Higher levels of single parenting skills, including cooperation between parents, have been associated with more pro-social behavior and less internalized pathology (Stolberg and Bush, 1985). These parental/familial variables are conceptualized as being interrelated. For example, parenting competence may be negatively influenced by intraspousal hostility (Hetherington, 1979).

Changes in both the child's and custodian's lives comprise environmental influences on child adjustment and have been associated with depression, hostility, anxiety, behavior pathology and poor self-esteem (Sandler, Wolchik and Braver, 1984; Stolberg and Anker, 1983; Stolberg and Bush, 1985). Excessive life change may make demands for rapid acquisition of new skills leading to frustration and may be associated with reduced support from the environment.

Divorce must be viewed as a sequence of stages and not as a life event whose characteristics are constant over time (Stolberg, Kiluk and Garrison, 1986). Time since separation has been found to be a mediator of children's outcome in the studies that have attempted to measure its adjustive role (Guidubaldi, Perry, Cleminshaw and McLaughlin, 1983; Wallerstein and Kelly, 1980). Children show substantial improvement in their adjustment after two years of separation (Hetherington, 1979). An initial drop in parenting skills and a high rate of environmental change have been postulated to contribute to the initial adjustment difficulties (Hetherington, 1979; Kurdek, Blisk and Siesky, 1981).

The great variety of influences on adjustment suggests that divorce is a dynamic, multifaceted phenomenon whose effects vary over time (Stolberg, Kiluk and Garrison, 1986). A concurrent investigation of influencers from more than one adjustment sphere, rather than the more commonly chosen methodologies that tap only one domain, may shed more accurate light on the adjustment process. Therefore, this study was undertaken to examine the effects of parental and environmental variables on adjustment. Furthermore, adjustment was more broadly construed to include cognitive, behavioral and affective elements. The relationships of the adjustment variables and the predictor variables to time were investigated to learn more about how the adjustment process proceeds over time.

METHOD

Subjects

Subjects were 23 boys and 16 girls whose natural parents were divorced and not remarried. Family income ranged from $12,000 to $53,000 with a mean of $27,000. Parents were separated an average of 37.5 months (range of 5 to 60 months). Twenty-eight were in mother custody; 3 were in father custody and 8 were in joint custody. Parents and children did not suffer from serious chronic illness or disability and parents had never been imprisoned.

Subjects were recruited through newspaper ads (9), newsletters to Parents Without Partners (3), daycare centers (6), a local parochial school (6) and from other sources (faculty, other subjects, churches) (7). Eight additional subjects were recruited by offering support groups for children at the end of the research study in exchange for participation.

Subjects and their families were assessed to be within normal limits on standardized measures of single parenting skills (Single Parenting Questionnaire) and affect (Affect Questionnaire). Parents reported less hostility than subjects in other studies (Stolberg and Bush, 1985). The mean parent reported child behavior problem score was one standard deviation above the standardization sample mean on the Child behavior Checklist (Achenbach and Edelbrock, 1979). This latter result may be reflective of divorce-related processes and not a poorly distributed sample (see Table 1).

TABLE 1. Means, Standard Deviations and Ranges of Covariate, Dependent and Independent Variables

	Mean	Standard Deviation	Minimum	Maximum
Covariate				
Age	7.6	1.6	6.0	11.0
Dependent Variables				
Myths About Divorce	1.9	1.9	0.0	6.0
Affect Questionnaire				
Happy	136.4	35.1	95.0	310.0
Angry	118.5	46.1	60.0	300.0
Fearful	88.6	34.4	10.0	165.0
Child Behavior Checklist				
Internalizing	64.0	11.3	40.0	81.0
Externalizing	61.8	11.9	41.0	85.0
Independent Variables				
Single Parenting				
Questionnaire	53.3	4.3	41.7	60.0
O'Leary Porter Scale of				
Overt Hostility	9.8	6.4	3.0	32.0
Divorce Events Schedule				
Good Events	16.7	4.8	7.0	26.0
Bad Events	5.5	3.0	1.0	13.0

Instruments and Variables

Divorce Study Questionnaire

The Divorce Study Questionnaire, specifically designed for this study, contains items in three areas; (1) demographic data, (2) exclusion criteria (e.g. "Have you, your child or your child's other parent: had any serious/chronic physical illness?"), and (3) contact with the nonresidential parent. Only the demographic and exclusion criteria information were used in this study.

O'Leary-Porter Scale of Overt Marital Hostility (OPS) (Porter and O'Leary, 1980)

The OPS is a 20-item inventory from which 10 embedded items are scored. The scored items ask how often different expressions of hostility (quarrels, physical abuse) occurred in the presence of the child in question (e.g., "How often do you and your former spouse display hostility in front of *this* child? never, rarely, occasionally, often, very often"). Test-retest reliability was .96 over two weeks, on a sample of 14 families. Correlation with the Short Marital Adjustment Test was .63 (Locke and Wallace, 1959). The OPS was used to measure the current level of overt hostility between former spouses.

Single Parenting Questionnaire (SPQ)

The SPQ consists of 88 items designed to assess dimensions of single parenting (e.g., "How often does your child come and talk to you about a problem?") (Stolberg and Ullman, 1985). Parents rate items on a four-point frequency of occurrence scale which is randomly keyed from least to most or most to least. Dimensions assessed include parental warmth, discipline/control, support systems and enthusiasm for parenting. Test-retest reliability over a two-week period ranged from .40 to .67 for 234 subjects, (Stolberg and Ullman, 1985). Inter-rater reliability, was significant at the $p < .05$ level for the Total score. Validity was demonstrated by significant correlations between SPQ scales and Fisher Divorce Adjustment Scale scores ($r = .44$, $p < .05$ for the Total score). In a previous study on a divorced sample, all pro-social behavior scales of the Achenbach Child Behavior Checklist were associated with all SPQ scales (Stolberg and Bush, 1985). The Total score was used in the current study.

Divorce Events Schedule-Children (DES-C)

The DES-C (Sandler, Wolchik, Braver and Fogan, 1985) assesses the occurrence of and subjective evaluation of events commonly found in the lives of children of divorce. The child indicates whether the events occurred "more often," "less often" or "as often as usual" during the last three months (e.g., "Mom is strict," "You move to a new house," "Dad does things that need to get done for you [like make lunch]"). The event is rated as good, bad or neutral. The degree of "goodness" or "badness" is rated on a one to seven scale. Test-retest reliabilities for total numbers of positive and negative events were .77 and .87, respectively over a two-week period. For the current study, standard procedures were changed to require rating the occurrence of an event during the last two years rather than during the last three months. Weighted scores were used to measure Total Good Events and Total Bad Events.

Child Behavior Checklist-Parent Report (CBCL-P) (Achenbach, 1978)

The CBCL contains 118 items (e.g., "Confused," "In a fog," "Cries a lot") which the parent rates on a three-point scale (less than average to more than average or not true to often true) or lists the requested information. The behavior checklist yields normed scores on nine behavior problem scales, two overall pathology factors (Internalizing, Externalizing) and three social competence scales. Higher scores are keyed to higher frequencies of occurrence and represent either greater pro-social skills or greater maladaptation (Achenbach, 1978). Test-retest reliability averaged between .82 for boys and .88 for girls between 6 and 11 for mother report over a two-week period ($p < .001$). Inter-parent reliability for all scales averaged .79 for boys and .63 for girls aged 6 to 11 ($p > .01$) (Achenbach and Edelbrock, 1979). All narrow band scales, Internalizing and Externalizing pathology scales and the three positive social behavior scales have been shown to distinguish disturbed boys from normals at the statistically significant level ($p < .01$) (Achenbach, 1978). Only the Internalizing and Externalizing dimensions were used in this study.

Myths About Divorce (MAD)

The Myths About Divorce Scale (Warren, 1985) is a 15-item forced-choice questionnaire that asks children to indicate their perceptions about divorce-related conditions in the family (e.g., "Some kids think they can love both parents at the same time" or "Some kids think they can't love both parents anymore"). Each item is presented as a pair of sentences with an accompanying stick figure drawing. The Total score indicates the number of maladaptive cognitions endorsed.

Affect Questionnaire (AQ)

The AQ is a 53-item instrument for measuring children's self-reported affect in specified, emotional, non-divorce situations (Garrison and Stolberg, 1982). The child is asked to distribute ten tokens among "happy," "sad," "angry," and "scared" in response to a short story (e.g., "You are playing ball and running. One of the players on the other team trips you"). The score for each emotion is the total number of tokens for that emotion. Only the happy, anger and fear scores were used in this study. Emotionally disturbed boys scored significantly higher than normal boys on the Anger scale (F $(1,27) = 12.490, p < .01$) and significantly lower on sadness (F $(1,27) = 10.41, p < .01$). Test-retest reliability was high (in the .90s for anger, happiness and sadness and moderate (in the 80s) for fear.

Procedure

Parents who agreed to participate in the study were given a package of questionnaires to complete either before they came with their child for the child interview or while they were waiting for their child during the interview. Families who participated in the support

groups as compensation were required to complete the questionnaires before the groups began. The researcher assisted the children
in completing the child report scales.

RESULTS

Data were analyzed in two steps. The relationships among independent variables were analyzed by means of a Pearson Product
Moment Correlation Matrix. As expected, longer time since separa-
tion was associated with lower intraspousal hostility (OPS) ($r = -.34, p < .05$) and lower child-reported rates of good events ($r = -.42, p < .01$). Lower levels of hostility were also associated
with higher levels of parenting skills ($r = .29, p < .05$). Good
events and hostility were positively correlated ($r = .31, p < .05$)
but were not significantly related with variance due to time since
separation removed.

Next, the relationship among independent and dependent variables was examined by means of hierarchical multiple regression
equations. For each of the six dependent variables (MAD, happy,
angry, fearful, and parent-reported internalizing and externalizing
behavior pathology), separate multiple regression equations were
generated for each parent variable (hostility, parenting skills) and
each environmental variable (child-reported good and bad events).
The co-variates, sex and age, were forced into the equations in the
first step. The parent or environmental variable was entered in the
second step. Months since separation was forced into the equation
in the third step. In the fourth step of each equation, the interaction
of time since separation by the parental or environmental variable
was tested at the .05 criterion for entry. Thus, for each dependent
variable, four multiple regression equations were generated, one for
each independent variable.

Statistically significant interactions of the parent or environmental variable by time since separation were further investigated by
plotting the mean value of the dependent variable at nine different
points. The points chosen were the mean value, plus one standard
deviation, and minus one standard deviation for the parent or environmental variable paired with the mean time since separation (37.5
months), plus one standard deviation (53.5 months) and minus one

standard deviation (23.5 months). Standardized beta weights from the multiple regression equations were used to calculate standardized values of the dependent variable. These standardized values were converted into raw scores and are given in Tables 2 and 3. For each independent variable that interacted with the sex of the child, six data points were calculated. These points represent the values of the dependent variable at the mean value, plus one and minus one standard deviation of the parent or environmental variable for boys and for girls. These values are given in Table 4.

Hostility

Hostility, with variance due to age and sex removed, accounted for 10% of the variance in parent reported externalized behavior pathology (Fc (3,32) = 4.36, $p < .01$) with high hostility associated with high internalized behavior. A significant interaction between hostility and months since separation was found for parent-reported internalized behavior and child-reported anger (Fc (5,30) = 5.97, $p < .05$; Fc (5,29) = 4.48, $p < .05$, respectively). Plotting mean behavior scores by hostility separately for recent, intermediate and distant separation (21.5, 37.5 and 53.5 months, respectively) suggested that increased hostility was related to higher levels of parent-reported externalized behavior for children of recently separated parents, only. (See Table 2.)

A significant parent hostility by months since separation interaction was found for child-reported anger (Fc (5,29) = 4.48, $p < .05$). Greater hostility was associated with increased child-reported anger at recent separation. The reverse relationship was found at distant separation, with greater hostility being associated with lower child-reported anger. (See Table 2.)

Parenting Skills

Parenting skills accounted for 21% of the variance in parent-reported externalized behavior pathology (Fc (3,33) = 10.97, $p < .005$) and 17% of the variance in parent-reported internalized pathology (Fc (3,33) = 8.75, $p < .005$), both above and beyond variance due to age and sex. Parenting skills also accounted for by sex and age (Fc (3,32) = 4.1, $p < .05$). All three of these relationships were in the positive direction.

TABLE 2. Predicted Values of Dependent Variables with Significant Time Since Separation by Hostility Interactions

| | Time Since Separation | | |
| | Recent | Intermediate | Distant |
	21.5 months	37.5 months	53.3 months
Independent Variable	Dependent Variable		
Hostility	Externalizing Behavior		
3.4	48.4	61.3	58.8
9.9	58.8	58.9	60.1
16.4	70.1	58.1	60.1
Hostility	Anger		
3.4	95.9	109.3	120.8
9.9	117.6	110.7	101.1
16.4	137.2	111.6	83.9

Note. Predicted values were derived from regression equation beta weights and converted to raw scores

Environmental Events

Good Events

Good events had no significant direct effects but interacted with sex of child to influence parent-reported externalizing and internalizing behavior pathology and fear (Fc (5,29) = 26.36, p < .001; Fc (5,29) = 5.84, p < .05; Fc (5,29) = 5.91, p < .05, respectively). For the two behavior pathology measures, higher levels of good events related to lower level of behavior pathology for boys. Girls, however, show the opposite relationship. Higher levels of

TABLE 3. Predicted Values of Myths About Divorce at Three Levels of Bad Events and Time Since Separation

| | Time Since Separation | | |
| | Recent | Intermediate | Distant |
	21.5 months	37.5 months	53.3 months
Independent Variable	Dependent Variable		
Bad Events	Myths About Divorce		
2.5	1.9	1.9	2.4
5.5	1.0	2.0	2.4
8.5	0.1	1.5	7.3

Note. Predicted values were derived from regression equation beta weights and converted to raw scores.

good events were associated with higher levels of behavior pathology. Good events was positively related to fear for boys and negatively related to fear for girls. Boys and girls showed no difference in fear at high levels of good events.

Bad Events

Bad events accounted for 19% of unique variance for child-reported anger (Fc $(3,31)$ = 3.98, $p < .05$). Bad events and anger were positively related. Bad events interacted with months since separation to predict myths about divorce (MAD) (Fc $(5,29)$ = 5.95, $p < .05$). For children of recently divorced parents, higher levels of bad events appeared to be associated with fewer misconceptions about divorce. At a moderate length of separation, cognitions about divorce appeared to be unrelated to bad events. At more distant separation a sharp increase in MAD occurred between the intermediate and high level of bad events producing the highest level of MAD across all conditions. At low levels of bad events,

TABLE 4. Predicted Values of Dependent Variables for Good Events by Sex Interactions Derived from Regression Equations

Independent Variable	Boys	Girls
	Dependent Variables	
Good Events	Externalizing Pathology	
11.9	62.8	49.7
16.7	47.6	62.5
21.5	38.0	75.5
	Internalizing Pathology	
11.9	56.0	58.8
16.7	51.0	62.8
21.5	47.0	74.0
	Fear	
11.9	68.0	110.3
16.7	91.4	98.3
21.5	105.2	92.2

there appeared to be no difference in level of MAD across the three separation groups.

Time Since Separation

Months since separation interacted with individual, parental and environmental variables in the prediction of some cognitive, affective and behavioral dependent variables. These effects have been described under the headings for each dependent variable and are summarized in Tables 2 and 3.

DISCUSSION

The importance of examining predictor variables from both the parental and environmental spheres is supported by the number of significant relationships found. The interactions between both parental and environmental variables and time since separation adds further to our understanding of the divorce adjustment process. It appears that some variables such as single parenting skills are potent predictors of adjustment across all five years of separation studied. Other variables such as hostility showed direct effects that varied with time.

Hostility decreased at longer separation. Parents may have had less to fight about and may have buried the hatchet on issues left from the marriage. This may, however, represent a sample bias, with parents still experiencing high hostility several years after separation being too drained to participate in a research study. The inverse relationship between hostility and parenting skills may occur because hostility interferes in co-parenting. There will likely be fewer parenting discussions that lead to an agreed upon course of action. Parents may even sabotage each other's efforts. Previous studies have found that parents whose intraspousal hostility reaches the level of physical abuse are also likely to abuse their children (Pagelow, 1984). Less "abusive" intraspousal hostility may also be related to hostility directed towards the child. Thus, the positive relationship between intraspousal hostility and child pathology may be partly mediated by hostility towards the child.

The effect of hostility on parent-reported externalizing behavior is consistent with the literature on more recently separated families (Emery, 1982; Stolberg and Bush, 1985). Even at 5 years post-separation, children witnessing high intraspousal hostility model that aggressive behavior. Hostility doesn't affect internalizing behavior until distant separation. After several years of this hostility, children become anxious, depressed and withdrawn. Children may have given up the hope that home life will improve. Internalization may be a response to the ineffectiveness of externalizing behavior as a long-term strategy for distracting parents from their own disagreements.

The relationship of hostility to child-reported anger may shed some light on the relationship of hostility to behavior. At recent separation, children responded to more situations with more anger when they themselves have witnessed more interparent hostility. The decrease in child-reported anger at higher levels of hostility for children at distant separation suggests that they may be denying or repressing anger. The higher internalized behavior scores may be a reflection of this unexpressed anger. Children gave more angry responses at low levels of hostility, possibly because they felt more free to express anger.

These results taken together suggest that "burying the hatchet" is not only necessary for current adjustment but for the future as well. With low hostility, children at distant separation showed lower internalized pathology scores compared to their counterparts at recent separation. Continued low hostility may allow children to recover from the effects of divorce.

Higher rates of bad events are related to more child-reported anger (Sandler, Wolchik and Braver, 1984). However, at recent separation, experiencing some bad events was, in this study, related to a better understanding of divorce. Children who see their parents disagree about issues such as money or see mom cry more may have evidence that divorce is between parents and about parents. By distant separation, high "bad events" has the opposite relationship to understanding divorce. Many bad events at several years post separation suggests that the family is having difficulty achieving environmental stability. Parents in such an unstable environment may actually have less time for the child. In fact, some of the maladaptive cognitions endorsed may reflect accurate, though painful, observations. When the separation occurred years before the bad event, it may be more difficult for the child to associate the two. Without this association available to the child, it may be very easy for the child to take bad events as evidence that they are unloved or unimportant.

The interaction of good events by sex of child in the prediction of both behavior variables and fear was initially confusing. On the two behavioral measures, girls, but not boys, responded in a counterintuitive direction to good events. Because the instrument used (the CBCL) was factored and normed separately for boys and girls, it can't be assumed that a particular score indicates the same level of pathology for boys and girls. Nevertheless, the direction of effects suggests that girls may be better behaved with fewer good events. It is possible that maturity demands are higher for girls when the environment is less favorable. Girls may feel free to act out more under better environmental conditions. While boys may have fewer behavior problems when there are more good events, they reported more fear. Perhaps boys are more free to express fear under good conditions. They don't have to "be strong for mom."

Events tapped in this study are related to mother, father, school and peers, among other things. Differences in the impact of events in one particular category may help explain gender differences in effects of overall good events. For example, contact with the non-custodial parent may be more important for the positive adjustment of boys than girls both in mother custody (Santrock and Warshak, 1983). Because most of the children in this study lived with their mothers, differences in the impact of overall good events may reflect differences in sensitivity to activities with the father. While girls said they liked visiting their fathers, something about these visits may have affected mothers' ratings of behavior pathology. For example, girls who learn to play rougher may be viewed as more problematic.

The importance of parental (hostility, parenting skills) and environmental (good and bad events) variables in promoting children's behavioral, affective and cognitive adjustment is reinforced by this study. Perhaps more importantly, some of these effects were different for children at different times since separation. However, this was not a longitudinal study and did not use pre-divorce data for comparison. Therefore, causal inferences are weak at best. One of the most important outcomes of this study may be the demonstration of the need for a prospective study investigating changes in the potency of parental and environmental variables as time since separation increases.

Prevention efforts directed at reducing parental hostility and increasing parenting skills may be effective in increasing behavioral, affective and cognitive adjustment of children. It may also be advisable to allow the child to experience some of the realities of divorce in order to bolster his or her understanding of divorce (reducing self-blame, etc.). However, environmental stability needs to be achieved in order to prevent future behavior problems. This suggests preventive programming designed to occur even as the parents make the decision to separate.

REFERENCES

Achenbach, T. (1978). The child behavior profile: I. Boys aged 6-11. *Journal of Consulting and Clinical Psychology, 46* 478-488.

Achenbach, T., and Edelbrock, C. (1979). The child behavior profile: II. Boys aged 12-16 and girls age 6-11 and 12-16. *Journal of Consulting and Clinical Psychology, 47*, 223-233.

Emery, R.E. (1982). Interpersonal conflict and the children of discord and divorce. *Psychological Bulletin, 92*, 310-330.

Garrison, S.R., and Stolberg, A.L. (1982). Modification of anger in children by affective imagery training. *Journal of Abnormal Child Psychology, 11*, 115-129.

Guidubaldi, J., Perry, J., Cleminshaw, H.K., and McLaughlin, K. (1983). The legacy of parental divorce: A nationwide study of family status and selected mediating variables on children's academic and social competences. *School Psychology Review, 12*, 300-323.

Hetherington, E.M. (1979). Divorce: A child's perspective. *American Psychologist, 34*, 851-858.

Hetherington, E. M., Cox, M., and Cox, R. (1978). The aftermath of divorce. In J.H. Stevens, Jr., and M. Mathews (Eds.), *Mother-child, father-child relations* (pp. 149-176). Washington, D.C.: National Association for the Education of Young Children.

Kurdek, L. (1981). An integrative perspective on children's divorce adjustment. *American Psychologist, 35*, 856-866.

Kurdek, L., and Berg, B. (1983). Correlates of children's adjustment to their parents' divorce. In L. Kurdek (Ed.), *New directions in child development: Children and divorce* (pp. 47-60). San Francisco: Jossey-Bass.

Kurdek, L., Blisk, D., and Siesky, A.E. (1981). Correlates of children's adjustment to their parents' divorce. *Developmental Psychology, 17*, 565-579.

Neal, J.H. (1983). Children's understanding of their parents' divorce. In L.A. Kurdek (Ed.), *New directions for child development: Children and divorce* (pp. 3-14). San Francisco: Jossey-Bass.

Pagelow, M.D. (1984). *Family violence.* New York: Prager Press.

Porter, B., and O'Leary, K.D. (1980). Marital discord and childhood behavior. *Journal of Abnormal Child Psychology, 8*, 287-295.

Sandler, I.N., Wolchik, S.A., and Braver, S.L. (1984). The *effects of divorce events and changes on child maladaptation.* Unpublished manuscript, Arizona State University.

Sandler, I.N., Wolchik, S.A., Braver, S.L., and Fogan, S.B. (1986). Significant events of children of divorce: Towards the assessment of risky situations. In S.M. Auerbach and A.L. Stolberg (Eds.), *Issues in clinical and community psychology: Crisis intervention with children and families.* Washington, D.C.: Hemisphere.

Stolberg, A.L., and Anker, J.M. (1983). Cognitive and behavioral changes in children resulting from parental divorce and consequent environmental changes. *Journal of Divorce, 7*, 23-41.

Stolberg, A.L., and Bush, J.P. (1985). A path analysis of factors predicting children's divorce adjustment. *Journal of Clinical Child Psychology, 14*, 49-54.

Stolberg, A.L., Kiluk, D., and Garrison, K.M. (1986). A temporal model of divorce adjustment with implications for primary prevention. In S.M. Auerbach and A.L. Stolberg (Eds.), *Issues in clinical and community psychology: Crisis intervention with children and families.* Washington D.C.: Hemisphere.

Stolberg, A.L., and Ullman, A.J. (1985). Assessing dimensions of single parenting: The Single Parenting Questionnaire. *Journal of Divorce, 8*, 31-45.

Wallerstein, J.S., and Kelly, J.B. (1980). *Surviving the break-up: How children and parents cope with divorce.* New York: Basic Books.

Warren, N. (1985). personal communication.

Warshak, R., and Santrock, J. (1983). The impact of divorce in mother custody and father custody homes: The child's perspective. In L. Kurdek (Ed.), *New directions in child development: Children and divorce* (pp. 29-46). San Francisco: Jossey-Bass.

Young, D.M. (1983). Two studies of children of divorce. In L.A. Kurdek (Ed.), *New directions for child development: Children and divorce* (pp. 61-70). San Francisco: Jossey-Bass.

The Impact of Divorce on Children's Academic Performance

Steven H. Kaye

SUMMARY. The academic performance of children of divorce was studied through a retrospective longitudinal design. The school records of 234 children of divorce and 223 children from intact families were examined and grades and achievement test scores in English and mathematics were recorded for five consecutive years. The results showed that children of divorce had poorer achievement test scores in the immediate aftermath of divorce. Their grades, on the other hand, did not seem to be adversely affected. By the fifth year following divorce, sex differences were pronounced with divorce adversely affecting the grades and achievement test scores of boys but not girls. The results were discussed in terms of their implications for research on divorce and academic performance as well as research on divorce and children in general.

Each year approximately 1.1 million children in the United States are added to the rolls of those touched by divorce. Based on the trends in the divorce rate between 1960 and 1978, Glick (1979) predicts that by 1990, 11 percent of all children will be living with a divorced parent and 32 percent of all children will have experienced a divorce. The large numbers of children experiencing a divorce has

Steven H. Kaye, PhD, is on the staff of the Counseling Service, Office of Student Services, University of Texas Health Science Center at San Antonio, TX 78284.

The author wishes to thank the Northside Independent School District for their cooperation with this research project. He also wishes to thank Michael Hogan for his help with the data analysis, David Schneider and George Bishop for their thoughtful comments, and Jaqui Freund, Laura Hudson, Anita Mancini, and Mary Osborne for their help in collecting the data. The research was supported in part by a faculty research grant from the University of Texas at San Antonio.

not gone unnoticed by social scientists and there has been increasing attention devoted to the impact of divorce on children's social, emotional, and intellectual development (e.g., Hess & Camara, 1979; Hetherington, Cox, & Cox, 1982; Wallerstein & Kelly, 1980). The present study examines the impact of divorce on one aspect of children's functioning, namely, academic performance.

The impact of divorce on children's academic performance has been examined in a number of studies (see Hetherington, Camara, & Featherman, 1983; Shinn, 1978 for comprehensive reviews of this literature). The results of this research suggest that divorce adversely affects children's grades and achievement test scores. For example, Blanchard and Biller (1971) found that father-absent third grade boys had lower Stanford Achievement Test scores and grades than father-present boys with highly available fathers. Santrock (1972) found that early father absence (0 to 2 years) due to divorce, separation, or desertion, had a negative effect for both sexes on Stanford Achievement Test scores. The Institute for Development of Educational Activities (1980) examined the school records of 18,000 students and concluded that one-parent children had lower academic achievement than their two-parent peers. The results of previous research on divorce and academic performance also suggest that divorce more adversely affects the academic performance of boys and more adversely affects quantitative as opposed to verbal skills (Hetherington, Camara, & Featherman, 1983; Shinn, 1978).

Although the impact of divorce on children's academic performance has received considerable attention, there has been a neglect of a number of important issues. One such issue, the onset issue, concerns the relationship between divorce and the first detectable change in children's academic performance. When is the impact of divorce on children's academic performance first seen? A second and related issue, the duration issue, concerns the length of time divorce affects children's academic performance. How long does divorce affect the academic performance of children? A third issue which has been neglected is the relationship between academic performance and the child's age at the time of the divorce. Are children of certain ages more vulnerable to the impact of divorce on academic performance? In addition to these three issues, the impact of divorce on the academic performance of boys versus girls and the impact of divorce on particular school subjects merit attention. The present study examined these five issues, making the following hypotheses:

1. Children of divorce will begin to show poorer academic performance in the immediate aftermath of divorce (in the first year following divorce). The rationale behind this hypothesis is that divorce is a disorganizing event which sets in motion a number of changes, for example, new relationships with each parent (Hetherington, Cox, & Cox, 1982; Wallerstein & Kelly, 1980). Children are likely to be preoccupied by these changes and to have problems concentrating at school and completing school assignments (Hess & Camara, 1979; Wallerstein & Kelly, 1980). The net result will be poorer academic performance. In addition, in the immediate aftermath of divorce, the custodial parent may have less time to help children with their homework or attend school-related functions. This may result in a decreased emphasis on school-related performance and poorer academic performance (Hetherington, Camara, & Featherman, 1983).

2. The poorer academic performance of children of divorce will extend for two to three years. After this time there will be no differences in the academic performance of children from divorced and intact families. The rationale behind this hypothesis is that the family system reorganizes and restabilizes itself following divorce. This process of establishing a new equilibrium is often difficult and extends for several years (Hetherington, Cox, & Cox, 1982; Wallerstein & Kelly, 1977). However, once a re-equilibrium is established, children of divorce will not differ in their academic performance from children from intact families.

3. The younger the child, the more likely divorce will adversely affect academic performance. This hypothesis rests on several bases. First, as children become older their understanding of interpersonal relationships increases (Shantz, 1983) and level of interpersonal reasoning has been shown to be positively related to children's adjustment to divorce (Kurdek, Blisk, & Siesky, 1981; Kurdek & Siesky, 1980). Second, older children are more likely to have a wider array of coping strategies and to use them more flexibly (Murphy & Moriarty, 1976; Kelly & Wallerstein, 1977). Third, older children are more likely to have social networks involving the

peer group and the school which can moderate the adverse effects of divorce. Finally, younger children, particularly early elementary-school-age children are being initiated into the social and intellectual world of the school. Consequently, they may be most vulnerable to the impact of divorce on academic performance.

4. Divorce will adversely affect the academic performance of boys more than girls. This hypothesis derives from research showing a positive relationship between father-son identification and intellectual development (see Radin, 1981 for a review of this literature). Since 90 percent of children of divorce live with their mothers (Glick, 1979), divorce is likely to adversely affect father-son identification which, in turn, is likely to adversely affect the son's academic performance.

5. Children of divorce will show poorer quantitative skills than children from intact families. This hypothesis is based on the rationale that divorce creates anxiety and interferes with concentration and persistence. Anxiety and difficulties in concentration and persistence, in turn, are considered to adversely affect quantitative performance (Hetherington, Cox, & Cox, 1982; Nelson & Maccoby, 1966). The impact of divorce on verbal skills is less clear but verbal skills may be enhanced, presumably from greater exposure to the mother's more verbal cognitive style (Hetherington, Camara, & Featherman, 1983).

METHOD

Subjects

Four hundred and fifty-seven children, 234 from divorced families and 223 from intact families were the subjects of the present study. The children were divided into three age levels based on age at the time of divorce. The three age levels were 6 and 7, 8 and 9, and 10, 11, and 12 years of age. Within each age level and each family type there were roughly equal numbers of boys and girls and equal numbers of Hispanic and Anglo children. Hispanic children were included in the study because Hispanics constitute 54% of the population of the city in which the research was conducted (Bureau of the Census, 1983). Table 1 presents the number of children from di-

Table 1

Characteristics of Sample

	Family Type		
	Divorced (n = 234)		Intact (n = 223)
Group	n		n
Sex			
Boys	121		113
Girls	113		110
Ethnicity			
Anglo	129		124
Hispanic	105		99
Age			
6 and 7 years	69 M = 7.04 SD = 0.57		61 M = 7.07 SD = 0.58
8 and 9 years	77 M = 8.95 SD = 0.54		77 M = 8.94 SD = 0.55
10, 11, and 12 years	88 M = 11.21 SD = 0.88		85 M = 11.29 SD = 0.92

vorced and intact families in terms of sex, ethnicity, and age. All children in the study attended schools in the same school district and all children from divorced families were in the custody of their mothers. No siblings were included in the study.

Children of divorce were identified through a search at the county courthouse of all civil cases between January 1, 1977 and May 31, 1979. This search through 60,000 pages of court documents produced a pool of approximately 3,000 children of divorce. A roster of all children in this school district in which the research was conducted was then examined to see which children were on both lists. Those children on both lists (approximately 15% of the original pool) formed the sample of children of divorce in the present study.

The sample of children from intact families was selected from class rosters. These children were matched on age (within a month for the great majority), sex, and ethnicity with children from divorced families. To minimize the variability attributable to socio-economic status (SES), the matched pair of children attended the same school. Court and school records were subsequently examined as a way of checking that children considered to be from intact families were indeed from intact families. If court or school records showed that the child had experienced a divorce, the child was dropped from the sample of children from intact families and a replacement was found. Since it was possible for a child to have experienced a divorce while living outside the county (court records are by county) and for the school to have no record of the divorce, a small but undetermined number of children were probably misidentified as children from intact families. As a result of this misidentification, differences between children from divorced and intact families are likely to be underestimated in the present study.

Information on the SES of the subjects' parents could not be obtained from school records and attempts to use census data to estimate SES proved unsuccessful. However, some information on the SES of the sample came from the number of children receiving free or reduced-cost lunches. In the 1979-80 school year 42% of children of divorce received free or reduced-cost lunches compared to 24% of children from intact families. This finding suggests that children of divorce grow up in less affluent surroundings than children from intact families, a finding consistent with Colletta's (1983) research showing economic stress to be a frequent concomitant of divorce. In the 1979-80 school year 46% of Hispanic children received free or reduced-cost lunches compared to 23% of Anglo children. This finding suggests that the Hispanic children in the sample came from families with lower incomes than did Anglo children.

Procedure

The basic procedure in the research was to examine school records and chart the grades and achievement test scores in English and mathematics of children from divorced and intact families. Achievement test scores from 1977-78 to 1980-81 came from the Science Research Associates achievement test series (1978). Achievement test scores from 1981-82 and 1982-83 came from the Iowa Tests of Basic Skills (1979). Grades and achievement test scores were charted for five consecutive years.

RESULTS

Analyses were conducted separately on children's grades and achievement test scores. Grades were converted into grade point averages (A = 4, B = 3, C = 2, D = 1, F = 0) and on the assumption that achievement test scores in the normative samples formed normal distributions, percentiles were converted into standard scores.

Grades

Two analyses of children's grades were performed, one looking at grades over five years and one looking at grades in the fifth year following divorce (for the first analysis, $n = 264$ with 134 children of divorce and 130 children from intact families; for the second analysis, $n = 405$ with 206 children of divorce and 199 children from intact families). The latter analysis was deemed necessary because a number of children had fifth year grades but did not have grades for five consecutive years. School records, unfortunately, were often incomplete.

Children's grades in the five-year period following divorce were analyzed through a repeated measures analysis of variance. The between-subject factors were age (6 and 7 years old, 8 and 9 years old, 10, 11 and 12 years old), sex, ethnicity (Anglo, Hispanic), and family type (divorced, intact). The within-subject factors were years (first, second, third, fourth, fifth) and subject matter (English, mathematics). As might be expected a number of significant main effects and interactions were found. In order to make the results more readable, only the main effects and interactions involving family type are described in detail. No attempt is made to analyze interactions which did not involve family type since these interactions are not relevant to the central purposes of the paper.

The analysis of grades in the five-year period following divorce showed significant main effects for family type, $F(1, 240) = 5.64$, $p < .05$, sex, $F(1, 240) = 22.84$, $p < .001$, ethnicity, $F(1, 240) = 7.00$, $p < .01$, age, $F(2, 240) = 24.72$, $p < .001$, subject matter, $F(1, 240) = 11.48$, $p < .01$, and years, $F(4, 960) = 42.41$, $p < .001$. Children from intact families had higher grades than children from divorced families (means of 2.83 vs. 2.54); girls had higher grades than boys (means of 2.91 vs. 2.44); Anglo children had higher grades than Hispanic children (means of 2.76 vs. 2.58); and younger children had higher grades than older children (means of 3.04, 2.91, and 2.34 for the 6- and 7-, 8- and 9-, and 10-, 11-, and 12 year olds respectively). In addition, grades in English were superior to grades in math (means of 2.72 vs. 2.64) and grades declined as the child spent more years in school (means of 3.00, 2.90, 2.66, 2.50, and 2.35 for the first, second, third, fourth, and fifth years).

Significant interactions were also found between year and family type, $F(4, 960) = 2.45$, $p < .05$, year and age, $F(8, 960) = 4.83$, $p < .001$, subject matter and sex, $F(1, 240) = 5.46$, $p < .05$, subject matter and age, $F(2, 240) = 3.14$, $p < .05$, and age, year, and subject matter, $F(8, 960) = 3.87$, $p < .001$. Figure 1 presents the year by family type interaction, the one interaction relevant to the hypotheses of the study. As can be seen from inspection of the figure, there is no support for the hypothesis that differences in grades appear in the immediate aftermath of divorce and not in later years. On the contrary there seems to be a fan-shaped pattern with differences in grades increasing over time.

A difference in grades between children from divorced and intact families was also seen in the analysis of variance of children's grades in the fifth year following divorce. This analysis showed significant main effects for family type, $F(1, 381) = 8.30$, $p < .01$, sex, $F(1, 381) = 19.17$, $p < .001$, ethnicity, $F(1, 381) =$

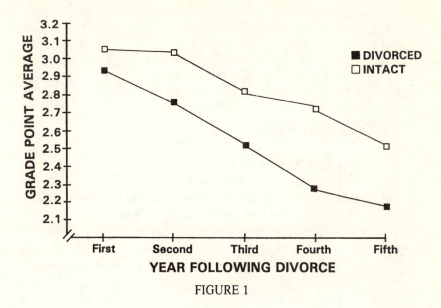

FIGURE 1

14.07, $p < .001$, and age, $F(2, 381) = 24.74, p < .001$. Children from intact families had higher grades than children from divorced families (means of 2.50 vs. 2.25). Thus, contrary to expectations, differences in grades between children from divorced and intact families were seen five years following divorce. In addition, girls had better grades than boys (means of 2.60 vs. 2.15); younger children had better grades than older children (means of 2.76, 2.47, and 1.98 for the 6- and 7-, 8- and 9-, and 10-, 11-, and 12-year olds respectively); and Anglo children had better grades than Hispanic children (means of 2.50 vs. 2.21).

Significant interactions were also found between family type and sex, $F(1, 381) = 5.48, p < .05$, sex and age, $F(2, 381) = 3.69, p < .05$, and subject matter and age, $F(2, 381) = 7.82, p < .001$. Once again, to aid readability, only the family type by sex interaction will be analyzed since it is the only interaction relevant to the hypotheses of the study. Analysis of the family type by sex interaction (Winer, 1971) showed that girls from divorced families had higher grades than boys from divorced families (means of 2.58 vs.

1.92) but girls from intact families did not differ in grades from boys from intact families (means of 2.62 vs. 2.39). This pattern of findings supports the hypothesis that divorce adversely affects the academic performance of boys more than girls. In fact, the grades of girls do not appear to be affected at all by divorce.

Achievement Test Scores

Analysis of children's achievement test scores was rendered difficult by a change from the Science Research Associates (SRA) to the Iowa Tests of Basic Skills (ITBS) series of achievement tests in 1981-82. Since it was considered unwise to treat scores from the two tests as equivalent, two analyses were performed. The first analysis (n = 238 with 116 children of divorce and 122 children from intact families) looked at the SRA total reading and total math subtest scores in the first two years following divorce. This analysis examined the impact of divorce on achievement test scores in the first years following divorce. The second analysis (n = 191 with 94 children of divorce and 97 children from intact families) looked at ITBS vocabulary, reading, and total math subtest scores in the fifth year following divorce. This analysis examined the longer term impact of divorce on achievement test scores. Both analyses used standard scores on the achievement tests as the dependent measure.

Children's achievement test scores in the first two years following divorce were analyzed through a repeated measures analysis of variance. The between-group gfactors were age, sex, ethnicity, and family type. The within-group factors were years and subject matter. The analysis showed significant main effects for family type, $F(1, 214) = 4.21, p < .05$, sex, $F(1, 214) = 7.70, p < .01$, ethnicity, $F(1, 214) = 27.04, p < .001$, and subject matter, $F(1, 214) = 14.38, p < .001$. Children from intact families had higher achievement test scores than children from divorced families (means of .39 vs. .20). This finding supports the hypothesis that divorce adversely affects the achievement test scores of children in the first years following divorce. In addition, girls had higher achievement test scores than boys (means of .42 vs. .18); Anglo children had higher achievement test scores than Hispanic children (means of .58 vs .04); and achievement test scores in reading were superior to achievement test scores in math (means of .39 vs. .22).

Significant interactions were also found between year and ethnicity, $F(1, 214) = 8.11, p < .01$, year, ethnicity, and sex, $F(1, 214) = 10.55, p < .01$, year, ethnicity, sex, and age, $F(2, 214) = 3.38$, $p < .05$, and year, sex, subject matter, family type, and age, $F(1, 214) = 4.64, p < .05$. The one interaction relevant to the hypotheses of the study (the year by sex by age by subject matter by family type interaction) was uninterpretable.

Analysis of achievement test scores in the fifth year following divorce showed significant main effects for age, $F(2, 167) = 4.16$, $p < .05$, ethnicity, $F(1, 167) = 7.83, p < .01$, and subject matter, $F(2, 334) = 3.85, p < .05$. Anglo children had higher achievement test scores than Hispanic children (means of .49 vs. .01); vocabulary scores were superior to reading scores which were superior to math scores (means of .31, .25, and .22 respectively); and 8- and 9-year olds were superior to 6-and 7-year olds who were superior to the 10-, 11-, and 12-year olds (means of .41 vs. .23 vs. .16).

Significant family type by sex, $F(1, 167) = 4.04, p < .05$, subject matter by sex, $F(2, 334) = 3.96 p < .05$, and family type by sex by age by ethnicity, $F(2, 167) = 3.79, p < .05$, interactions were also seen. Analysis of the family type by sex interaction showed that girls from divorced families had higher achievement test scores than boys from divorced families (means of .34 vs. .02) but boys from intact families had higher achievement test scores than girls from intact families (means of .50 vs. .17). This pattern of findings is similar to the family type by sex interaction in the analysis of fifth year grades. Both analyses support the hypothesis that divorce adversely affects the academic performance of boys more than girls. The family type by sex by age by ethnicity interaction was uninterpretable.

DISCUSSION

The findings of the present study indicate that the impact of divorce on children's academic performance depends upon the sex of the child, the number of years following the divorce, and the way in which academic performance is measured. In the immediate aftermath of divorce, boys and girls from divorced families show poorer performance on achievement tests than children from intact families. Their grades, on the other hand, do not seem to be adversely affected. In the fifth year following divorce, both the grades and achievement test scores of boys from divorced families seem to be adversely affected. In contrast, no adverse effects on grades and achievement test scores seem to appear for girls.

This patterning of results is complicated. Why should achievement test scores but not grades be affected for both sexes in the immediate aftermath of divorce? One possibility is that teachers give children extra help and support with their classroom assignments in the immediate aftermath of divorce. A second possibility is that teachers take into account the stress the child is under when assigning grades to children of divorce. It may also be that achievement tests, given only once a year for a period of several days, create greater anxiety in an already anxious child.

The striking sex differences in the fifth year following divorce may be mediated by the adverse effects on boys of the loss of a male model of problem solving and achievement. They may also be mediated by changes in boys' self-control. Following divorce, boys may be more disruptive in the classroom and consequently they may receive less support from teachers for academic difficulties and they may devote less time to mastering school work. The net result is poorer academic performance. Support for this explanation comes from research showing boys from divorced families to be more disruptive and aggressive in the classroom than boys from intact families (Felner, Stolberg, & Cowen, 1975; Felner, Ginter, Borke, & Cowen, 1981; Hetherington, Cox, & Cox, 1982). There is also evidence that boys from divorced families are less likely to complete school assignments and to be prepared and attentive in class (Hess & Camara, 1979; Hetherington, Cox, & Cox, 1982).

Divorce may have a differential impact on the academic performance of the sexes but it does not appear to differentially affect particular school subjects. It seems that anxiety and difficulties in concentration depress performance in the quantitative and verbal areas to an equal degree. Divorce also does not appear to deferentially affect the academic performance of children of different ages.

The hypothesis that divorce is more likely to adversely influence the academic performance of younger as opposed to older children received no support from the present study. On the contrary, younger children from both intact and divorced families had higher grades than older children. This superior performance is probably attributable to less variation in grades at the younger ages. Teachers seem to be less likely to give Ds and Fs to elementary school children.

The findings of the present study on divorce and ethnicity were consistent from analysis to analysis and somewhat surprising. Although there is evidence that the family life of Hispanic children differs from Anglo children (Alvirez & Bean, 1976), there was little evidence in the present study for differential effects of divorce on Anglo and Hispanic children. Divorce appeared to affect the academic performance of Anglo and Hispanic children in similar ways. The present study did find that Anglo children had superior grades and achievement test scores. However, it needs to be emphasized that ethnicity and SES were confounded in the present study and that the superior performance of the Anglo children in the present study is probably attributable to their higher SES. Future research on divorce and ethnicity needs to unconfound SES and ethnicity.

Implications for Future Research

The present study has a number of implications for research on divorce and children's academic performance and for research on divorce and children in general. With respect to research on divorce and children's academic performance, the present study highlights the necessity of considering both grades and achievement test scores and for looking at academic performance over time. In addition, the present research suggests that special attention be paid to the child's classroom behavior and work habits because disruptive behavior and poor work habits may have a pronounced impact on children's grades. These grades, may in turn, affect children's attitudes about schooling and their motivation to learn (Hetherington, Camara, & Featherman, 1983).

With respect to research on divorce and children in general, the present study suggests that a crisis model of divorce is only partially correct. While it is the case that the period following the divorce is a time of disequilibrium for the family (Hetherington, Cox, & Cox, 1982; Kelly & Wallerstein, 1977), the impact of divorce on children may continue once the family has achieved some type of equilibrium. Unresolved issues related to the divorce may accumulate over time and the impact of this "unfinished business" may not be seen until several years after the divorce. It therefore appears that a crisis model of divorce needs to be complemented by a cumulative stress model which focuses on the problems which persist or gradually increase following a divorce, for example, the decreased availability of the father (Hetherington, Cox, & Cox, 1982; Wallerstein & Kelly, 1980).

The findings of the present study also suggest that more attention needs to be paid to the differential effects of growing up in mother- and father-custody families. All the children of divorce in the present study were in the custody of their mothers. The poorer academic performance of boys may be related to this custody arrangement, with boys having greater difficulty than girls adjusting to the absence of their fathers and to the presence of new men in their mothers' lives (Hess & Camara, 1979; Hetherington, Cox, & Cox, 1982; Wallerstein & Kelly, 1980). That custody arrangements matter can be seen from the research of Santrock, Warshak, and Elliot (1982). They found that children of divorce showed better social adjustment when the same-sexed parent had custody.

Finally, the results of the present study indicate the necessity for both in-depth studies of small samples of children and larger survey-type studies. The present study related the academic performance of children of divorce to a number of key demographic variables. The present study, however, did not examine several other important variables, for example, the quality of the mother-child, father-child, and mother-father relationships. These family processes are strongly related to the social, emotional, and intellectual functioning of children (e.g., Hess & Camara, 1979; Hetherington, Cox, & Cox, 1982; Jacobson, 1978a, 1978b, 1978c; Pett, 1982; Raschke & Raschke, 1979; Wallerstein & Kelly, 1980) and they are probably best studied by sensitive interviewers working closely with a small number of families.

REFERENCES

Alvirez, D., & Bean, F. (1986). The Mexican American family. In C. H. Mindel & R. W. Habenstein (Eds.), *Ethnic families in America* (pp. 271-292). New York: Elsevier.

Blanchard, R. W., & Biller, H. B. (1971). Father availability and academic performance among 3rd grade boys. *Developmental Psychology, 4,* 301-305.

Bureau of the Census. (1983). *Census tracts: San Antonio, Texas* (Department of Commerce Report No. PHC80-2-319). Washington, DC: U.S. Government Printing Office.

Colletta, N. D. (1983). Stressful lives: The situation of divorced mothers and their children. *Journal of Divorce, 6*(3), 19-31.

Felner, R. D., Ginter, M. A., Borke, M. F., & Cowen, E. L. (1981). Parental death or divorce and the school adjustment of young children. *American Journal of Community Psychology, 9,* 181-191.

Felner, R. D., Stolberg, A., & Cowen, E. L. (1975). Crisis events and school mental health referral patterns of young children. *Journal of Consulting and Clinical Psychology, 43,* 305-310.

Glick, P. C. (1979). Children of divorced parents in demographic perspective. *Journal of Social Issues, 35*(4), 170-182.

Hess, R. D., & Camara, K. A. (1979). Post-divorce family relationships as mediating factors in the consequences of divorce for children. *Journal of Social Issues, 35*(4), 79-96.

Hetherington, E. M., Camara, K. A., & Featherman, D. L. (1983). Achievement and intellectual functioning of children in one-parent households. In J. T. Spence (Ed.), *Achievement and achievement motives: Psychological and sociological approaches* (pp. 208-284). San Francisco: Freeman.

Hetherington, E. M., Cox, M., & Cox, R. (1982). Effects of divorce on parents and children. In M. E. Lamb (Ed.), *Nontraditional families: Parenting and child development* (pp. 233-288). Hillsdale, NJ: Erlbaum.

Institute for Development of Educational Activities. (1980). *The most significant minority: One-parent children in the schools.* Washington, DC: National Association of Elementary School Principals. (ERIC Document Reproduction Service No. ED 192 438)

Iowa Tests of Basic Skills. (1979). Chicago: Riverside.

Jacobson, D. S. (1978a). The impact of marital separation/divorce on children: I. Parent-child separation and child adjustment. *Journal of Divorce, 1,* 341-360.

Jacobson, D. S. (1978b). The impact of marital separation/divorce on children: II. Interparent hostility and child adjustment. *Journal of Divorce, 2,* 3-19.

Jacobson, D. S. (1978c). The impact of marital separation/divorce on children: III. Parent-child communication and child adjustment, and regression analysis of findings from overall study. *Journal of Divorce, 2,* 175-194.

Kelly, J. B., & Wallerstein, J. S. (1977). Brief interventions with children in divorcing families. *American Journal of Orthopsychiatry, 47,* 23-36.

Kurdek, L. A., Blisk, D., & Siesky, A. E. (1981). Correlates of children's long-term adjustment to their parents' divorce. *Developmental Psychology, 17*, 565-579.

Kurdek, L. A., & Siesky, A. E. (1980). Children's perceptions of their parents' divorce. *Journal of Divorce, 3*, 339-378.

Murphy, L. B., & Moriarty, A. E. (1976). *Vulnerability, coping, and growth.* New Haven: Yale University Press.

Nelson, E. A., & Maccoby, E. E. (1966). The relationship between social development and differential abilities on the scholastic aptitude test. *Merrill-Palmer Quarterly, 12*, 269-289.

Pett, M. G. (1982). Correlates of children's social adjustment following divorce. *Journal of Divorce, 5*(4), 25-39.

Radin, N. (1981). The role of the father in cognitive, academic, and intellectual development. In M. E. Lamb (Ed.), *The role of the father in child development* (2nd ed.) (pp. 379-427). New York: Wiley.

Raschke, H. J., & Raschke, V. J. (1979). Family conflict and children's self-concepts. *Journal of Marriage and the Family, 41*, 367-374.

Santrock, J. W. (1972). Relation of type and onset of father-absence on cognitive development. *Child Development, 43*, 455-469.

Santrock, J. W., Warshak, R. A., & Elliot, G. L. (1982). Social development and parent-child interaction in father-custody and stepmother families. In M. E. Lamb (Ed.), *Nontraditional families: Parenting and child development* (pp. 289-314). Hillsdale, NJ: Erlbaum.

Science Research Associates Achievement Series. (1978). Chicago: Science Research Associates.

Shantz, C. U. (1983). Social cognition. In J. H. Flavell & E. M. Markman (Eds.), *Handbook of child psychology: Volume 3. Cognitive development* (pp. 495-555). New York: Wiley.

Shinn, M. (1978). Father absence and children's cognitive development. *Psychological Bulletin, 85*, 295-324.

Wallerstein, J. S., & Kelly, J. B. (1977). Divorce counseling: A community service for families in the midst of divorce. *American Journal of Orthopsychiatry, 47*, 4-22.

Wallerstein, J. S., & Kelly, J. B. (1980). *Surviving the breakup.* New York: Basic Books.

Winer, B. J. (1971). *Statistical principles in experimental design* (2nd ed.). New York: McGraw-Hill.

Effects of Post-Divorce Relationships on Child Adjustment

Daniel E. Shybunko

SUMMARY. This study examined how parent-child and interparent relationships affect child adjustment after at least two years of parental separation. Fifteen mother-custodial divorced families and 15 intact families with children from 9-12 years of age completed child adjustment and family relationship assessments. Each child's teacher completed an assessment of school adjustment. No significant difference was found between divorced and intact family groups on the quality of parent-child relationships or child adjustment, even when there is a conflictual interparent relationship.

Increasingly, the view has emerged in the divorce literature that psychological adjustment is moderated less by the intact or separated nature of a household, than by process variables such as the quality of parent-child and interparent relationships. A number of researchers have called for a focus on these various family relationships as they relate to children's adjustment to the divorce process (Ellison, 1983; Hess & Camara, 1979; Hodges, Buchsbaum, & Tierney, 1983; Wallerstein & Kelly, 1980).

Several questions arise. Are parent-child relationships necessarily impaired by the divorce process, and to what degree? Does a positive parent-child relationship with either parent buffer a child

Daniel E. Shybunko, PhD, is on the faculty of the University of Tennessee, Knoxville.

This study was a doctoral dissertation at the University of Tennessee, Knoxville, and was supported in part by the Department of Psychology.

The assistance of Leonard Handler, PhD, Wesley Morgan, PhD, Gary Peterson, PhD, Robert Wahler, PhD, and Judge Bill Swann is gratefully acknowledged.

299

against the effects of divorce or parental discord? Is a child's positive relationship with the custodial mother as important as a good relationship between the child and the noncustodial father?

There is evidence that the divorce process results in a number of changes in the parent-child relationship. In addition to more conflict and increased salience of the custodial mother, divorced parents often experience a period of diminished capacity to parent. This is characterized by inconsistency, the making of fewer maturity demands, less effective communication, and a tendency to be less affectionate (Hetherington, Cox, & Cox, 1978). The disturbance is usually sharpest between mothers and sons. Fathers often tend to become less nurturant and more detached from their children (Hetherington, 1979).

The first year post-divorce appears to be the most traumatic time of change for both parents and children (Kolevzon & Gottlieb, 1983). After a period of approximately two years, most divorced families find that their relationships stabilize, children manifest fewer symptoms, and many have recovered to their previous level of functioning (Kurdek, Blisk, & Siesky, 1981; Hetherington, Cox, & Cox, 1978; Wallerstein & Kelly, 1980).

Parent-child relationships have been shown to affect child adjustment to divorce more than the level of parental discord. A positive parent-child relationship, even with only one parent, has been found to greatly mitigate the negative effects of divorce (Hess & Camara, 1979). While some studies have found that the child's relationship with the noncustodial father is of equal importance and separate from the relationship with the custodial mother (Hess & Camara, 1979), other studies suggest that only a very good relationship with the mother has any mitigating effect (Hetherington, Cox, & Cox, 1979) or that good contact with a parent is beneficial only in the context of a positive interparent relationship (Kurdek & Blisk, 1983).

There is considerable support for the notion that the degree of parental conflict affects children's adjustment to divorce (Ellison, 1983; Emery, 1982; Hodges, Buchsbaum, & Tierney, 1983; Jacobson, 1978; Parish & Nunn, 1981; Nelson, 1981).

A variety of methodological weaknesses have been identified in the divorce research (Emery, 1982; Kanoy & Cunningham, 1984;

Kitson & Raschke, 1981; Kulka & Weingarten, 1979; Kurdek, 1983; Levitan, 1979; White & Mika, 1983). There has clearly been a need for divorce research to employ more random approaches to sampling rather than the frequent use of clinical, self-selected, or otherwise potentially unrepresentative samples. Furthermore, variables that have been found to moderate adjustment need to be addressed, such as child's age, sex, birth order, family size, length of separation, parent's stability, and socioeconomic status.

The selection of children in the 9-12 year, "later school age" group has been suggested by Wallerstein and Kelly's (1980) observation that these children appeared especially vulnerable to depression and anger during the first year of the separation, along with exhibiting a more pronounced deterioration in relationships with fathers than any other age group.

The purpose of this study was to examine the psychological adjustment of children who have experienced divorce. While the literature suggests that divorce is certainly stressful for families, especially during the first year, there is considerable evidence that the effects are short-term or minimal (Berg & Kelly, 1979; Crossman, Shea, & Adams, 1980; Hodges, Wechsler, & Ballantine, 1978; Kulka & Weingarten, 1979; Reinhard, 1977). Thus, it is hypothesized that the divorce process does not necessarily interfere with normal psychological growth and adjustment.

An additional focus of this study was to examine to what degree parent-child and interparent relationships affect child adjustment. Past research suggests that children's adjustment to divorce is influenced by the quality of the relationship with each parent and the interparent relationship.

METHOD

Subjects

The sample included 15 divorced and 15 intact families. A family in this study was comprised of one child and both parents in the case of an intact family, or a child and at least the custodial mother in the case of a divorced family.

Divorced families were identified from legal records of the local court. Families were contacted initially by a letter explaining the study, and then contacted by telephone to determine if they were interested in participating. Intact families were randomly drawn from the same classrooms as the divorced family children, and similarly contacted. A payment of ten dollars was made to each participating family.

Families were selected by the following criteria: parents in the intact families and custodial mothers in the divorced families had to have been married only once, and to have a child between the ages of 9 and 12 years at the time of the study. Only one child was used per family. In addition, only divorced families with custodial mothers who had been separated for at least two years were selected. The period of separation was measured from the date of actual physical separation rather than the date of the divorce decree. The period of separation ranged from 2 years, 0 months, to 9 years, 11 months, with a mean of 3.73 years.

Families were excluded from the study if the custodial mother had remarried, or where the children or parents had a history of emotional disorders (prior to the separation in the case of the divorced families). The level of emotional disturbance required for exclusion was a degree of impairment in adaptive functioning that had necessitated a psychiatric hospitalization.

The divorced group children included nine males and six females with a mean age of 10.3 years. The intact group children included eight males and seven females with a mean age of 10.2 years. The divorced group included five first-born, eight second-born, and two third-born children. The intact group included eight first-born, five second-born, one third-born, and one sixth-born child.

The divorced and intact groups included identical distributions of 12 mothers working outside of the home and 3 mothers not working outside of the home. Of the divorced mothers, nine were employed full-time and three were employed part-time while seven of the intact family mothers were employed full-time and five were employed on a part-time basis.

Using Hollingshead's (1977) four-factor procedure to assess social status, the mean social status score for both the divorced and intact family groups fell in the Medium Business, Minor Professional, and Technical level. Further, both groups demonstrated a similar distribution of social status. All subject families were Caucasian.

Measures

This study used two measures of family relationships and two measures of child adjustment.

Measures of Family Relationships

1. Family Relationship Inventory (FRI). The FRI (Nash, Morrison, & Taylor, 1982) is a self-report instrument that yields a self-appraisal and a portrayal of feelings toward spouse, siblings, children, parent, or any significant other. These relationships are directly assessed. An individual assigns each of 50 descriptions (with a positive or negative connotation) to some member of the family or to him/herself. This yields a positive or negative valence score of each relationship, along with a self-appraisal. Test-retest reliability and validity data have been reported by Nash, Morrison, and Taylor (1982).

2. Family Environment Scale (FES). The FES (Moos, 1974) is a 90-item paper and pencil test which measures 10 aspects of family environments. These scales are further grouped into three dimensions: Relationships, Personal Growth, and Systems Maintenance. Of particular interest in this study was the Relationship dimension, which includes the Cohesion, Conflict, and Expressiveness scales. Test-retest reliability and validity data are reported by Moos and Moos (1981). The FES has been used extensively to explore characteristics of different types of families. A number of studies have used the FES in comparing divorced and intact families (Reinhard, 1977; Slater, Stewart, & Linn, 1983).

Measures of Child Adjustment

1. Child Behavior Checklist (CBCL). The CBCL (Achenbach & Edelbrock, 1983) consists of 20 social competence and 118 behavior problem items. The CBCL items are scored on a 0-1-2 scale by parents and teachers. The Teacher's Report Form of the CBCL lists behavior problems in the same format as the CBCL. However, some questions are adapted for the school environment and teachers

are asked to base ratings on the previous two months, rather than the six-month period specified on the CBCL. Extensive clinical and normative testing has been done with the CBCL. Interparent, inter-interviewer, and test-retest reliabilities are reported by Bartko (1976). Achenbach and Edelbrock (1983) present data supporting the validity of the CBCL.

2. Washington University Sentence Completion Test for Measuring Ego Development (WUSCT). The WUSCT was developed by Loevinger and Wessler (1970) and is based on the authors' proposed sequence of normal ego development. The use of lower levels of ego functioning implies the use of impulsive and self-protective mechanisms, while the upper levels of ego functioning are indicated by autonomous self-critical thought, with a tolerance for ambiguity and configural complexity. The WUSCT identifies qualitative differences in successive stages of ego development. Every response to an incomplete sentence stem is matched against the sequence of qualitative stages and is assigned to the level it most closely resembles. Data regarding the validity and reliability of the WUSCT are reported by Loevinger and Wessler (1970) and Redmore and Waldman (1975) respectively.

Procedure

Families were administered the various assessment instruments at either the University Psychological Clinic or at their homes, whichever was more convenient. After completing an information questionnaire, parents were asked to complete the FRI, FES, and CBCL in that order. At the same time the child was asked to complete the FRI, FES, and the WUSCT. The FRI and FES items were presented orally.

Upon the parent signing a release of information, the child's teacher was contacted, met at the school, and requested to complete the Teacher's Report Form of the CBCL.

After completion and scoring of the instruments, interested families were provided with a feedback session. This session involved a summary, explanation, and discussion of the family's relationship assessment. Eight families (four divorced, four intact) took advantage of the feedback session.

RESULTS

After a traditional group-difference approach, a multiple regression analysis of the data was performed to determine which variables (mother-child relationship, father-child relationship, mother-father relationship, child's sex, marital status, or FES scales) would best predict child adjustment. The predictor variables were applied to each of the four adjustment measures: Social Competence, parent-rated Behavior Problems, teacher-rated Behavior Problems, and Ego Development. In order to determine if the effects revealed in the combined sample were more or less powerful in the divorced family, an additional multiple regression was applied to the divorced family data separately.

This study found that when otherwise equivalent divorced and intact families were compared, little significant difference was evident in either the rated quality of the parent-child relationships or in child adjustment. In spite of the expectedly more negative relationship between divorced parents compared with married couples, the quality of the parent-child relationships in the divorced families were found to be as positive as in the intact families. Furthermore, although the divorced families were found to be less cohesive than the intact families, the degree of expressiveness and conflict was quite similar.

Divorced and intact family children exhibited little differences with regard to measures of adjustment. The groups did not differ significantly on measures of social competence, parent-rated behavior problems, or ego development. However, the divorced family children were found to have a significantly higher level of behavior problems than intact family children when rated by teachers.

Comparison of Divorced and Intact Groups on Relationship Variables

The three relationship variables derived from the FRI yielded scores ranging from -18 to $+20$. For purposes of analysis, a constant of $+20$ was added to all of the relationship scores. Consequently a score of 20 would be considered neutral, a score above 20 would be considered a positively rated relationship, and a score below 20 would be considered a negatively rated relationship.

The mother-child score was acquired from the child's FRI rating of his/her mother, while the father-child score was acquired from the child's rating of his/her father. The mother-father score was derived from the mother's FRI rating of her husband or ex-husband. It is important to note that the "relationship scores" are more accurately the child's or mother's perception of a particular relationship rather than a measure of a specific dimension of the relationship.

Table 1 presents the divorced and intact group means for each relationship. The divorced and intact family groups did not differ significantly on measures of the mother-child or father-child relationship. Divorced and intact family group means for both relationships would be considered positive, with the mother-child relationship for both groups being rated as somewhat more positive than the father-child relationship. Not surprisingly, the mother-father relationship in the divorced families was rated significantly more negative than the mother-father relationship in the intact family (t (28) = 6.86, p < .01).

The relationship scores from the FES represented the mean of the mother and child scores on each relationship scale. These means are presented in Table 2. There was no significant difference between the divorced and intact family groups on either the Expressiveness or Conflict scale. However, the groups did differ on the Cohesion scale. The intact family group reported a significantly higher level

Table 1

Comparison of Mean Relationship Scores by Marital Status

Relationship	Divorced	Intact	t
Mother-Child	30.3	29.9	.26
Father-Child	22.9	25.6	1.51
Mother-Father	15.9	27.9	6.86*

*p < .01.

Table 2

<u>Comparison of Mean Family Environment Scale Scores by</u>

<u>Marital Status</u>

Relationship Scales	Divorced	Intact	<u>t</u>
Cohesion	51.1	59.4	2.57*
Expressiveness	48.6	49.8	.42
Conflict	55.3	49.3	1.73

*<u>p</u> < .05.

of cohesion compared with the divorced family group (t (28) = 2.57, p < .05).

Comparison of Divorced and Intact Family Groups on Adjustment Variables

The Social Competence and parent-rated Behavior Problem scores were derived from the mother's responses on the CBCL. The teacher-rated CBCL yielded an additional Behavior Problems score. Table 3 presents a comparison of the divorced and intact family group means on the adjustment measures.

There was no significant difference between the divorced and intact groups on either measures of Social Competence or parent-rated Behavior Problems. However, the divorced group did demonstrate a significantly higher level of Behavior Problems compared with the intact group as rated by the teachers (t (28) = 2.84, p < .01).

The distribution of Ego Development scores is shown in Table 4. These scores were drawn from each child's responses to the

Table 3

Comparison of Mean Adjustment Scores by Marital Status

Adjustment Measure	Divorced	Intact	t
Social Competence	50.9	57.3	1.67
Behavior Problems (P)	57.9	52.1	1.82
Behavior Problems (T)	59.2	52.1	2.84*

*$p < .01$.

Table 4

Distribution of Ego Development Levels by Marital Status

Level	Divorced	Intact
I2 (Impulsive)	8	3
Delta (Self-Protective)	4	9
Delta/3 (Transitional)	1	3
I3 (Conformist)	1	0
I3/4 (Transitional)	1	0

WUSCT. A Yates Corrected chi-square was applied to the data comparing the frequency of 12 (Impulsive) levels of ego development for the divorced and intact group children with the frequency of Delta (Self-Protective) or higher levels. The marital status of a child's family and the child's level of ego development were found to not be significantly related, chi-square $(1, N = 30) = 2.30$, $p > .05$.

Multiple Regression Analysis

The multiple regression analysis revealed the father-child relationship as the best predictor of Social Competence. It was found that 14% of the total variance in Social Competence was attributed to the rated quality of the father-child relationship, $F(1,25) = 4.46$, $p < .05$. Of the variance in Social Competence attributed to the predictor variables, 74% of this was due to the father-child relationship.

Marital status was found to predict a significant 16% proportion of the total variance in teacher-rated Behavior Problems, $F(1,25) = 5.57$, $p < .05$. Of the variance in teacher-rated Behavior Problems attributed to the predictor variables, 58% was due to the marital status variable.

The relationship or marital status variables did not predict a significant proportion of the variance in any other measure of adjustment. Similarly, none of the FES variables predicted a significant degree of the variance in adjustment.

When a multiple regression analysis was performed on solely the divorced family data, the trend seen with the combined data with regard to the role of the father-child relationship became more prominent. Due to the past research noting the effect of sex upon adjustment to divorce, the variable of child's sex was added to the three relationship variables in this analysis. These variables predicted a significant 64% of the variance in Social Competence, $F(4,10) = 4.45$, $p < .05$. The father-child relationship variable emerged as a strong predictor of Social Competence in the divorced family group, $F(1,10) = 12.51$, $p < .01$. Of the variance in Social Competence attributed to the predictor variables, 70% was due to the father-child relationship variable.

DISCUSSION

The results of this study support the hypothesis that for this particular age group, after a period of at least two years, the divorced process does not necessarily produce impaired parent-child relationships or impaired child adjustment. There was no significant difference between divorced and intact family groups in the rated quality of parent-child relationships or in measures of children's adjustment in social competence, parent-rated behavior problems, or ego development.

These findings were not unexpected. A number of studies have also found that the quality of interaction among members of divorced families does not differ greatly from that of many intact families (Hess & Camara, 1979; Hodges, Buchsbaum, & Tierney, 1984; Reinhart, 1977). In spite of the expectedly more negative relationship between divorced parents compared with married couples, the quality of the parent-child relationships in the divorced families were found to be as positive as in the intact families. These findings are consistent with previous research (Hess & Camara, 1979) in concluding that parental discord does not necessarily determine the quality of the parent-child relationships. This suggests that a positive parent-child relationship can be maintained in the postdivorce family, even in the context of an acrimonious or conflictual interparent relationship.

The groups did differ with regard to teacher-rated behavior problems, a pattern which has been previously reported. Hess and Camara (1979) found that children from divorced families demonstrated a tendency toward exhibiting greater stress, less productive work styles, and more aggressive behavior than their peers from intact families. These results suggest that even after a marital separation of two years, school adjustment is still likely affected by the divorce process. Children of divorced families are more likely than intact family children to be inattentive, aggressive, or socially unpopular.

In general however, the finding of little significant differences between divorced and intact family children in either the rated quality of parent-child relationships or adjustment may reflect the restabilization process in parent-child relationships and adjustment that has been described by Hetherington, Cox, and Cox (1978) and Wallerstein and Kelly (1980).

The process of divorce appears to involve an initial and often temporary regression in adaptive functioning not unlike the process of bereavement. Changes, symptoms, problems, or characteristics seen at one point in time do not necessarily indicate permanent change or impairment but rather the response of an individual or family system to a crisis. With time, the initial and often expected conflicts in parent-child relationships tend to wane.

The results are more equivocal regarding the hypothesis that adjustment is influenced more by the quality of family relationships than by marital status. While other studies (Hess & Camara, 1979) report that parent-child relationships were the best predictors of child adjustment, the present results are less clear. Unlike Hess and Camara (1979), marital status was found in the present study to actually be a good predictor of teacher-rated behavior problems. Although the combined family relationship variables did not prove to be powerful predictors of child adjustment in general, the father-child relationship was found to be a good predictor of social competence regardless of marital status. Moreover, the importance of the father-child relationship increased dramatically in the divorced family. This supports the view (Hetherington, Cox, & Cox, 1978) that availability of the father is associated with positive adjustment and social relations, especially with boys.

The ability of the father-child relationship to predict social competence tends to illuminate the critical role of this relationship in facilitating the development of social competence in children (Blanchard & Biller, 1971; Epstein & Radin, 1975; Weinraub, 1978).

This study has implications for both psychological intervention and judicial mediation with divorcing families. It is important to recognize divorce as a process of gradual family redefinition and restabilization. This process has the potential for risk as well as for the forging of a healthy, productive, post-divorce family. The courts and clinicians can play a role in facilitating the development of that new family structure. Emphasis should be placed on supporting and maintaining the parent-child relationship, especially the father-child relationship. Accordingly, the present study does not support the concept of the sole "psychological parent" and supports liberal visitation for the noncustodial parent.

In the divorce process, families and relationships do not end, they change. How children and families negotiate these changes determines to what extent a stable, healthy, post-divorce family is created. This study supports the healthy potential of the post-divorce family, and affirms the continuing importance of family relationships.

REFERENCES

Achenbach, T. M. & Edelbrock, C. (1983). *Manual for the child behavior checklist and revised child behavior profile.* Burlington, VT: Queen City Printers.

Bartko, J. J. (1976). On various interclass correlation reliability coefficients. *Psychological Bulletin, 83,* 762-765.

Berg, B. & Kelly, R. (1979). The measured self-esteem of children from broken, rejected, and accepted families. *Journal of Divorce, 2,* 363-369.

Blanchard, R. & Biller, H. B. (1971). Father availability and academic performance among third-grade boys. *Developmental Psychology, 4,* 301-305.

Crossman, S. M. & Adams, G. R. (1980). Divorce, single parenting, and child development. *The Journal of Psychology, 106,* 205-217.

Ellison, E. A. (1983). Issues concerning parental harmony and children's psychosocial adjustment. *American Journal of Orthopsychiatry, 53,* 73-80.

Emery, R. E. (1982). Interparental conflict and the children of divorce and discord. *Psychological Bulletin, 92,* 310-330.

Epstein, A. S. & Radin, N. (1975). Motivational components related to father behavior and cognitive functioning in preschoolers. *Child Development, 46,* 831-839.

Hess, R. D. & Camara, K. A. (1979). Post-divorce family relationships as mediating factors in the consequences of divorce for children. *Journal of Social Issues, 35,* 79-96.

Hetherington, E. M. (1979). Divorce: A child's perspective. *American Psychologist, 34,* 851-858.

Hetherington, E. M., Cox, M., & Cox, R. (1978). The aftermath of divorce. In J. H. Stevens & M. Mathews (Eds.), *Mother-child, father-child relationships* (pp. 149-176). Washington, DC: National Association for the Education of Young Children.

Hetherington, E. M., Cox, M., & Cox, R. (1979). Family interaction and the social, emotional, and cognitive development of children following divorce. In V. Vaughn & T. Brazelton (Eds.), *The family: Setting priorities.* New York: Science and Medicine.

Hodges, W. F., Buchsbaum, H. K., & Tierney, C. W. (1983). Parent-child relationships and adjustment in preschool children in divorced and intact families. *Journal of Divorce, 7,* 43-58.

Hodges, W. F., Wechsler, R. C., & Ballantine, C. (1979). Divorce and the preschool child. *Journal of Divorce, 3,* 55-69.

Hollingshead, A. B. (1977). *Four factor index of social status.* Unpublished manuscript, Yale University, New Haven.

Jacobson, D. S. (1978). The impact of marital separation/divorce on children: Interparent hostility and child adjustment. *Journal of Divorce, 2,* 3-19.

Kanoy, K. W. & Cunningham, J. L. (1984). Consensus or confusion in research on children and divorce: Conceptual and methodological issues. *Journal of Divorce, 7,* 45-71.

Kitson, G. C. & Raschke, H. J. (1981). Divorce research: What we know; What we need to know. *Journal of Divorce, 4,* 1-37.

Kolevzon, M. S. & Gottlieb, S. J. (1983). The impact of divorce: A multivariate study. *Journal of Divorce, 7*, 89-98.

Kulka, R. A. & Weingarten, H. (1979). The long-term effects of parental divorce on adult adjustment. *Journal of Social Issues, 35*, 50-78.

Kurdek, L. A. (1983). Concluding comments. In L. A. Kurdek (Ed.), *Children and divorce. New directions for child development* (pp. 83-87). San Francisco: Jossey-Bass.

Kurdek, L. A., & Blisk, D. (1983). Dimensions and correlates of mothers' divorce experiences. *Journal of Divorce, 6*, 1-24.

Kurdek, L. A., Blisk, D., & Siesky, A. E. (1981). Correlates of children's long-term adjustment to their parents' divorce. *Developmental Psychology, 17*, 565-579.

Levitin, T. E. (1979). Children of divorce; An introduction. *Journal of Social Issues, 35*, 1-25.

Loevinger, J. & Wessler, R. (1970). *Measuring ego development*. Vol. 1. San Francisco: Jossey-Bass.

Moos, R. (1974). *Combined preliminary manual for the family, work, and group environment scales*. Palo Alto, CA: Consulting Psychologists Press.

Moos, R. & Moos, B. (1981). *Family environment scale manual*. Palo Alto, CA: Consulting Psychologists Press, Inc.

Nash, L., Morrison, W. L., & Taylor, R. M. (1982). *Family relationship inventory*. Los Angeles, CA: Psychological Publications.

Nelson, G. (1981). Moderators of women's and children's adjustment following divorce. *Journal of Divorce, 4*, 71-83.

Parish, J. S. & Nunn, G. D. (1981). Children's self-concepts and evaluations of parents as a function of family structure and process. *The Journal of Psychology, 107*, 105-108.

Redmore, C. & Waldman, E. (1975). Reliability of a sentence completion measure of ego development. *Journal of Personality Assessment, 39*, 236-243.

Reinhard, D. W. (1977). The reaction of adolescent boys and girls to the divorce of their parents. *Journal of Clinical Child Psychology*, 21-23.

Reinhart, G. (1977). One-parent families: A study of divorced mothers and adolescents using social climate and relationship styles. *Dissertation Abstracts International, 38*, 2881B.

Slater, E. J., Stewart, K. J., & Linn, M. W. (1983). The effects of family disruption on adolescent males and females. *Adolescence, 18*, 931-942.

Wallerstein, J.. S. & Kelly, J. B. (1980). *Surviving the breakup*. New York: Basic Books.

Weinraub, M. (1978). Fatherhood: The myth of the second-class parent. In J. H. Stevens & M. Mathews (Eds.), *Mother/child father/child relationships*. Washington, DC: National Association for the Education of Young Children.

White, S. W. & Mika, K. (1983). Family divorce and separation: Theory and research. *Marriage & Family Review, 6*, 175-192.

The Effect of Children's Family Type on Teachers' Stereotypes

Joseph Guttmann
Marc Broudo

SUMMARY. The main purpose of this study was to investigate teachers' stereotypic perceptions of the effects of different family types on the functioning of children. Seventy-six Israeli teachers were asked to evaluate the academic, social and emotional levels of functioning of a fictitious fifth grade boy who was variously described to them as being from an intact, remarried, divorced or conflicted family. Three main results were obtained. First, teachers expected the child from the intact family to function better academically, socially, and emotionally than the child from the conflicted family. Second, teachers expected similar levels of academic, social, and emotional functioning in a case of both the child of divorced parents and the child from the remarried family. Third, three dimensions differentiated between teachers' expectations when the child was described as coming from an intact, remarried or conflicted family but did not do so as regards the child of divorced parents. These results are discussed in the context of teacher-student interactions and their potential to trigger a process of self-fulfilling

Joseph Guttmann, PhD, is on the faculty of the School of Education, Haifa University, Mt. Carmel, Haifa, Israel. Marc Broudo, PhD, is on the faculty of the University of British Columbia.

315

prophecy. The findings are also considered in reference to the doubt-
ful validity of studies in which teachers' evaluations are used as
measures of children's adjustment to the divorce or remarriage of
their parents.

Teachers' stereotypes regarding children from different types of
family may have an influence on the cognitive, social, and emotional functioning of children. The stereotypes and expectations of
teachers may affect the quality of teacher-student interactions and
set in motion the process of self-fulfilling prophecy (Good, 1982;
Meichenbaum, Bowers, and Ross, 1969; Rist, 1970; Rosenthal and
Jacobson, 1968). Rist (1970) has analyzed the factors that are critical for both the development of teachers' expectations of pupils and
the process by which such expectations influence the classroom experiences of teachers and pupils. According to Rist, teachers' expectations in this matter are significantly determined by a variety of
characteristics subjectively attributed to particular pupils. Among
these characteristics is the child's family constellation.

The effect of family constellation on the development and the
psychological welfare of children is a cornerstone in the various
theories of child development. According to these, the risk of psychological maladjustment increases drastically in children when
they are raised either in the absence of a parent or in an unhappy
home. In their systematic reviews of the relevant research, Blechman (1982) as well as Adams, Miller, and Schrepf (1984) have
raised serious doubts as to whether these theories have been adequately confirmed. They cite numerous studies whose results support the contentions of these theories but which have been found to
be methodologically inadequate in a variety of ways. One such
methodological inadequacy is the reliance on teachers' evaluations
for the purpose of judging children's behavior.

Teachers' evaluations have often been used by researchers to
judge and compare the functioning of children from different types
of family (Bronfenbrenner, 1961; Cortes and Fleming, 1968; Kellam, Ensminger, and Turner, 1977; LeCorgne and Laosa, 1976;
Santrock, 1972, 1977; Santrock and Tracy, 1978). In these studies,
teachers' ratings on various measures, such as leadership and social, emotional, and scholastic adjustment, have tended to favor
children from intact families over those from divorced or conflicted

families. The interpretations of studies of this sort are flawed as a result of a number of methodological problems (Herzog and Sudia, 1973; Blechman, 1982). In particular, the validity of rating-scale assessment techniques has been challenged on the grounds that the ratings may largely reflect the "implicit" personality theories of individual raters rather than the child's actual performance (Mischel, 1968, 1973). Blechman (1982) too questions the appropriateness of using teachers' ratings because of the stereotypes and biases of teachers about the effects of the family background of pupils. Indeed, the few studies that have compared teachers' ratings with the self-ratings of children (Hammond, 1979; Santrock, 1972, 1975), or with children's actual performance (Engemoen, 1967; Ferri, 1976), have revealed discrepancies between the compared sets of measures. For instance, Ferri (1976) asked teachers to rate parents' interest in their children's schoolwork, and has checked how often parents have visited school. Teachers rated single parents as being less interested in their children's schoolwork, whereas in actual fact single parents did not differ from other parents in the frequency of their school visits. Santrock (1975) also found that the difference in moral conduct between children from intact and divorced families was only "in the eyes of the beholders"—i.e., in teachers' ratings.

The reasons for the discrepancy between data based on teachers' ratings and on direct observation are not clear. Teachers' ratings may accurately reflect their knowledge of the children's behavior over a long period of time, and may therefore be less influenced by temporary situational variables than by experimentally induced ratings of a hypothetical child. Thus it might be argued that teachers' evaluation reflect actual family type differences and do not derive from unfounded stereotypes. But some of the better controlled studies have shown that when variables referring to environmental and individual differences are controlled—such as family income, reasons for the father's absence, age, and I.Q.—then family type accounts for very little, if any, of the variance in the dependent measures (Adams and Horovitz, 1980; Bane, 1976; Covell and Turnbull, 1982; Engemoen, 1967; Fowler and Richards, 1978; Herzog, 1974; Herzog and Sudia, 1973; Hunt and Hunt, 1975; Langner, 1963).

Teachers' ratings may also represent the implicit theory of the teacher-raters, and reflect their misperceptions or stereotypes of children. To determine whether this is indeed the case, teachers should be asked to evaluate children from different family types while controlling for personal and background information. In the present study, teachers' perceptions of children from intact, divorced, remarried and conflicted families are compared under such conditions. This study enlarges the scope of earlier research which has compared teacher's stereotypes of the scholastic, social, and emotional functioning of the children of divorced and intact families (Santrock and Tracy, 1978; Guttmann, Geva, and Gefen, 1984). It tests whether the discrepancies mentioned above can be attributed to teachers' stereotypes. It also attempts to determine whether teachers differentiate in their expectations of children on the basis of family types. Finally, it concerns itself with the composition of these stereotypes.

METHOD

Subjects

The subjects consisted of 76 women teachers who were enrolled in extension courses at Haifa University, in Israel. They ranged in age from 26 to 44 ($M = 38$), and had accumulated from 4 to 22 years of teaching experience ($M = 14$). Eighty-seven percent of the subjects were married, 7.8% were divorced, 2.6% were widowed, and 2.6% were single.

Materials

The stimulus material for the experiment consisted of a questionnaire introduced by a written description of a fictitious boy in which the experimental variable of family type was manipulated. This introduction stated that the purpose of the study was to examine "the reliability of teachers' expectations of the level of a child's scholastic, social, and emotional functioning when only a limited amount of information about the child is made available." The subjects were instructed to read the description of the boy carefully, and then to rank him in regard to 28 characteristics, each on a 1-5 scale representing a range of evaluation from negative (1) to positive (5). Nine of the characteristics were related to scholastic performance (e.g., receives good grades–receives poor grades; invests much effort in studies–invests little effort in studies; diligent–not diligent; able to concentrate–unable to concentrate). Ten of the characteristics were related to social behavior (e.g., socially active in class–socially passive in class; likes to be with friends–does not like to be with friends; trusts friends–does not trust friends; gets along with others–does not get along with others). Finally, nine characteristics were related to the child's emotional functioning (e.g., happy–sad; outgoing–withdrawn; optimistic–pessimistic; self-confident–insecure).

The fictitious boy, who was named Ori, was described as "an 11-year-old fifth-grader who lives in the city with his parents and a 13-year-old brother and 8-year-old sister." His family was depicted as a middle-class Israeli family living in a three-bedroom apartment located in a pleasant neighborhood. His father was given out to be an engineer working at the local electric company, and his mother was described as a registered nurse employed at a nearby hospital. Ori was portrayed as being of average intelligence, in good physical health, and of average height and weight.

While these personal and background characteristics were kept in constant in the introduction, four different family types were inserted that corresponded to the four experimental conditions of the study:

1. Intact — "lives with both parents."
2. Divorced — "lives with his mother, who has been divorced four years."
3. Remarried — "lives with his mother, who was divorced four years ago and has remarried, and with his stepfather as well for the past two years."
4. Conflicted — "lives with both natural parents, who do not get along and are in constant conflict."

Procedure

The experimental procedure followed a between-subject design. The sample was randomly divided into four groups, each of which comprised 19 subjects and was assigned an experimental condition consisting of one of the four Family Type descriptions. Eight subjects objected that the information given about Ori was insufficient to allow them to fill out the questionnaire. The experimenter acknowledged the difficulty and did not insist that the subjects fill out the questionnaire. In all, five persons chose not to participate in the experiment.

RESULTS

Cronbach's Alpha reliability test of each dimension yielded reasonably high Alpha coefficients (i.e., .81 for the Academic, .79 for the Social, and .75 for the Emotional dimension). For each subject an average score was computed for each dimension to represent the subject's evaluation of the fictitious child's functioning (see Table 1).

A mixed factorial multivariate analysis was performed to deter-

Table 1

Means and Standard Deviations of the Subjects' Evaluations

of the Fictitous Child's Academic, Social and Emotional

Functioning in the Four Family Types.

		Academic	Social	Emotional
Divorced	M	3.22	3.35	3.09
	S.D.	.53	.50	.59
Remarried	M	3.23	3.17	3.22
	S.D.	.47	.51	.41
Conflicted	M	2.92	2.69	2.48
	S.D.	.49	.54	.46
Intact	M	3.38	3.82	3.72
	S.D.	.42	.43	.40
Total M		3.18	3.26	3.13

mine a possible differential effect of the variables of the subjects' family and occupational background. The analysis yielded no significant results. Therefore the data of the subjects within each experimental condition was pooled.

The 4 × 3 (Family Type × Dimensions of Functioning) ANOVA, with the second factor being a repeated measure factor, yielded a significant Family Type main effect ($F(3,72) = 4.58; p < .01$) and a Family Type × Dimensions of Functioning interaction ($F(6,144) = 22.63; p < .001$). Scheffe's Post-Hoc analysis for paired comparisons revealed (1) a significant difference between the Intact family type and the other three family types (i.e., the child from the Intact family was ranked as functioning better overall than the child from the Divorced, or Remarried, or Conflicted family); (2) a significant difference between the Conflicted family type and both the Divorced and the Remarried family types (i.e., the child from the Conflicted family was ranked as functioning worse overall than the child from either the Divorced or Remarried family); (3) no difference was found between the Divorced and Remarried family types.

To obtain an understanding of the source and meaning of the significant interaction (see Figure 1) three one-way ANOVA were performed, one for each dependent variable (each at .016 Alpha level of significance). The results revealed significant effect of Family Type on the subjects' evaluations of the fictitious child's functioning Academically ($F(3,72) = 8.63; p < .01$), Socially ($F(3,72) = 17.42; p < .01$), and Emotionally ($F(3,72) = 26.18; p < .01$). Tukey's Post-Hoc pair-wise comparisons showed:

1. Subjects evaluated the academic functioning of the child from the Intact family as significantly better than that of the child from the Conflicted family.
2. Subjects evaluated the social functioning of the child from the Intact family as significantly better than that of the child from any of the three other family types, and they evaluated the social functioning of the child from the Divorced family as better than that of the child from the Conflicted family. No differences were found between the child from the Divorced and the Remarried family, nor between the child from the Remarried and the Conflicted family.

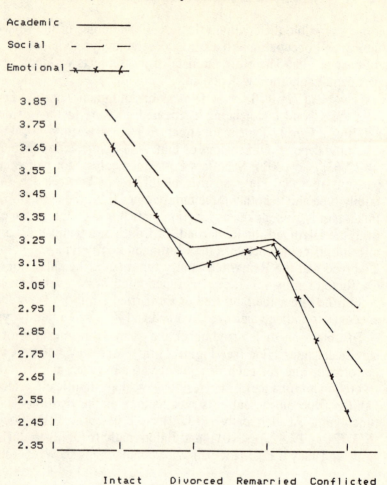

Figure 1. Interaction of the Four Family Type with the Three Dimensions of Functioning.

3. Subjects evaluated the emotional functioning of the child from the Intact family as significantly better than that of the child from any of the three other family types, and they evaluated the emotional functioning of the child from the Divorced and the Remarried family as better than that of the child from the

Conflicted family. No difference was found between the child from the Divorced and the Remarried family.

For the purpose of comparisons between the three dimensions of functioning within each family type, four one-way ANOVA were performed (each ANOVA at .0125 Alpha level of significance). The results revealed significant differences in the subjects' evaluations between the three dimensions of the child's functioning within the four family types: Divorced ($F(2,72) = 5.42$; $p < .01$); Conflicted ($F(2,72) = 8.54$; $p < .01$); and Intact ($F(2,72) = 9.38$; $p < .01$). The results of paired t-tests showed:

1. Subjects evaluated the social functioning of the child of divorced parents as better than his emotional functioning.
2. Subjects evaluated the academic functioning of the child from the Conflicted family as better than his social and emotional functioning, and his social functioning as better than his emotional functioning.
3. Subjects evaluated the social and emotional functioning of the child from the Intact family as better than his academic functioning.

Of the various results obtained by the discriminant analysis it is the percentage of matched Actual and Predicted membership in an experimental condition which is of particular interest. Table 2 presents these Actual-Predicted matching percentages.

The results indicated a relatively high and statistically significant ($X2(9) = 28.6$; $p < .01$) within-group uniformity and between-group differentiation in the subjects' patterns of response. That is, the three dimensions of functioning differentiated among the four family types. This is very obvious for three of the four family types: Remarried, Conflicted, and Intact families. The percentages of correct classification of Actual and Predicted membership were as follows: 68% for the child from the Remarried family; 75% for the child from the Conflicted family; 60% for the child from the Intact family; and only 28% for the child from the Divorced family.

Table 2

Precentage of Correctly Classified Predicted Experimental

    Conditions' Memberships.

Actual Group	Predicted Group Membership				Total
	1	2	3	4	
Divorced	28%	28%	22%	22%	100%
Remarried	16%	68%	0	16%	100%
Conflicted	5%	20%	75%	0	100%
Intact	15%	25%	0	60%	100%

DISCUSSION

The overall results of this study show that teachers' evaluations of children's social and emotional functioning vary systematically in accordance with the family background of the children. However their evaluations of children's academic functioning is not similarly affected. The results also show that teachers do not differentiate between children from divorced and remarried families, and that they perceive both as functioning better socially and emotionally than children from conflicted families but worse than those from intact families. Finally, the results show a relatively high degree of between-teacher agreement regarding the cognitive, social and emotional profiles of the children of intact, remarried and conflicted families, but considerable disagreement concerning the same profiles in the case of the children of divorced parents. The latter point is made evident in the nearly equal division of subjects' predicted group memberships into the four actual group-memberships.

One of our initial assessments points to the apparent sensitivity of the dependent measures in reflecting teachers' differentiation between the family types. Given an adequate measuring instrument, teachers make the relatively sophisticated choice of discriminating between the different dimensions of their composite attitudes or expectations regarding children from the different types of family. The high degree of agreement among teachers is indicative of their adherence to clear and socially agreed upon stereotypic images of the children of intact, remarried, and conflicted families when only a limited amount of background information is made available. The high degree of disagreement among the teachers in regard to children from divorced families may reflect a transitional stage in the process of the change of attitudes in Israeli society toward divorce in general, and toward the children of divorced parents in particular. Some of our subjects (22%) attributed to the child from the divorced family similar characteristics to those of the child from the intact family; and the same percentage of subjects attributed to the child from the divorced family similar characteristics to those of the child from the conflicted family. Apparently the teachers had no clear image in their mind of the social and emotional profiles of children of divorced parents.

Noteworthy is the similarity which was found in the evaluations deriving from the teachers' stereotypic images between the child of divorced parents and the child from the remarried family. This may have been the consequence of their perception of second marriage as having a detrimental effect on children. But it might also be attributed to their perception of divorce as not being very harmful to children. Although the social and emotional functioning of the child of the divorced and remarried family types was evaluated as significantly worse than that of the child from the intact family, the child of both these family types was perceived as functioning better than the child from the conflicted family. These findings would appear to reflect the belief of teachers that although having an intact family is best for children, they are better off living with divorced parents than in a conflicted family. This interpretation is in agreement with the findings of earlier studies regarding the differences and similarities between children from these family types (Burchinal, 1964; Landis, 1960; Nye, 1957).

The results of the present study show that teachers expect a similar level of academic functioning of children from the four types of family background. This is an unexpected finding, particularly as regards the comparison between the child from the divorced family and the child from the intact family. Differences in teachers' stereotypic expectations concerning the scholastic performance of children of these two family types were found by Santrock and Tracy

(1978) as well as Guttmann, Geva, and Gefen (1984), the latter of whom used a sample of Israeli teachers. The absence of difference revealed in the present study may be an indication of the changing attitudes among Israeli teachers in the course of the last three years, and of their increasingly sophisticated understanding of the impact of divorce on children — i.e., the likelihood of there being more of a negative effect on their social and emotional functioning and less on their academic performance.

One of the more important implications of our results concerns the validity of studies which use teachers' evaluations as the sole measure of children's functioning. The findings show that teachers form differential sets of behavioral expectations on the basis of a child's family background alone. Thus if teachers' evaluations are used, there is a danger of false conclusions being arrived at concerning the effects of different family types on children. Since teachers appear to be predisposed to rank children from divorced, remarried, and conflicted families more negatively on social and emotional measures than children from intact family, considerable caution should be observed in interpreting the results of studies that rely on teachers' evaluation. So, for example, findings that children of divorced parents are at psychological risk, or that they have serious problems of social and emotional adjustment, may have to be reevaluated in the case of studies grounded on teachers' ratings. The need of more research is indicated for determining the stability and persistence of teachers' stereotypes in this regard over time, with a greater quantity of behavioral data being provided for the subjects. In the meantime, teachers' stereotypic differential expectations of pupils from different family backgrounds should be considered as an intervening variable that may bias research results.

REFERENCES

Adams, P.L. and Horovitz, J.H. (1980) Coping patterns of mothers of poor boys. *Child Psychiatry and Human Development* 10, 144-155.

Adams, P.L., Milner, J.R. and Schrepf, N.A. (1984) *Fatherless children*. New York: John Wiley & Sons.

Bane, M. (1976) Marital disruption and the lives of children. *Journal of Social Issues* 32, 103-117.

Blechman, E.A. (1982) Are children with one parent at psychological risk? A methodological review. *Journal of Marriage and the Family* February, 179-195.

Bronfenbrenner, U. (1961) Some familial antecedents of responsibility and leadership in adolescents. In L. Petrullo and B.M. Bass (Eds.) *Leadership and interpersonal behavior*. New York: Holt, Rinehart & Winston, 239-273.

Burchinal, L.G. (1964) Characteristics of adolescents from unbroken home, broken, and reconstituted families. *Journal of Marriage and the Family* 36, 44-51.

Cortes, C.F. and Fleming, E.S. (1968) The effects of father absence on the adjustment of culturally disadvantaged boys. *Journal of Special Education* 2, 413-420.

Covell, K. and Turnbull, K. (1982) The long-term effects of father absence in childhood on male university students' sex-role identity and personal adjustment. *Journal of Genetic Psychology* 141, 271-276.

Engemoen, L. (1967) The influence of membership in a broken home on test performance of first grade children. *Dissertation Abstracts*. No. 9-A, 27-28.

Ferri, E. (1976) *Growing up in a one parent family: A long term study of child development*. Windsor, Berkshire (England): NPER.

Fowler, P.C. and Richards, H.C. (1978) Father absence, educational preparedness and academic achievement: A test of the confluence model. *Journal of Educational Psychology* 70, 595-601.

Good, T.L. (1982) How teachers' expectations effect results. *American Education* December, 25-32.

Guttmann, J., Geva, N. and Gefen, S. Teachers' and school children's stereotypic perception of "the child of divorce". Unpublished manuscript, Haifa University, 1984.

Hammond, J.M. (1979) Children of divorce: A study of self-concept, academic achievement, and attitudes. *The Elementary School Journal* 80, 55-62.

Herzog, J.D. (1974) Father-absence and boys' school performance in Barbados. *Human Organization* 33, 71-83.

Herzog, E. and Sudia, C.E. (1973) Children in fatherless families. In B.M. Caldweel and H.N. Ricciuti (Eds.) *Review of child development* Vol 2. Chicago: University of Chicago Press.

Hunt, L.L. and Hunt, J.G. (1975) Race and the father-son connection: The conditional relevance of father absence for the orientations and identities of adolescent boys. *Social Problems* 23, 35-52.

Kellam, S.G., Ensminger, M.E. and Turner, R.J. (1977) Family structure and the mental health of children. *Archives of General Psychiatry* 34, 1012-1022.

Landis, J.T. (1960) The trauma of children when parents divorce. *Marriage and Family Living* 22, 7-13.

Langer, T. (1963) Broken homes and mental disorder. *Public Health Reports* 78, 921-926.

LeCorgne, L.L. and Laosa, L.M. (1976) Father absence in low income Mexican American families: Children's social adjustment and conceptual differentiation of sex role attributes. *Developmental Psychology* 12, 470-471.

Meichenbaum, D.H., Boweres, K.S. and Ross, R.R. (1969) A behavioural analysis of teacher expectancy effects. *Journal of Personality and Social Psychology* 13, 306-316.

Mischel, W. (1973) Toward a cognitive social learning reconceptualization of personality. *Psychological Review* 80, 252-283.

Nye, F.I. (1957) Child adjustment in broken and in unhappy unbroken homes. *Marriage and Family Living* 19, 356-361.

Rist R.C. (1970) Student social class and teacher expectations: The self fulfilling prophecy in ghetto education. *Harvard Educational Review* 40, 4110-4150.

Rosenthal, R. and Jacobson, L. (1968) *Pygmalion in the classroom*. New York: Holt, Rinehart & Winston.

Santrock, J.W. (1975) Father absence perceived material behavior and moral development in boys. *Child Development* 46, 753-757.

Santrock, J.W. (1977) Effects of father absence on sex typed behaviors in male children: Reason for the absence and age of onset of the absence. *The Journal of Genetic Psychology* 130, 3-10.

Santrock, J.W. and Tracy, R.L. (1975) Effects of children's family structure status on the development of stereotypes by teachers. *Journal of Educational Psychology* 70, 754-757.

The Adversarial Legal Process
and Divorce:
Negative Effects
Upon the Psychological
Adjustment of Children

Graham S. Saayman
R. Vanessa Saayman

SUMMARY. This study investigated the effects of the adversarial legal process per se upon the psychological adjustment of children of divorce. A highly controlled sample, including 23 fathers and 39 mothers, divorced for an average of 2.8 years, and a total of 103 children, was investigated. Parents were interviewed independently to assess the family system pre- and post-divorce. Divorce, as a

---

Graham S. Saayman, PhD, is Professor of Psychology, University of Cape Town, Rondebosch, South Africa 7700. R. Vanessa Saayman, BA, B Soc Sci, is a Research Assistant, University of Cape Town.

Financial assistance rendered by the Human Sciences Research Council towards the cost of this research is hereby acknowledged. Opinions expressed or conclusions reached are those of the authors and are not to be regarded as those of the Human Sciences Research Council. We thank Mr. Frank Bokhorst for advice concerning the statistical analysis of results and Mr. Trevor Blow for assistance in developing the questionnaire on the legal aspects of divorce.

329

function of the adversarial process, was categorized and entered, together with the age of child and the measures of family functioning, into a multiple linear regression. The Rutter A (2) Scale measured child adjustment. The ROLES dimension of family functioning, both pre- and post-divorce, as well as an acrimonious divorce, contributed significantly to the psychological maladjustment of children, indicating that the adversarial process does not "serve the best interests" of the child. It is recommended that the adversary process be replaced by a system of divorce mediation, via Family Courts.

INTRODUCTION

There is a widespread opinion that the adversarial legal system escalates conflict and hostility between spouses in the crisis of the divorce process (Brown, 1982). This implies that (i) divorce is necessarily deleterious to the adjustment of parents and children and that (ii) the adversarial system compounds these effects. Whereas negative consequences of divorce for a significant proportion of parents and children have been substantially demonstrated (Wallerstein and Kelly, 1980; Wallerstein, 1985), evidence for hypothesis (ii) above, focussing specifically upon the act of divorce per se, is deficient. Indeed, an investigation failed to demonstrate any significant impact upon *parental adjustment* to marital separation attributable to the adversarial system (Spanier and Anderson, 1979). Nevertheless, negative evaluations of the adversarial system, as it applies to divorce, by professionals from a variety of disciplines, are so consistent, and the rate of divorce so alarming, that alternatives in the form of "family mediation" (Blades, 1985) via Family Courts have been implemented in North America and Europe.

The aim of the present study was, therefore, to investigate the hypothesis that divorce proceedings per se, conducted within the adversarial system, are inimical to the psychological adjustment of children. However, the factors known to influence the development of personality are multiple and complex. The family, in particular, has a powerful influence upon child development and this is pivotal in court decisions concerning maintenance, custody and access taken "in the best interests" of children of divorce (Goldstein et al., 1980).

In assessing the effects of divorce proceedings per se upon the adjustment of children, it is consequently essential to include in the equation an assessment of family functioning *prior to* divorce. Secondly, whereas divorce entails a radical *restructuring* of the family, legal, financial and parental obligations persist, whilst the bonds established in the context of primal family relationships retain their potency (Derdeyn, 1977). An assessment of family functioning in the *post-divorce* situation is also therefore necessary. Moreover, much of the early research on divorce was conceptually flawed in that "linear, unidirectional causal models accompanied by relatively static, single variable approaches" were typically used (Levitin, 1979, p. 2). The conceptual framework of family systems theory is necessary to assess the extent to which "all family members are simultaneously and systematically affected by divorce" (Beal, 1979, p. 140). Thus, in the present study, the role of the family system, both pre- and post-divorce, was assessed by means of a highly researched and sophisticated model of family functioning. The statistical analysis employed, multiple linear regression, simultaneously assesses the contributions of the independent factors entered into the equation which predicts child adjustment (Blechman, 1982). The analysis determines whether or not these variables act independently, or whether their effects combine or overlap. It was thus possible to assess the unique contribution of the adversary process per se upon child adjustment. A preliminary report on this investigation has been published elsewhere (Saayman and Saayman, 1985).

METHODOLOGY

Subjects

Sixty-two parents (23 fathers and 39 mothers, with an average age of 38.5 and 36.9 years respectively at the time of divorce) were interviewed. Included were 15 mothers and 15 fathers who agreed that their ex-spouses be interviewed separately by two researchers. The data, analyzed independently, provided an estimate of their shared perceptions of the marriage and the process of divorce. The average length of marriage was 12.1 (range 2-24) years. Couples had been divorced for an average of 2.8 (range 1-11) years. Seventy-four percent of the divorces had been granted under the "no fault" legislation of the Divorce Act (Hahlo and Sinclair, 1980). There were 103 children with an average age of 9.8 (range 1-23) years at the time of divorce. Sixty-one were boys and 42 were girls. All of the mothers and 6 fathers were custodial parents.

Strict controls produced a small but highly homogeneous sample, an essential prerequisite for the study. Subjects were white, predominantly English-speaking volunteers, varying in socioeconomic status from the lower to the upper levels of the middle-class range. A preliminary questionnaire enabled the exclusion of parents with a history of psychiatric or debilitating physical illness or substance abuse. The custodial parents were not disadvantaged with respect to instrumental and affective needs: a financially deprived single-parent, lacking emotional support from adult peers, has limited resources for maintaining and nurturing children (Bloom et al., 1979; Glasser and Navarre, 1965). Custodians described adequate emotional support from sources such as family, new relationships and church groups. Whereas income tended to decline after divorce, none of the parents reported major financial problems.

Subjects were obtained from three sources: divorce-oriented workshops, responses to a standardized letter sent to addresses obtained from the court records, and responses to a brief, factual press report requesting the participation of volunteers. To control for "perceived demand effects" (Orne, 1962), subjects were told that their experiences would contribute to an understanding of divorce, that the researchers had no clear-cut expectations concerning the outcome of the study and that their confidentiality would be strictly safeguarded.

Interview

Parents were interviewed individually in their homes. Interviews lasted between 1 1/2 and 2 hours, were tape-recorded and transcribed onto scoring sheets. Rutter and co-workers have demonstrated the interview as a reliable means of gathering family data, whether the spouses are interviewed conjointly or separately (Brown and Rutter, 1966; Rutter and Brown, 1966; Quinton et al., 1976).

The interview proceeded in three stages and in the first two was semi-structured and retrospective. In stage one, interviewees ranked, in order of priority, problems central to divorce, providing their perceptions of the development of the family and of the dissolution of the marriage. Family functioning prior to divorce was then systematically assessed: each interviewee was asked the same, structured questions derived from the McMaster Model of Family Functioning (Epstein et al., 1981). Questions focussed on Problem Solving, Communication, Roles and Affective Responsiveness (see below).

Stage two examined the process of divorce. Subjects described events from the time a decision was made to consult a lawyer. A standard series of questions, derived from pilot interviews concerning experiences of divorced persons, as well as from consultations with members of the legal profession, probed the nature of the divorce experience.

Stage three examined family functioning and the quality and quantity of the communication of the ex-spouses in the post-divorce situation. Subjects were then asked to complete, in their own time, but within the next few days, a series of questionnaires providing measures of (i) family functioning (The Family Assessment Device [Epstein et al., 1983]), (ii) the post-divorce coparental relationship (Ahrons, 1981) and (iii) child adjustment (Rutter et al., 1970). These were posted to the researchers.

Measures of Family Functioning

In stage one of the interview, the researcher employed an interview format derived from some of the categories of the McMaster Model of Family Functioning, which comprises six dimensions: Problem Solving, Communication, Roles, Affective Responsiveness, Affective Involvement and Behavior Control (Epstein and Bishop, 1981). Family functioning is rated on each dimension on the seven-point scales of the McMaster Clinical Rating Scale (Epstein et al., 1982), ranging from "severely disturbed" (point 1), through "non-clinical/healthy" (point 5) to "superior" (point 7).

Parents were also asked to complete the *Family Assessment Device* (Epstein et al., 1983), a questionnaire assessing the six dimensions of the Model described above, together with a seventh scale *General Functioning*, rating the overall health/pathology of the family. Scores range from 1.00 (healthy) to 4.00 (unhealthy). The parents completed the questionnaire, in their own time, in two ways: (i) retrospectively on the family as it was immediately before action to institute divorce proceedings and (ii) on the post-divorce family, at the time of interview. Family functioning, assessed via the interview, was rated independently of the scored questionnaire.

Child Adjustment

The Rutter Scale A (2) (Rutter et al., 1970), completed by parents, discriminates between children who have emotional and behavioral disorders and those who do not. A score of 13 or more designates disorder, determinable as either antisocial or neurotic in nature. The scale is used throughout the entire school-age period (5-16 years). Of the total 103 children in the sample, 83 fell within this age-range and, accordingly, only data from this sub-sample were entered into the statistical analysis.

Age of Child at Time of Divorce

Since the age of the child at the time of divorce may influence subsequent emotional and behavioural adjustment (Kalter and Rembar, 1981), the age of children at the time of divorce was entered into the regression analysis.

Post-Divorce Coparental Relationship

Extreme interparental conflict prior to, during and after divorce has a negative impact upon the emotional adjustment of children (Anthony, 1974; Rosen, 1977; 1979; Westman et al., 1970). The interview and Family Assessment Device measured aspects of this variable but an additional index was derived from the work of Ahrons (1981). This was a five-point scale measuring the frequency and content of post-divorce parental interactions as well as the quality of the relationship, in terms of conflict and support, generated by parental responsibilities.

Divorce Category

The "adversarial" nature of divorces may vary from the "do-it-yourself" variety to protracted and traumatic contests for the spoils of marriage. *"Divorce Category"* measures the degree of interparental turbulence *surrounding the divorce process per se*, employing objective, concrete indices such as uncontested *vs.* contested divorce, variations in duration and costs, use of one or more lawyers and degree of anger and hostility generated once the process was initiated. Each divorce was allocated to one of three Divorce Categories, ranging in degree of acrimony from (1) *neutral* through (2) *intermediate* to (3) *negative*.

Legal Arbitration

Arbitration was defined as the framework provided by the lawyers to solve problems constructively for the benefit of the whole family, with particular emphasis upon *the best interests of the children*. Standard questions included items such as: Lawyer's attitude to client and spouse (supportive, neutral, antagonistic); response to client's affective state (empathically dealt with, ignored, manipulated to escalate antagonism); escalated client's initial claims thus provoking hostility and mistrust of spouse; explored whether or not to pursue divorce action; suggested counselling or marital psychotherapy; legal rights and obligations supportively defined; mediated and defused rather than polarized conflicts; acted genuinely in the best interests of the children.

Arbitration was rated on a scale of 1-5, measuring the extent to which the attitude, style, technique and approach of the lawyer(s) approximated the above definition. Rating was facilitated by the emphatic views of subjects concerning the quality of professional services received. Point 1 represents *negative arbitration* (lack of mediation, confrontational attitude with respect to spouse, escalation of antagonism), point 3 *moderate arbitration* (neutral attitude to client's affect and spouse, focus on reality issues) and point 5 *supportive arbitration* (constructive mediation, defused negative affect, genuine focus on child's best interests).

Number of Lawyers

The measures of the adversary process (Divorce Category and Legal Arbitration) are subject to possible bias via the approach to divorce of individual lawyers: the repeated inclusion of a limited number of individual lawyers with reputations as "divorce specialists" in the sample might distort the measures employed. Systematic control was not possible, but post hoc analysis revealed that a total of 89 lawyers was consulted. In 20 instances, the same lawyer was involved in the divorce proceedings of two or more couples, whilst in 17 cases subjects either did not recall or refused to disclose the names of their attorneys. Thus, in at least 52 cases, the measures of the adversary process were independent of the possible influence of the approach of individual lawyers.

RESULTS

Child Adjustment Scores

The mean of the total score on the Rutter scale was 7.9 with a standard error of 0.70, indicating that, on average, children in this sample fell within the normal range. However, 23.5% of the children were designated as "neurotic" and 22.4% as "antisocial."

Multiple Linear Regression

The following variables were entered into the statistical analysis to assess their contributions to child adjustment, as measured via the Rutter scale: (i) The seven dimensions of the Family Assessment Device (ii) Age of child at time of divorce (iii) Post-divorce coparental relationship (iv) Divorce Category and (v) Legal Arbitration.

Two separate analyses of the data, employing the multiple linear regression technique, were performed from the perspectives of family functioning (i) *prior to* and (ii) *post-divorce*. Both analyses yielded significant results and the same two variables emerged as significant predictors of the psychological adjustment of children: the *Roles* dimension of family functioning as measured by the Family Assessment Device and *Divorce Category*.

Prediction of child adjustment (via the Rutter scores), in terms of standardized regression weights, was as follows: (i) *Prior to divorce*, Child Adjustment = 0.18 (Divorce Category) + 0.38 (Roles), F = 8.11; df 2, 80; p < 0.005 and (ii) *Post-divorce*, Child Adjustment = 0.20 (Divorce Category) + 0.25 (Roles), F = 3.73; df 2, 80; p < 0.05.

The analysis did not identify any other variables entered into the equation, over and above Roles and Divorce Category, as having a significant effect upon child adjustment (Table 1).

Family Functioning Pre- and Post-Divorce

The means and standard errors of each of the scales of the Family Assessment Device are shown in Table 2. In each case, post-divorce mean values showed a decrease with respect to pre-divorce levels, that is towards the *healthy* (point 1) range of the scales. The results of a Hotelling's T test for differences between means (Winer, 1962) indicate that all of these decreases were highly significant (p < 0.0001).

Comparisons of Perceptions of Ex-Spouses

The means and standard errors of the data derived from the Interview on family functioning prior to divorce, from each scale of the Family Assessment Device, both pre- and post-divorce, from the Rutter Scale and from the Post-divorce Coparental Relationship for the 30 ex-spouses, are shown in Table 3. The results of *t* tests for differences between means showed no significant differences for any of the measures.

DISCUSSION

A significant proportion of children in this study were identified as "neurotic" (23.5%) or "antisocial" (22.4%). It is pivotal to note that the negative influence of the adversarial process upon children ("Divorce Category"), is *statistically independent* of the effects of the family category "Roles," also a major determinant of child adjustment—although the effect of Roles was more reliable than the effect of Divorce Category (Table 1). Consequently, this

Table 1. Values of F-to-remove (*) and of F-to-enter of each variable at step two of the regression analysis, both before and after divorce.

	Roles	Divorce Category	Legal Arbitration	Age of Child	Problem Solving	Communication	Affective Responsiveness	Affective Involvement	Behaviour Control	General functioning	Co-parental Relationship
Prior to divorce	13,9*	3,1*	0,1	0,4	1,9	0,5	1,0	0,1	0,7	0,5	0,5
Post-divorce	5,4*	3,4*	0,2	1,4	0,9	0,2	1,0	0,8	0,0	0,0	0,6

Table 2. Means ($\pm$ S.E.) of each of the dimensions of the family categories schema, as measured by the FAD, prior to and post-divorce.

	Problem Solving	Communication	Roles	Affective Responsiveness	Affective Involvement	Behavior Control	General Functioning
Prior to divorce	2,63$\pm$0,06	2,69$\pm$0,06	2,51$\pm$0,05	2,66$\pm$0,07	2,53$\pm$0,05	2,15$\pm$0,05	2,62$\pm$0,07
Post-divorce	1,99$\pm$0,07	2,03$\pm$0,06	2,24$\pm$0,05	2,01$\pm$0,09	2,14$\pm$0,05	1,86$\pm$0,06	1,98$\pm$0,07

Hotelling T^2 = 79,51; F Value = 10,24   P < 0,0001

339

Table 3. Means ($\pm$ S.E.) of measures of family functioning from 30 ex-spouses, derived from the Interview (Clinical Rating Scale), Family Assessment Device prior to and post-divorce and Child Adjustment Scores (Rutter Scale)

Clinical Rating Scale and Rutter Scale

	Problem Solving	Affective Communication	Roles (Instrumental)	Roles (Affective)	Affective Responsiveness	Rutter Scale
Fathers	2,4$\pm$0,24	2,93$\pm$0,18	3,9$\pm$0,23	3,00$\pm$0,24	3,47$\pm$0,27	7,67$\pm$1,27
Mothers	2,3$\pm$0,25	2,87$\pm$0,16	4,0$\pm$0,22	3,13$\pm$0,19	3,33$\pm$0,27	7,94$\pm$1,21

Family Assessment Device prior to divorce

	Problem Solving	Communication	Roles	Affective Responsiveness	Affective Involvement	Behavior Control	General Functioning
Fathers	2,72$\pm$0,12	2,80$\pm$0,15	2,37$\pm$0,11	2,89$\pm$0,13	2,55$\pm$0,11	2,19$\pm$0,13	2,59$\pm$0,16
Mothers	2,4$\pm$0,10	2,62$\pm$0,11	2,57$\pm$0,11	2,5$\pm$0,10	2,56$\pm$0,13	2,11$\pm$0,11	2,49$\pm$0,11

Family Assessment Device post-divorce

	Problem Solving	Communication	Roles	Affective Responsiveness	Affective Involvement	Behavior Control	General Functioning
Fathers	2,07$\pm$0,13	2,10$\pm$0,13	2,05$\pm$0,10	2,21$\pm$0,17	2,08$\pm$0,11	1,81$\pm$0,14	2,09$\pm$0,15
Mothers	1,98$\pm$0,22	2,05$\pm$0,17	2,23$\pm$0,10	1,94$\pm$0,20	2,22$\pm$0,14	1,82$\pm$0,11	1,98$\pm$0,18

investigation confirms the prediction that *the adversarial legal system per se* has a negative impact upon the psychological adjustment of children of divorce and therefore supports the principle of establishing mechanisms for divorce mediation via Family Courts.

It is not surprising that the comprehensive Roles category is significantly related to the psychological adjustment of children since this important dimension encompasses a variety of recurrent behaviors necessary for the maintenance of the family. It depends upon the collaboration of parents to ensure that essential tasks are allocated and accomplished, including provision of food and shelter and the routine management of the system. It also implies that children receive supervision and emotional support. Moreover, the individual development of the adults must not be overlooked. In many cases, one of the parents had been overburdened with an inequitable share of tasks, frequently distributed in a nonreflective manner: the husband as sole breadwinner and the wife in the traditional housekeeper role. Thus, the parents struggled to maintain an equitable balance between financial demands and adequate attention to marital and family relationships, often at the expense of their own development. Such imbalance poisons the marriage, with escalating confrontation concerning the basic issue of *"who makes the rules."* This dynamic then reverberates upon the adjustment of the children, setting up a spiral of negative transactions. Parental control splits and deviant behaviour of children further imbalances the system. Problems become insoluble, and the marriage crumbles.

However, it is surprising indeed that the stringent statistical analysis also identifies a significant relationship between a negative divorce, a relatively short-term process, and the psychological maladjustment of children. Moreover, this relationship exists irrespective of the individual attitudes and approaches to divorce of a reasonable sample of lawyers. Thus, whether lawyers approach divorce as empathic, impartial family counsellors, or as gladiators doing battle on behalf of their clients, this has no significant bearing upon the psychological adjustment of the children. This suggests that it is the *very structure of the adversarial system* which is potentially damaging to children of divorce. Indeed, results do little more than to illustrate a truism: if the legal system specifies antagonism and confrontation as its modus operandi, then its implementation cannot but generate negative effects in a significant proportion of instances, irrespective of whether or not its administrators attempt to apply the rules with the benignity demanded, somewhat paradoxically, by its objectives, namely, to function in the best interests of the child (Group for the Advancement of Psychiatry, 1980).

The majority of the divorces in the present study took place under the "no fault" legislation, yet they ranged in degree of acrimony and hostility from minimum, in the "do-it-yourself" type divorces (Category 1), through to divorce involving protracted litigation in an atmosphere of intense hostility (Category 3). The present study confirms Rosen's (1977; 1979) findings that "interparental turbulence" is a major determinant of the psychological maladjustment of children of divorce. However, the simultaneous assessment of a variety of factors potentially capable of influencing child adjustment permits a finer analysis of the notion of "interparental turbulence." The regression analysis indicates that severe interparental turbulence at the *very time of divorce* exerts a negative influence upon children. This is supported by the fact that no relationship was found between child adjustment and a negative emotional atmosphere (as measured by the family category "Affective Responsiveness") in the family ether *prior to*, or *after* divorce. Similarly, the contribution of the Post-divorce Coparental Relationship (Ahrons, 1981) was lost in the regression analysis. It should be noted, however, that *extreme* interparental hostility (physical assault in the presence of the child) prior to separation is a strong predictor of child maladjustment (Jacobson, 1978). Similarly, active marital discord and lack of affection are associated with child maladjustment, " . . . but a good relationship with one parent can go some way toward mitigating the harmful effect of a quarrelsome unhappy home" (Rutter, 1971, p. 255). Nevertheless, our findings consistently implicate interparental hostility at *the time of divorce* as a predictor of child maladjustment. Precisely how this effect is mediated is beyond the scope of this report, but the work of Anthony (1974), Rosen (1977; 1979) and Westman et al., (1970) suggests that the *denigration* of one parent by the other has a severe impact upon intrapsychic processes in the child. Other investigators report that the psychosocial adjustment of the divorcee is an important moderator of the psychological adjustment of her children (Hetherington et al., 1977; Nelson, 1981).

Concerning the methodology of this study, the data derived independently from the 30 ex-spouses on the Family Assessment Device, Rutter Scale, and the ratings of the interview, give a strong indication of the reliability of these measures, since there were no significant differences between the scores of the ex-spouses on any of these instruments (Table 3). Moreover, the strong agreement between the perceptions of the ex-spouses on the development and termination of the marriage indicates that the study has considerable validity, despite the problematic nature of the retrospective method (Kazdin, 1965). Brown and Rutter (1966) have found similar agreements in the separate accounts of husbands and wives on aspects of family life.

Further, the results also have positive implications, since they suggest that the psychological adjustment of children need not necessarily be impaired by divorce *provided that* the roles necessary for effective family functioning are adequately fulfilled both prior to and after divorce. Conversely, children in *intact* families may suffer maladjustment to the extent to which the Roles dimension is inadequately fulfilled. Indeed, in support of this view is the finding that each measure of family functioning *improved* following divorce (Table 2). This is not surprising since divorce, by definition, implies an inability to adequately resolve marital and family problems, with consequent negative effects upon the vulnerable child. This improvement in family functioning post-divorce may have absorbed the contribution of the post-divorce coparental relationship to the child adjustment scores in the regression analysis, particularly as, in this highly controlled sample, custodial parents were adequately supported both financially and affectively by a variety of social networks. Further, and most importantly, extreme hostility between the parents at the time of divorce is an independent predictor of child maladjustment, and this is true, *even if* the Roles dimension is adequately fulfilled both prior to and after divorce. This applies to those cases where one or both parents *lose control* in response to the emotional stress of attempting to achieve an equitable divorce agreement. Most divorces are grievously painful, but, in certain cases, the loss of children and income may provoke a series of frantic attempts to redress the ensuing psychological imbalance, all of which merely serve to worsen the situation. For example, many fathers feel that they are offered *no option* in custody claims, particularly when demands are made to pay large sums of maintenance to make this "legalized robbery" possible. Consequently, in the Wallerstein and Kelly study (1980), many noncustodial parents " . . . lacking legal rights to share in decisions about major aspects of their children's lives . . . withdrew from their children in grief and frustration. Their withdrawal was experienced by the children as a rejection and was detrimental in its impact" (p. 310). In the case of many mothers, inadequate recompense for years of caring for children, running the household, often contributing financially both in terms of hard cash and cheap labour in setting up their husbands in early business ventures, may fuel enormous fires of emotional upheaval and resentment. In short, the full catastrophe of years of unhappy marriage is recapitulated in the arena of the adversarial process. In these Category 3 divorces, the "best interests of the child" can hardly be served. The financial costs and emotional stress are enormous, as parents attempt to drum up support for their own case. The repercussions upon the psychological adjustment of children are all too obvious (Hess and Camara, 1979).

Clearly, the adversarial system places lawyers, de facto, in a situation analogous to the family therapist and requires them, in the emotionally laden death throes of a marriage, to attempt to achieve the objectives of the mental health professional: the prevention of serious behavioural and emotional disorders in the children and the possibility of subsequent psychiatric disorders in adulthood (Wiseman and Fiske, 1980). Indeed, lawyers are frequently called upon to deal with complex emotional reactions before they can begin to address the legal issues of divorce yet, importantly, they often feel professionally unprepared (Felner et al., 1982; Doane and Cowen, 1981). The adversarial process, therefore, frequently places the legal profession in an uncomfortable, if not an untenable position.

These results have implications for the establishment of Family Courts. Firstly, they may assist in the early identification of children most at risk: in those cases where family functioning is disturbed in the Roles dimension, and where parents are enmeshed in the degree of emotional turmoil defined by Divorce Category 3. Since the rate of divorce is exceptionally high, these findings may assist the Courts in achieving a cost-effective system of mediation by providing a focus upon children potentially most vulnerable to the negative effects of divorce.

Secondly, they imply that a system of mediation will require, in order to be effective, the expertise of professionals who have available the precise skills which the problematic families in divorce contests lack: the ability to facilitate *negotiation*. And this ability is dependent upon the skills required to conduct a series of impartial, objective and compelling *assessments* (child development, mental status examination, personality diagnosis, family functioning inter alia) which dissect out in percise detail the options available to the family. Clinical experience and previous research indicate that in the "treatment" stage of family therapy, the therapist assists the family to negotiate a contract where negotiation is defined as the "ability to verbalize clearly and directly the options available and thus to allocate, *on the basis of mutual agreement*, both instrumental and affective tasks to appropriate family members" (Cunningham and Saayman, 1984). Significantly, the present study suggests that it is precisely this ability which is either impaired during pre- and post-divorce family functioning (Roles) or else is susceptible to the adverse effects of the divorce process (Divorce Category). In the latter case, it would seem that the structure of the adversarial arena, when encountered by a significant proportion of *personalities* (see Kressel et al., 1980 for a typology of divorcing couples), sets in motion a destructive series of provocative and confronting challenges and demands, instigating an escalating spiral of animosity, which enmeshes all parties concerned. Thus, it is particularly in these cases that a different system, employing mediation strategies via Family Courts, would be recommended and it is likely that the type of intervention then required would most closely resemble divorce therapy.

REFERENCES

Ahrons, C.R. (1981). The continuing coparental relationship between divorced spouses. *American Journal of Orthopsychiatry, 51,* 415-428.

Anthony, E.J. (1974). Children at risk from divorce: A review. In E.J. Anthony (Ed.), *The Child in His Family: Children at Psychiatric Risk* (Vol. 3). New York: John Wiley & Sons.

Beal, E.W. (1979). Children of divorce: A family systems perspective. *Journal of Social Issues, 35,* 140-154.

Blades, J. (1985). *Family Mediation.* New Jersey: Prentice-Hall.

Blechman, E.A. (1982). Are children with one parent at psychological risk? A methodological review. *Journal of Marriage and the Family, February,* 179-195.

Bloom, B.L., White, S.W., & Asher, S.J. (1979). Marital disruption as a stressful life event. In G. Levinger & O.C. Miles (Eds.), *Divorce and Separation: Context, Causes, and Consequences* (pp. 184-200). New York: Basic Books.

Brown, D.G. (1982). Divorce and family mediation: History, review, future directions. *Conciliation Courts Review, 20,* 1-4.

Brown, G.W., & Rutter, M. (1966). The measurement of family activities and relationships: A methodological study. *Human Relations, 19,* 241-263.

Cunningham, A., & Saayman, G.S. (1984). Effective functioning in dual-career families: An investigation. *Journal of Family Therapy, 6,* 365-380.

Derdeyn, A.P. (1977). Children in divorce: Intervention in the phase of separation. *Pediatrics, 60,* 20-27.

Doane, J.A., & Cohen, E.L. (1981). Interpersonal help-giving of family practice lawyers. *American Journal of Community Psychology, 9,* 547-558.

Epstein, N.B., & Bishop, D.S. (1981). Problem-centered systems therapy of the family. In A.S. Gurman & D.P. Kniskern (Eds.), *Handbook of Family Therapy* (pp. 444-482). New York: Brunner/Mazel.

Epstein, N.B., Baldwin, L.M., & Bishop, D.S. (1982). McMaster Clinical Rating Scale. Brown/Butler Family Research Program. Providence, Rhode Island.

Epstein, N.B., Baldwin, L.M., & Bishop, D.S. (1983). The McMaster Family Assessment Device. *Journal of Marital and Family Therapy, 9,* 171-180.

Felner, R.D., Primavera, J., Farber, S.S., & Bishop, T.A. (1982). Attorneys as caregivers during divorce. *American Journal of Orthopsychiatry, 52,* 323-336.

Glasser, P., & Navarre, E. (1965). Structural problems of the one-parent family. *Journal of Social Issues, 21,* 98-109.

Goldstein, J., Freud, A., & Solnit, A.J. (1980). *Beyond the Best Interests of the Child.* London: Burnett Books.

Group for the Advancement of Psychiatry, Committee on the Family. (1980). *Divorce, Child Custody and the Family, Volume X, Publication No. 106.* New York: Mental Health Materials Center.

Hahlo, H.R., & Sinclair, J.D. (1980). *The Reform of the South African Law of Divorce.* Cape Town: Juta and Co., Ltd.

Hess, R.D., & Camara, K.A. (1979). Post-divorce family relationships as mediating factors in the consequences of divorce for children. *Journal of Social Issues, 35*, 79-97.

Hetherington, E.M., Cox, M., & Cox, R. (1977). The aftermath of divorce. In J.H. Stevens, Jr. & M. Mathews (Eds.), *Mother-Child, Father-Child Relations*. Washington, D.C.: NAEYC.

Jacobson, D.S. (1978). The impact of marital separation/divorce on children: II. Interparent hostility and child adjustment. *Journal of Divorce, 2*, 3-19.

Kalter, N., & Rembar, J. (1981). The significance of a child's age at the time of parental divorce. *American Journal of Orthopsychiatry, 51*, 85-100.

Kazdin, A.E. (1965). Research methods in clinical psychology. In B. Wolman (Ed.), *Handbook of Clinical Psychology*. New York: McGraw-Hill.

Kressel, K., Jaffee, N., Tuchman, B., Watson, C., & Deutsch, M. (1980). A typology of divorcing couples: Implications for mediation and the divorce process. *Family Process, 19*, 101-116.

Levitin, T.E. (1979). Children of divorce: An introduction. *Journal of Social Issues, 35*, 1-25.

Nelson, G. (1981). Moderators of women's and children's adjustment following parental divorce. *Journal of Divorce, 4*, 71-83.

Orne, M.T. (1963). On the social psychology of the psychological experiment: With particular reference to demand characteristics and their implications. *American Psychologist, 17*, 776-783.

Quinton, D., Rutter, M., & Rowlands, O. (1976). An evaluation of an interview assessment of marriage. *Psychological Medicine, 6*, 577-586.

Rosen, R. (1977). Children of divorce: What they feel about access and other aspects of the divorce experience. *Journal of Clinical Child Psychology, Summer*: 24-27.

Rosen, R. (1979). Some crucial issues concerning children of divorce. *Journal of Divorce, 3*, 19-25.

Rutter, M. (1971). Parent-child separation: Psychological effects on the children. *Journal of Child Psychology and Psychiatry, 12*, 233-260.

Rutter, M., & Brown, G.W. (1966). The reliability and validity of measures of family life and relationships in families containing a psychiatric patient. *Social Psychiatry, 1*, 38-53.

Rutter, M., Tizard, J., & Whitmore, K. (1970). *Education, Health and Behaviour*. London: Longman.

Saayman, G.S., & Saayman, R.V. (1985). Negative effects of the adversarial legal system upon the psychological adjustment of children of divorce: An empirical study. *Natal University Law and Society Review, 1*, 43-53.

Spanier, G.B., & Anderson, E.A. (1979). The impact of the legal system on adjustment to marital separation. *Journal of Marriage and the Family, 41*, 605-613.

Wallerstein, J.S. (1985). The overburdened child: Some long-term consequences of divorce. *Social Work, 30*, 116-123.

Wallerstein, J.S., & Kelly, J.B. (1980). *Surviving the Breakup: How Children and Parents Cope with Divorce*. New York: Basic Books, Inc.

Westman, J.C., Cline, D., Swift, W.J., & Kramer, D.A. (1970). Role of child psychiatry in divorce. *Archives of General Psychiatry, 23*, 416-420.

Winer, B.J. (1962). *Statistical Principles in Experimental Design*. New York: McGraw-Hill.

Wiseman, J.M., & Fiske, J.A. (1980). Lawyer-therapist team as mediator in a marital crisis. *Social Work, 25*, 442-445.